AF576411

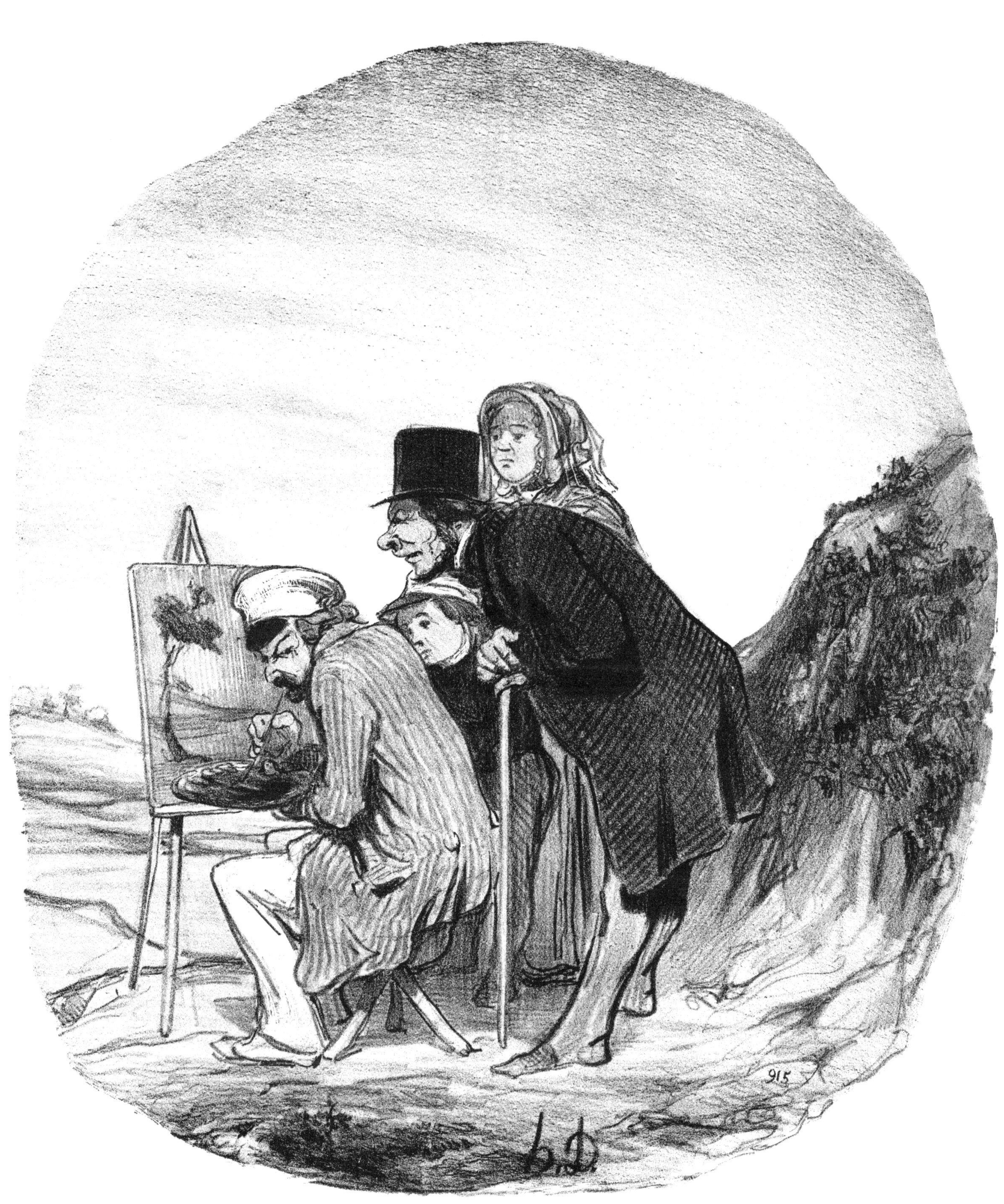
915

DAUMIER

120 GREAT LITHOGRAPHS

EDITED BY

Charles F. Ramus

DOVER PUBLICATIONS, INC.
NEW YORK

To My Wife,
Katherine Davis Ramus

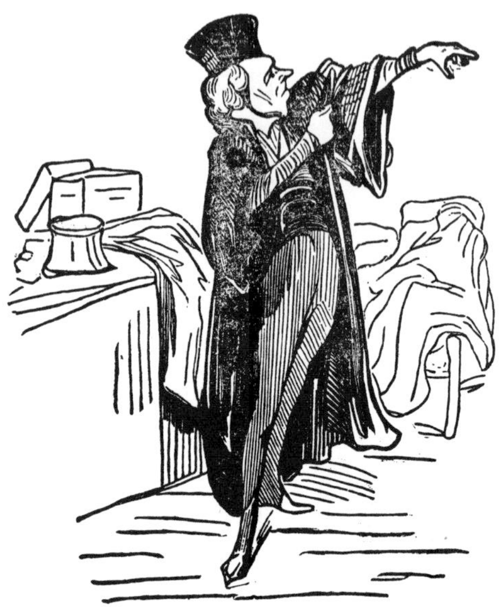

"Lawyer Pulling Up His Sleeve." B.155. From *Le Charivari,* Apr. 15, 1839.

Published in Canada by General Publishing Company, Ltd., 30 Lesmill Road, Don Mills, Toronto, Ontario.
Published in the United Kingdom by Constable and Company, Ltd.

Daumier: 120 Great Lithographs is a new work, first published by Dover Publications in 1978.

International Standard Book Number: 0-486-23512-2
Library of Congress Catalog Card Number: 77-83928

Manufactured in the United States of America
Dover Publications, Inc.
180 Varick Street
New York, N.Y. 10014

LIST OF ILLUSTRATIONS

mother is in the heat of composition), from *Les Bas-bleus*

45. Monsieur, pardon si je vous gêne ("Pardon me, sir, if I disturb you"), from *Les Bas-bleus*
46. Femme de lettre humanitaire (Humanitarian woman of letters), from *Les Bas-bleus*
47. Mon cher ami, ne croyez pas ("My dear friend, don't think"), from *Les Carottes*
48. Ce qu'on appelle dîner au restaurant (What is known as dining in a restaurant), from *Les Etrangers à Paris*
49. Grandes eaux à Versailles (All fountains on at Versailles), from *Les Etrangers à Paris*
50. Mon cher monsieur, il m'est absolument impossible ("My dear sir, it is absolutely impossible for me"), from *Les Gens de justice*
51. Il défend l'orphelin et la veuve (He defends the orphan and the widow), from *Les Gens de justice*
52. Grand escalier du Palais de justice (Main staircase of the Palace of Justice), from *Les Gens de justice*
53. Le danger de vouloir visiter (The danger of choosing to visit), from *Pastorales*
54. Et dire que c'est aujourd'hui la St Médard! (And to think that today is Saint Médard's Day!), from *Pastorales*
55. Une course au coucou (A trip in the post-chaise), from *Pastorales*
56. Un jeune homme en train d'acquérir (A young man in the process of acquiring), from *Professeurs et moutards*
57. C'est demain la fête de sa femme (Tomorrow is his wife's birthday), from *Les bons Bourgeois*
58. Dites donc, Ravignard ("Say, Ravignard"), from *Les bons Bourgeois*
59. Votre tableau me plairait assez ("I'd be quite satisfied with your picture"), from *Les bons Bourgeois*
60. Mais si, ma femme ("Oh, yes, dear"), from *Les bons Bourgeois*
61. Oh! la . . . la ("Ow . . . ow"), from *Les bons Bourgeois*
62. Un jour de congé (A day off), from *Les Papas*
63. Un père est un cheval (A father is a horse), from *Les Papas*
64. Seule manière de faire poser un enfant (The only way to make a child pose), from *Les Papas*
65. De ce côté-là vous voyez la tour ("In this direction you view the Tower"), from *Locataires et propriétaires*
66. Brigand de propriétaire ("This robber of a landlord"), from *Locataires et propriétaires*
67. Je ne loue pas aux gens qui ont des enfants! ("I never rent to people who have children!"), from *Locataires et propriétaires*
68. Nayades de la Seine (Naiads of the Seine), from *Les Baigneuses*
69. Ma p'tite me donne bien du mal ("My little one gives me plenty of trouble"), from *Les Baigneuses*
70. Tiens . . . vla un homme qui s'est déguisé en femme! ("Well! . . . there's a man disguised as a woman!"), from *Tout ce qu'on voudra*
71. Inconvénient d'avoir un parent (The disadvantage of having a relative), from *Tout ce qu'on voudra*
72. Dire que je n'ai pas pu tirer ("Just think, I haven't seen a thing to shoot at"), from *Quand on a du guignon*
73. Ma femme reste bien long-temps à ce banquet ("My wife has really been a long time at that banquet"), from *Les Femmes socialistes*
74. Un parricide (A parricide), from *Actualités*
75. Empire, Orléanisme et Légitimité (Empire, Orleanism and Legitimacy), from *Idylles parlementaires*
76. Belle dame, voulez-vous bien accepter mon bras? ("Fair lady, will you accept my arm?"), from *Actualités*
77. Un monsieur qui s'enflamme (A gentleman who gets hot), from *Les Parisiens en 1852*
78. Aux Champs-Elysées (On the Champs-Elysées), from *Croquis musicaux*
79. Oui, madame Fribochon ("Yes, Madame Fribochon"), from *Actualités*
80. Un jour où l'on ne paye pas (Free-admission day), from *Le Public du Salon*
81. Qui diable se serait jamais douté ("Who the devil would ever have suspected"), from *Actualités*
82. Bigre! . . . j'ai eu tort ("Confound it! I was wrong"), from *Actualités*
83. Des dames d'un demi-monde (Women of the half-world), from *Actualités*
84. Modes du printemps de 1855 (Spring fashions, 1855), from *Actualités*
85. Comme quoi un jour d'entrée à quatre sous (Showing how, on a day when the admission is four sous), from *L'Exposition universelle*
86. Histoire de tuer le temps (Just to kill time), from *Actualités*
87. A la Bourse (At the Stock Exchange), from *Croquis parisiens*
88. Quinze centimes un bain complet (Fifteen centimes for a complete bath), from *Croquis parisiens*
89. Le mauvais côté des nouveaux omnibus (An unpleasant aspect of the new omnibuses), from *Croquis parisiens*
90. Ayant eu la fâcheuse idée (The unfortunate idea), from *Croquis d'été*
91. Divertissement aquatique (Aquatic amusement), from *Croquis d'été*

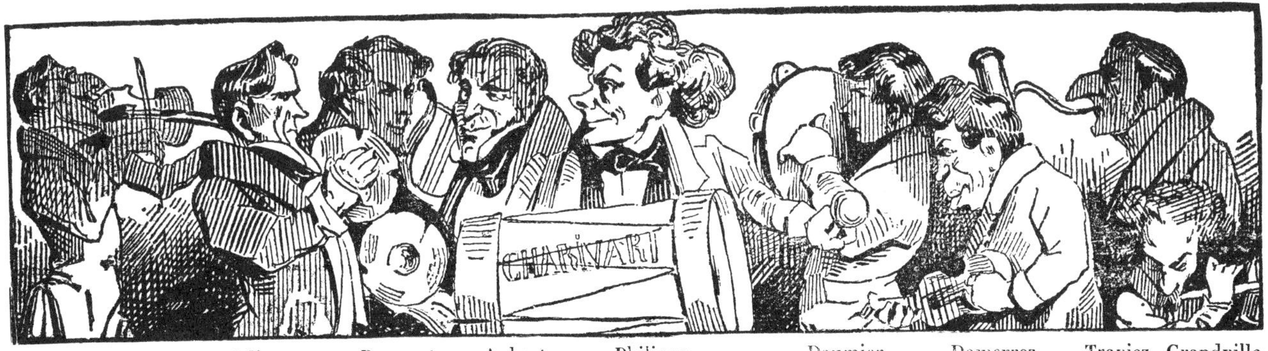

"The Orchestra of *Le Charivari*" (the masthead described on page xiv). B.6. From *Le Charivari*, Jan. 19/20, 1834.

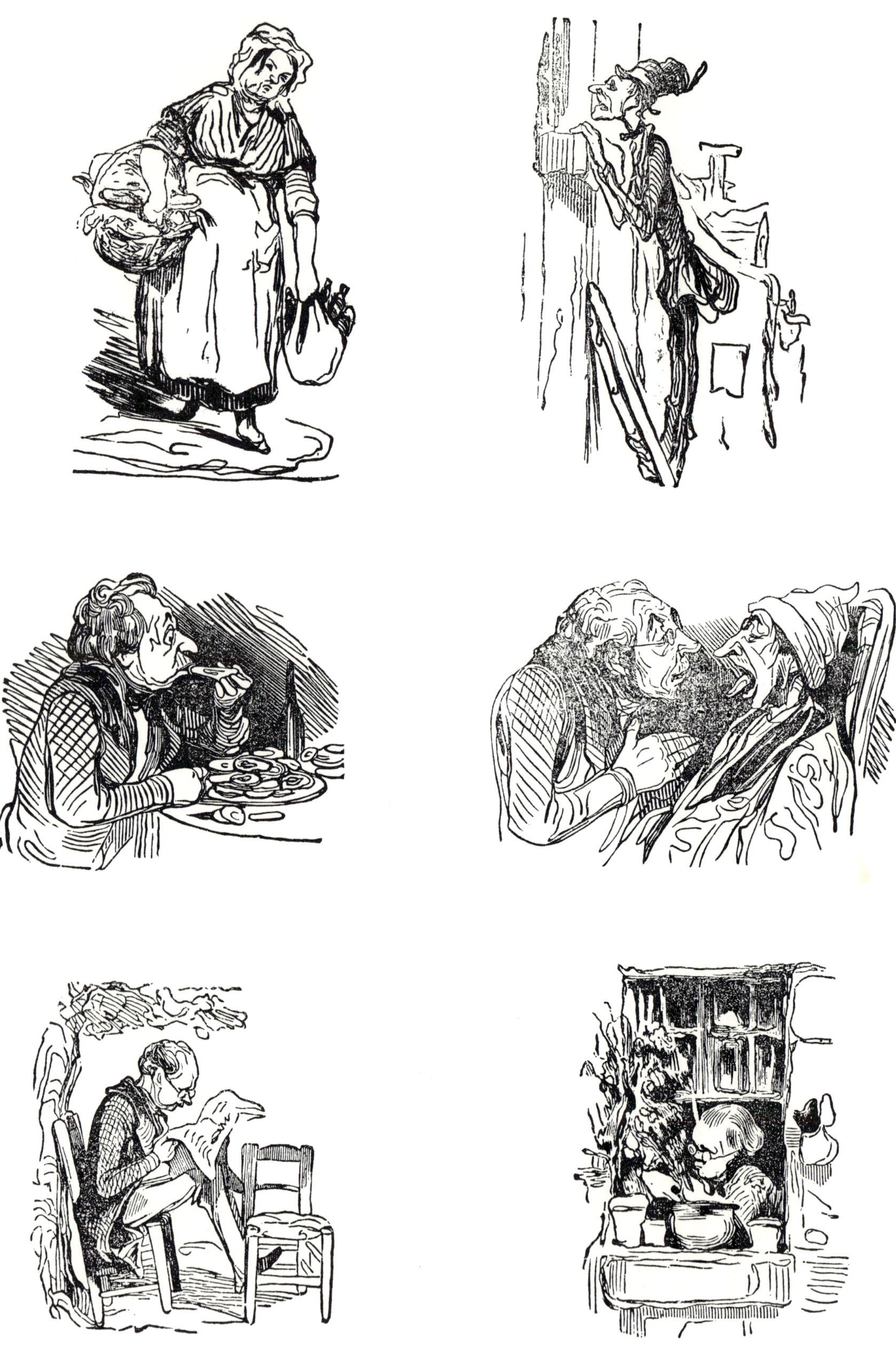

Illustrations from *Le Charivari.* TOP LEFT: "Housewife Returning from the Market." B.189. Mar. 14, 1839. TOP RIGHT: "Bertrand Bringing the Jailed Macaire Comforting Words and Files." B.251. June 29, 1839. CENTER LEFT: "Man Eating Oysters." B.146. Jan. 12, 1839. CENTER RIGHT: "Doctor and Patient." B.140. Dec. 20, 1838. BOTTOM LEFT: "Man Reading." B.249. June 28, 1839. BOTTOM RIGHT: "The Gillyflower Lover." B.198. Mar. 24, 1839. All the small figures (not the full-page plates) in this volume are wood engravings reproduced at original size. The B numbers are those of Bouvy's catalogue of Daumier's wood engravings (see Bibliography).

INTRODUCTION

Honoré-Victorin Daumier, the great French caricaturist of the nineteenth century, today is acclaimed as one of the preeminent satirists of all time. Born at Marseilles on February 26, 1808, he spent most of his life in Paris, retiring during his last months to his summer home at Valmondois outside the capital, where he died on February 11, 1879.

His father, Jean-Baptiste Daumier, a glazier, was encouraged by friends to launch out as a dramatic poet in Paris, where he went in April 1815. Toward the end of 1816 he sent for his wife Cécile, their two daughters and young Honoré. Jean-Baptiste gained some prestige and success with *Philippe II*, a tragedy performed in the winter season of 1817–1818, and also with a book of verse, *Les Veilles poétiques* (Poetic Vigils), published in 1823. In spite of the support of his friends, these activities brought in no money, and he continued his craft of glazier, with his shop on the street and living quarters at the rear. Life was very hard for this impecunious family, as seen in their ten changes of address from 1815 to 1830.

Growing up in this poor household, young Daumier, from the age of eight on, heard his father declaiming poems and rhymes upon arising in the morning, at table and upon going to bed. It was in this period, too, that Honoré began to absorb knowledge about the theater, storing away in his mind the plots of old dramas his father read aloud, just as a little later he was to observe various kinds of gestures, movements and lighting effects when he attended the playhouses. When his father's play was presented in a small theater on the Rue Chantereine, the boy of ten was present and, without a doubt, was influenced in his later work by this performance, for there he saw actors silhouetted against the darkness of the set, the Argand lamps glowing as footlights, the prompter hidden from the audience in his small box. The result of all this influence of the theater is seen in some 242 lithographs and wood engravings pertaining to stage productions and such related subjects as street singers, carnivals, circuses and puppets. Three such scenes appear in this volume as Plates 33, 96 and 104.

So far as is known, young Daumier had no education other than what he gained at home. He learned most from the streets of Paris and the Louvre Museum. He sauntered at will on the boulevards, the main thoroughfares and the blind.alleys and by observation, stimulated by his innate curiosity, he began to acquire an immense reservoir of information on people, gestures, characteristics and backgrounds. He doubtless learned to read and picked up considerable knowledge from listening to the discussions among his father's literary friends. For the rest of his life, he was to draw upon this piecemeal education.

Daumier's parents, in need of money, apprenticed him at about the age of 12 as errand boy to a notary. A Parisian urchin of this type appears in Plate 13. Among the various legends circulated about Daumier, it is said that, while working for this notary, he came in contact with the courts and at this early time acquired his lasting hatred for lawyers and judges. It is true that later, from July 1829 to May 1831, the family lived on the Rue de la Barillerie, near the Palais de Justice, where the young man had an excellent opportunity to observe these officials.

After Honoré lost his job as errand boy, his next position, gained through his father's literary connections, was that of a clerk in the Delaunay bookstore, one of the shops in the wooden galleries of the Palais-Royal, a property owned by the Duc d'Orléans, Louis-Philippe. In this bustling location the boy was able to observe the celebrities of the day.

In the period that followed, Daumier became more and more infatuated with art. Determinedly, he informed his parents that he wanted to become a painter. They were greatly concerned about his arguments and finally consulted the family friend Alexandre Lenoir, to whom Jean-Baptiste had dedicated a poem. Lenoir, founder and director of the Musée des Monuments Français, was distinguished in the art world not only as an archeologist, collector and connoisseur, but as a minor artist and follower of Jacques-Louis David. Heartily approving the young Daumier's decision and accepting him as pupil, he introduced Daumier to ancient, medieval and Renaissance art, and also to the work of Michelangelo, Rubens and Rembrandt, all of whom became idols of the young painter. Lenoir's teaching was academic, fundamentally sound, but dry. He set Honoré to copying Roman sculpture, particularly casts from Trajan's Column. Daumier soon tired of drawing casts and, preferring to work on his own with younger artists, entered the Académie Suisse, where for three hours each morning he learned to draw from live models. A classmate was Denis-Auguste Raffet, who acquainted him with the work of Nicolas-Toussaint Charlet, whom art students venerated as the lithographer of Napoleon's campaigns. Daumier also spent some time at the Atelier Boudin, working there, too, from live models. He still continued to haunt the Louvre and observe prints in shops and in the stalls of the *bouquinistes* along the quays of the Seine. Such prints as those by Louis-Léopold Boilly, Francisco Goya and Carle and Horace Vernet inspired him and taught him much.

When he was 14, Daumier began to make lithographs. This process, invented in 1798 by the German Aloys Senefelder, utilizes the mutual antipathy of water and grease. Drawing with a grease crayon on a finely ground slab of limestone, the artist can achieve a variety of tones from silvery grays to velvety blacks, a wider range than offered in any other print medium. In 1816 Count Charles Lasteyrie had opened in Paris the first lithograph shop with hand presses. A short time later a number of other shops opened, and the new medium soon became fashionable. The printing of lithographs became an important business, although color lithography was not developed until the 1870s.

Some say that Daumier at first disliked lithography, since his principal desire was to paint. Because of economic necessity, this yearning had to be stifled until the latter decades of his life. His first two lithographs, registered at the Ministry of the Interior on April 16 and September 12, 1822, are street scenes, the first representing three soldiers before a tent show of traveling performers, the second depicting a group of soldiers outside a town hall. The latter print was crudely hand-colored, doubtless by some employee at the printer's. These two prints are listed as A and B in the Daumier catalogue of Loys Delteil, the famous French cataloguer of nineteenth-century graphics.

Edwin De T. Bechtel, the New York lawyer, writer and connoisseur of prints, credits Daumier with three additional early lithographs: a family on a Sunday afternoon stroll, which appeared on December 24, 1822; the first political subject, on May 4, 1824; and a book illustration on May 19 of the same year. These five early prints are signed with the capital letters "H. D.," somewhat ornamented with curlicues, but their authenticity has been disputed by some skeptics since they are not marked with the famous "h. Daumier" or "h. D." (with lower-case "h") which Daumier was later to adopt as his signature (there are several variations in his early years).

By 1825, Daumier was an apprentice to Zéphirin Belliard, a publisher of prints and a popular but mediocre portraitist. Like any other *rapin* (art student), Daumier had among his tasks in the studio to prepare or "grain" the lithograph stones and to clean the rooms at the end of the day. He could not have liked the work he did there, copying portraits of simpering celebrities, putting tones in areas of sentimental compositions which pandered to royalist tastes, or drawing illustrations, alphabets and rebuses for children's publications. Nevertheless, he did learn much about contrasts of tones and the drawing of physical characteristics in portraits. He also drew some illustrations for a journal edited by one William Duckett, and during this time he must have produced many unsigned works that are as yet unidentified.

From about the time he was 15, Daumier had been seen in the editorial rooms of various republican papers, where he met artists and article writers, quite possibly including Charles Philipon. In 1830, Philipon became Daumier's editor, beginning to publish his drawings on July 22 of that year. The first of these, No. 1 in Loys Delteil's catalogue (or L.D. 1, to use the form of reference we shall adopt here), appeared in *La Silhouette*, Philipon's first journal, published 1829–1830. Philipon was a free-lance artist of sorts, endowed with more ideas than talent, but acquainted with a considerable number of artists, chiefly caricaturists. With the popularity of lithography continually growing, Philipon saw an opportunity to realize some of his ideas and brought from Lyons to Paris his brother-in-law Gabriel Aubert (1787–1847), a notary who had bankrupted himself through speculations. With Philipon as his silent partner, Aubert opened a shop at No. 15 Galerie Véro-Dodat, which for many decades remained one of the most successful print shops in Paris. From September 4, 1830, Aubert was to publish the greater part of Daumier's works, either singly or in albums, separately from their appearance in journals.

After some experience in publishing *La Silhouette* (a pot-pourri magazine which featured in each issue an original lithograph by such artists as Charlet and Charles-Joseph Traviès along with satiric articles by Philipon, Balzac and others), Philipon created the weekly periodical *La Caricature*, which first appeared on November 4, 1830. Philipon gathered around him young artists and writers with republican beliefs similar to his own who formed his *équipe* or "gang." Philipon served as manager and Aubert as publisher. The first 14 issues of *La Caricature* contained such amusing illustrations as opera costumes by Eugène Forest, grotesque shadows by Grandville (Jean-Ignace-Isidore Gérard), dancing crabs by Henry Monnier and "door and window" boudoir scenes by Achille Devéria. In the eighth number, December 23, 1830, the first political subjects appeared; these were by Alexandre Decamps and Raffet and still mild in comparison with the later vituperative excoriations to be produced by Traviès, Grandville and Daumier.

During Daumier's years of study and hackwork, he had observed the gathering storm of discontent with the Bourbon Restoration of Louis XVIII and Charles X. This dissatisfaction grew out of strict censorship, countless arrests, the Jesuit domination over Charles X, and his appointment to the Council of his favorite the Prince de Polignac, a rabid royalist who conceived the infamous Ordinances of 1830, one of the principal catalysts setting off the July Revolution. The Ordinances, issued on July 25, 1830, prohibited the publication of any journal of less than 25 pages without official authorization; dissolved the Chamber of Deputies and called for new elections; and restricted the franchise to the wealthiest 25 percent of the existing electors. The journalists retaliated with a manifesto calling on all France to resist, and there followed the riots in the streets during the "Three Glorious Days" (*les Trois Glorieuses*) of July 27, 28 and 29. (The revolution was actually engineered by the maneuverings of Talleyrand and the banker supporters of the Duc d'Orléans, Louis-Philippe of the younger Bourbon line.)

Daumier probably mounted one of the barricades which sprang up during the brief July Revolution. It is said that he had a scar on his forehead from one of the skirmishes against the reluctant troops of the elder Bourbon line. While the people carried on the fighting, the scheming and wily politicians pulled the strings. Charles X fled, and Louis-Philippe was made "King of the French," a somewhat less lofty title than that of earlier monarchs, who had been known as kings "of France and Navarre." The newspapers dubbed this neophyte king "the July Catastrophe" as he quickly surrounded himself with unpopular ministers and parasites, some of the usual turncoat debris, relics from 1789, from the Terror, the Directory, the Empire and the Restoration.

The Revolution of 1830 gained two important objectives: freedom from the dull, narrow-minded, Church-dominated royal court, and the relaxation of the censorship of Charles X's reign. During the several months required for the July Monarchy to become partially stabilized, the new regime was cautious where newspapers were concerned, particularly in August while the new Chamber of Deputies was rewriting the Charter. The government at first took care to observe one of the main provisions of the new Charter in regard to the press, that "every Frenchman has the right to express his opinions." Daumier and others took full advantage of this respite from censorship to draw many caricatures which previously would have been considered seditious. Among the 39 lithos Delteil lists as Daumier's before he joined the staff of Philipon, several had not been allowed to be published.

Daumier's first depiction of the new king showed Louis-Philippe shearing a flock of Republican sheep (L.D. 18). In another early caricature (L.D. 24), a Bonapartist mob around the Vendôme Column is being dispersed by Marshal Lobau squirting syringes. Actually, fire hoses were used, for the first time in history in such an incident. The syringe became one of the many symbols used to characterize the new ruler and his July Monarchy.

Louis-Philippe's reign was also to become known as the Juste-Milieu, the happy medium or middle-of-the-road regime, with the King preferring to do nothing rather than to arouse any dangerous situations. Proud of his rule of moderation, he stated in a speech in 1831: "We must not only cherish peace, we must avoid everything that might provoke war. As regards domestic policy, we will endeavor to maintain a *juste milieu*."

Within a few months, criticisms of the July Monarchy began to appear in the editorial pages of Philipon's weekly *La Caricature*, one of the three journals in Paris at that time that represented the opposition, the other two being the large dailies of power and authority, *Le National* and *La Tribune*. A little later *Le Charivari* was to join them, along with many smaller sheets that acted as gadflies biting at the usurping regime. Of them all, *La Caricature* was the most formidable, vitriolic and trenchant attacker of Louis-Philippe and his henchmen. The censors sent police almost daily to raid Aubert's newspaper offices and gallery, while several printers kept him supplied with more works of art to sell in order to pay the mounting fines. By August 1831 the republican papers had suffered 281 seizures, 251 trials, sentences totaling 1226 months and fines totaling 347,550 francs.

In its existence of almost five years, from November 4, 1830, to August 27, 1835, *La Caricature* published every Thursday an issue of four pages of text, with many sarcastic articles written by Philipon and his staff, plus a column titled "Pochades" (Rough Sketches), chiefly concerning current events. Each issue also contained two original lithographs printed on fine white paper (*blanc de chine*). These 524 lithos, some hand-colored as was the practice in the nineteenth century, were declared by Philipon to be "masterpieces" which he said were bound to increase in value. In most issues of *La Caricature*, Philipon gave an explanation of the litho along with the name of the artist. He failed to do so only when he was in prison serving one of his many sentences for "exciting contempt for the government and insulting the person of the King."

Philipon himself contributed ten drawings to *La Caricature*. One of his early abusive blasts, not published in the paper but offered for sale at Aubert's during the first week of May 1831, was titled "Soap Bubbles." It was an exasperating delineation of soap bubbles evaporating in the air, each labeled as one of the

"Promises of July" (1830). In reply, the police raided the print shop and confiscated the stone, and Philipon was brought to trial for sedition.

In his trial Philipon and his lawyer, reiterating that freedom of the press had been promised by the July Monarchy, insisted: "The pen is free, the crayon ought to be. . . . The promises of July have been a cruel hoax." The trial dragged on for months, with the day-to-day proceedings reported at great length by Philipon in *La Caricature*. Proclaiming as his motto "War on the abuses," Philipon protested: "It is the mission of caricature to probe, to investigate the ridiculous, to do justice." Nevertheless he was sentenced to prison in mid-July 1831.

During one of his numerous trials (November 14, 1832) Philipon quickly sketched a four-part transformation sequence, changing a front view of Louis-Philippe into a pear with a face by cleverly incorporating the king's wig and side whiskers as stem and leaves. This greatly amused the jury (*poire* means "fool" in French as well as "pear") but, although Philipon maintained that the pear was not an insult, that no limit should be placed on the freedom of artists and that there were similar resemblances to be found throughout nature, his arguments were to no avail and *La Caricature* was fined again! This symbol of Louis-Philippe was to become famous as an illustration in history books for generations to come.

Philipon's contribution to French journalism lies in his use of lithography as a medium for satiric caricature. He is also noted for his astute guidance and ability as an "idea man" for all his artists and writers. With his creative imagination and uncanny news sense, combined with a tenacious and combative persistence, he was one of the most resourceful of journalists. He continually invented for his papers new twists in lampooning the King and his confederates. In research of the articles, letters and columns that appeared in Philipon's several papers, the present writer has gleaned nearly 500 different references to Louis-Philippe, some merely pointed allusions easily understood at the time because of current events and popular phrases, others direct attacks as "the Crowned Pear," "the Muzzler of Liberty," "the Ugly Ogre of the System," "the Frightening Thought," "the Fatted Ox," "the Master Miser." One of the epithets, *Monsieur Chose*, can be translated as Mr. Nothing, Mr. What's-His-Name or Mr. Thingumbob, while the monarch, depicted in various occupations, was also dubbed "the Grocer," "the Farmer King" (clodhopper), "the Clown," "the Bleeder-Surgeon" and "the First Acrobat of Europe." Among many other terms Philipon contrived with which to bombard the hated regime were "the Financial Monarchy," "the Insatiable System" and "this paternal government under which we have the good fortune to be unfortunate."

The first record of Daumier's full acceptance on Philipon's staff is the rare lithograph "Gargantua" (L.D. 34), reviving the hero of the famous satire by Rabelais. The subject matter of this scatological rendering of a fat, pear-headed glutton seated on an enema chair in the Place de la Concorde (the Palais de Bourbon, where the Deputies met, is seen in the background) may have been conceived by the clever mind of Philipon, but the drawing shows the artist's own growing awareness of balanced composition and interpretation, and the print is signed with his soon-to-become-famous "h. Daumier."

"Gargantua" was published by Aubert and exhibited briefly for sale in the window of the print shop, with the words in the top margin "La Caricature (*Journal*)" and at the bottom "on sale at Aubert's." In the second state all these words were eliminated. Aubert must have withheld the publication of this lithograph from *La Caricature* for fear of another trial for the journal. In fact, after the print first appeared, on December 15, 1831, raids on Aubert's shop occurred for three days, the prints being seized by the "Gisquetaires," the police under Chief Gisquet. Daumier was brought to trail in February 1832, and given a sentence of six months in Sainte-Pélagie, the prison for political offenders, where Philipon had already been serving his sentences. Daumier's sentence was postponed but, like the publisher Aubert and the printer Delaporte, he was fined 500 francs.

The period between this trial for "Gargantua" and his actual arrest saw several of Daumier's political satires (L.D. 35–39) offered by Aubert but quickly censored and not allowed to appear in the paper. *La Caricature*, however, succeeded in printing a few others (L.D. 40–49). Doubtless, most of these works were created at Philipon's suggestion.

It is quite possible that Daumier might never have served a sentence for the publication of "Gargantua," but with the appearance of "The Washermen" (L.D. 39), after several other censored prints, his trial was revived. "The Washermen," printed on August 22, 1832, showed the Attorney-General Persil scrubbing the tricolor flag of the Republic while the minister d'Argout of the famous nose and old Marshal Soult hold the corners of the flag. The caption reads: "The blue will be all right, but this damnable red sticks like blood!" (An all-white flag was a symbol of the Bourbon monarchy.)

In its August 30 issue, *La Caricature* stated that Daumier had been arrested at his home in the Place de la Grève on August 27, before the eyes of his father and mother, of whom he was the sole support. He was taken to Sainte-Pélagie but was transferred to the private prison-hospital of Dr. Pinel through the influence of Philipon, who by this time was also serving a sentence there.

In that same August of 1832, just as Daumier was about to enter the prison and Philipon was recuperating at Dr. Pinel's, the manager's third publication, *L'Association mensuelle lithographique*, came off the press. Philipon had announced this new monthly in the pages of *La Caricature*. Subscribers would pay 12 francs a year and would receive every month a large lithograph with explanation. Philipon stated that he was initiating this project to build up a reserve fund to cover fines assessed against all the republican papers, since the government continued to ignore the new Charter's provision for freedom of the press. He further adivsed subscribers to look upon this as an investment, for in years to come the prints would be worth many times the modest charge of one franc! The first number of *L'Association* appeared with a sketch by Grandville, while five of Daumier's lithos were included in the 24 issues. The final issue, that of September 1834, contained his powerful "Rue Transnonain" (Plate 8).

Philipon, writing his weekly columns from Dr. Pinel's, began to call Daumier his "collaborator" and continued working out details of more projects to keep Daumier busy and his hand in practice. It is likely that Daumier then began the series of drawings for the wood-engraved mastheads to be used in the new daily *Le Charivari* (the term signifies a noisy, jangling mock serenade intended to harass an unliked party). While encouraging Daumier to prepare more drawings, Philipon was polishing up his rough ideas for this new four-page paper, which would have articles similar to those in *La Caricature*, columns by various writers and an original lithograph every day. An advance notice of this coming publication appeared in *La Caricature* on November 8, 1832.

Fired with enthusiasm after his release from Dr. Pinel's in January 1833, Daumier was more than ever the implacable enemy of the "majestic potentate" and his regime. He returned at once to lithographing the two lengthy series of portraits of the eminent men surrounding Louis-Philippe (a few of these bust portraits had already appeared in *La Caricature*, announced by Philipon as the beginning of a complete Gallery of Celebrities). As models for these drawings of the important ministers and deputies whom *La Tribune* had dubbed "the improstituted," Daumier had produced some 36 small busts in clay, exaggerating the outstanding features of each.

Stories have been circulated that Daumier sat in the press gallery of the Chamber of Deputies, clay in hand, forming these caricatured images. It is more likely that, as stated by the art critic Philippe Burty, who claimed to have heard it directly from Daumier, the artist modeled the busts from memory in his studio, where he also colored them. Maurice Gobin, in his *Daumier sculpteur*, relates that the busts were molded in raw earth and not baked but only dried, and it is surprising that they could have endured as well as they have. After using them as models for his lithographs, Daumier left them at the office of *La Caricature* for the use of other staff artists. This was at the request of Philipon, who was reported to have paid Daumier 15 francs each for the sculptures. Upon Philipon's death, his family kept the busts for some time, later selling them to the Parisian art dealer Maurice Le Garrec, whose family still owns them. Today these small models, ranging in size from four to nine inches, are extremely fragile, but fortunately have been cast in bronze in several editions.

In Daumier's lithographs based on these models, one notices the deep shadows accentuating knobby cheekbones, sharp noses and jutting chins. These interpretations are powerful and distilled representations of reality. In contrast to Daumier's portraits of these men, their academic counterparts in the Musée de Versailles, painted by Salon prize-winners of that time, present little more than idealized facades.

For many of the bust lithographs, Daumier contrived a symbolic coat of arms, sarcastically detailing the person's characteristics; these allusions and innuendoes were quite possibly suggested by Philipon. One of the most scathing depictions is that of André Dupin (Plate 2). Although only five of the bust portraits appeared in *La Caricature*, the series was continued in Philipon's new paper, *Le Charivari*, while the series of standing portraits, following the same sculptured models, ran for some time in *La Caricature*, though not consecutively.

Philipon had begun publication of his new daily journal, *Le Charivari*, on December 1, 1832. From this time on until his retirement 40 years later, Daumier was a constant contributor, except for the short period in the 1860s when he was temporarily dismissed. The early issues of *Le Charivari* were smaller than the tabloid size of *La Caricature*, containing four pages of text with some theater listings and two half-columns of terse comments titled "Carillon" (meaning a scolding or a noisy upbraiding) and "Echos" (this was a brief synopsis of current happenings). Both columns, succinctly edited, added continuously to the uproar the paper was causing; the squibs in "Carillon" are as fine examples of satire as are Daumier's trenchant and pithy caricatures.

It took clever planning to have *Le Charivari* appear regularly every morning. It was necessary to have an abundant supply of already printed lithographs, which at that time of course were printed singly. Among the principal artists contributing to Philipon's papers were Traviès and Grandville, whose work throws into relief the greater prints by Daumier. Political caricatures, on the average of two each week, alternated with views of cities and illustrations of current novels and plays. With a deadline schedule worked out weeks in advance, the editors could draw upon a vast supply of illustrations on various subjects and yet be ready for abrupt changes with the turn of events.

Because of the continuing increase in fines and the costs of labor and paper, Philipon experimented with many methods for cheaper and faster reproduction of the drawings for his papers. For some of his contributions to *Le Charivari*, Daumier began to use a lithographic ink called tusche for drawing on the stone; this gave a faster covering than the grease crayon for large dark areas.

Daumier's drawings for ten mastheads of *Le Charivari* began to appear in late 1833. These drawings on end-grain woodblocks were finished by professional engravers, as in the German Gothic period. Each masthead was used about a week at a time for several months during that winter. The woodblocks were later cut up, and details from them used for a long time afterwards as tailpieces and text fillers in books and other publications. The drawings included heads and shoulders of groups of the "improstituted" rascals in the government, except for one depicting the staff of the paper, Philipon's "gang." This wood engraving, "The Orchestra of *Le Charivari*; Nine Characters," appeared as a masthead for the paper in January 1834, with the names of the staff included: Forest, Julien, [Auguste] Bouquet, Aubert, Philipon in the center beating the drum, Daumier with tambourine, [Auguste] Desperrets, Traviès and Grandville.

In August 1834, Philipon again stepped up his vilifications of the "King of the Barricades" and his court, and *Le Charivari* began to include in the left margins of the "Carillon" column some minute wood engravings alongside many paragraphs, adding a visual impact to the biting comments on the regime. These tiny pieces, averaging less than half an inch square, were drawn and engraved anonymously, and were used repeatedly to symbolize Louis-Philippe and his confederates. Often the design is a pear with a top hat, a pear with an umbrella, a pear riding a bony nag, a crowned pear, a pear on a platter, a large frog on a leaf. The King's son Ferdinand is represented either as a scared rabbit running or as a peacock brandishing a sword. The two crossed syringes indicate Lobau, head of the National Guard. A powdered wig or a plumed bicorne hat denotes a Peer, the Scales of Justice a judge or lawyer, while various patterns of scissors stand for the continuing censorship. (Examples of Daumier's wood engravings appear in the text pages of this volume.)

On July 28, 1835, an attempt was made to assassinate the King, on his way with his entourage to a review. The radical Corsican Joseph-Marco Fieschi had constructed his "infernal machine," a battery of rifles arranged to fire all at once from a window as the King passed by. Louis-Philippe was only slightly bruised by a shot and escaped serious injury, although some 40 other persons were killed or wounded. This incident, along with the relentless war still being waged by Philipon and the other remnants of the republican press (the long trials of the defendants in a riot of April 1834 were still going on), was the final triggering off for the passage of the harsh September Laws. These laws of September 9, 1835, forbade any insult to the King, any arousal of hate or scorn of his person or of his constitutional authority, any attack against the government established by the Charter of 1830 or adherence to other forms of government, even the taking of the title of "republican." Imprisonments and fines were specified so that juries could decide on the punishments by simple majority. No paper or magazine was allowed to publish without depositing a bond, and no design—engraving, lithograph, medal or stamp—no emblem of whatever nature might be published, exhibited or put on sale without authorization of the Minister of the Interior. The restrictions applied likewise to any theatrical or similar entertainments, which would also require official authorization. Louis Blanc, in his history of the first ten years of Louis-Philippe's reign, sums up the effect of this censorship:

> The laws of September deprived accused persons of their most precious security against injustice. They falsified, rendered null and void, the institution of the jury. They brought within the same culpable category the actual commission of a crime and the discussion of a theory. They converted the power of the press into a weapon exclusively available to the wealthy bourgeoisie, stripping the poor man and his sacred interests of every possible organ of defense. A fine consummation of the glorious Revolution of July!

In August 1835 Daumier's last contribution to *La Caricature* appeared (L.D. 130). Tragically it summed up the total waste of effort on the part of the people, the fighters and the journalists, and the thousands who saw their hard-won victory of 1830 juggled away by nefarious bankers and politicians for the cause of the usurper Louis-Philippe. Daumier shows three patriots emerging from their tomb, which is designated "Died for Liberty, 27, 28, 29 July, 1830"; they exclaim bitterly: "It was certainly worthwhile getting killed!"

With the disastrous September Laws, Daumier was forced to abandon the political field and shift his emphasis to subjects in the social field. Turning to the human comedy, Daumier began his production for *Le Charivari* and several other journals that eventually totaled more than 3500 lithos that gently mocked the manners and morals, the happy days and the times of sadness and tribulation, of the poor and middle classes. While the early genre subjects lacked the powerful drawing of his brilliant portraits and his abusive political caricatures, they were carefully done, and the many different series soon began to show more freedom in drawing. As for his portraits of politicians, Daumier molded a number of small figurines of ordinary citizens to use as models for his drawings. Gobin's catalogue of Daumier's work shows some

19 of these sculptures, which obviously provided details of dress, gestures and poses that would appear in various lithographs.

One of the first genre series was *French Types*, not original in subject matter since other artists before Daumier, such as the sixteenth-century Swiss Jost Amman, had drawn tradesmen and craftsmen. The first print in the series, "The Little Law Clerk" (Plate 13), is one of the best, while "The Public Scrivener," "The Cook" and "The Butcher" give a good idea of its continuation. Daumier contributed two drawings a week on the average to *Le Charivari*, where, as in the earlier issues, his delightful lithos were found side by side with a miscellany by other artists: cityscapes, views, sentimental trivia and scenes from current dramas and novels, most of no great artistic worth. At times months separate the start and the end of a Daumier series, and often several series overlap. This is the case with *Sketches of Expressions*, which ran from January 1838 through March 1839, overlapping both *Caricaturana* and *Course in Natural History*.

The long series of *Caricaturana*, 100 lithos comprising the overall career of Robert Macaire, was begun by Daumier on August 20, 1836, and continued to November 25, 1838. Unfortunately, this famous series is at times somewhat tedious because of the lengthy captions concocted by Philipon. Without the superb drawings, the series would be almost uninteresting today. While it was running in *Le Charivari*, this set, depicting the typical business promoter, was extremely popular since a money-making craze was sweeping over France.

Because the reign of Louis-Philippe saw a great expansion of industry, many new businesses were springing up, while citizens were following the dictum uttered by François-Pierre-Guillaume Guizot during the Restoration: "Enrich yourselves!" There was great plundering of the public by this "kingdom of bankers," as Philipon called the governmental system. The financial mischief and skullduggery of the period were admirably displayed by Robert Macaire, adroit swindler, and his stooge Bertrand. The character of Robert Macaire, the archetype of charlatans, first portrayed by the talented and inventive actor Frédérick Lemaître, became through Daumier's drawings one of the most important caricatural symbols of the nineteenth century, the confirmation of the existence of widespread corruption in the governmental and business worlds.

The saga of Robert Macaire grew out of the melodrama *L'Auberge des Adrets (auberge* = inn), a stilted and boorish play which opened at the Ambigu-Comique in 1823. The colorless leading role was assigned to Lemaître, who, constantly adding changes in costumes and lines, made the role a great success. In this play and his own later play *Robert Macaire*, Lemaître enlarged his interpretation from that of a ragged tramp, a common thief with tattered frock coat and patched pants, to that of the dapper confidence man, the financial schemer, the juggler of joint-stock companies. Despite the September Laws which prohibited papers like Philipon's *La Caricature* and plays like Lemaître's *Robert Macaire*, the significance of the character could not be wiped out, and all speculation, peculation and corruption came to be known as "Macairism."

In his Daumier anthology *Financial and Businessmen*, Jean Adhémar explains the behind-the-scenes drama upon which Philipon based his captions: the big-business dealings of Emile de Girardin (1806–1881), the businessman and journalist who dipped his hand into many "get-rich-quick" schemes and founded a cheap, widely circulated paper, *La Presse*, which provided advertising for his many financial enterprises. Philipon made a studied assault upon Girardin in detailing the various chicaneries and promotions practiced by Robert Macaire. Daumier was to picture Macaire as an admirer of industry, a journalist, a vendor of mine stocks, a publisher, a stock-exchange speculator, a lawyer, a merchant of Bibles, a purveyor of all sorts of shady schemes for instant wealth (Plates 14 and 15).

Thackeray, in his *Paris Sketchbook* of 1840, was to write a penetrating appraisal of Macaire as the formidable rogue who, with a faithful companion, was

> giving the spectator a kind of "Beggar's Opera" moral. . . . The world was all before him where to choose, with no lack of opportunities for exercising his wit. There was the Bar with its roguish practitioners, rascally attorneys, stupid juries and foresworn judges; there was the Bourse with all its gambling, swindling and hoaxing, its cheats and its dupes; the Medical Profession and the quacks who ruled it alternatively; the Stage and the cant that was prevalent there; the Fashion and its thousand follies and extravagances. Robert Macaire had all these to exploit. Through all the empire, through all the ranks, the professions, the lies, crimes and absurdities of men, he made sport at will."

Daumier's *Caricaturana* lithographs were extremely popular, enjoying an unmatched success, with *Le Charivari's* subscriptions jumping to 3000 copies, while Aubert's shop was selling some 2500 individual prints and 6000 with text. The drawings, appearing in the paper two or three times a week, were already being sold in albums before the series ended, and by December 1838 the complete set of 100 in an album was offered for 45 francs in black and white or 55 francs hand-colored.

During the more than two years that Daumier worked on these lithos, he began to lose his rather dry and precise genre manner; his drawing became more loose, with added feeling, more expressive gestures, sharper accentuations. His personality as an artist began to appear under a different light, as his humanism took on a richer quality. *Caricaturana* was to become one of the most famous series he ever created.

Turning from the early influence of his classics-imbued father and his instruction under Lenoir in drawing from antique casts, Daumier had taken an anti-academic point of view. In many of the prints in the series *Sketches of Expressions* he particularly satirized the classic theater (Plate 16). The comic spoofs of mythological characters in the series *Ancient History* continue this attack upon the classic school (Plates 34–36). During the period from December 1841 to January 1843 Daumier drew several small series, *Silhouettes*, *Monomanias* and a second Robert Macaire set of 20 prints. There also appeared 15 half-length figures in *Tragico-Classical Faces*, again lampooning the classic theater.

During the 1840s, too, Daumier was producing his series on lawyers and judges which today is the favorite of print collectors, *The Men of Justice*. Daumier has often been accused of being too violent in his excoriations of the legal profession, but in these magnificent examples, as also in the lawyer prints appearing later in other series and shorter sets, he makes his caricatures superb works of art. In these versions of daily courtroom antics and corridor scenes, as well as in the watercolors and oils painted in his later life, Daumier shows the venal courts and the legal practitioners in a candid and virulent light. He portrays judges asleep during the trials, and emphasizes the arrogance of the double-tongued attorneys. In this series, Daumier is truly a member of the realist school, giving more than the mere surface procedure of a trial or the confrontation of opponents. His laughter is bitter when bailiffs search for evidence, when solicitors insult clients, when illiterate couples dictate letters to a public writer outside the courtroom, when a scornful lawyer refuses a prospective client or hypocritically defends either side (Plates 27 and 50–52).

Probably at the request of his editors at *Le Charivari*, Daumier drew a series on *The Bluestockings*, the "liberated" Frenchwomen giving their all to emulate the novelist George Sand, whom Thackeray called "our Pythoness of Paris." The French historian Dubreton wrote: "George Sand's novels had the effect of a revolution . . . but the women, not satisfied with fiction, adopted free-and-easy manners and acted George Sand literally" (Plates 44–46). Other series in the genre manner alternated and overlapped throughout this richest and most prolific peiod of Daumier's work, which continued through the latter years of Louis-Philippe's reign up to the Revolution of 1848.

This was an apparently happy time in Daumier's life, as on April 26, 1846, he married Marie-Alexandrine Dassy, a dressmaker he had known intimately for some seven years. Daumier was 38, his wife 24. He called her his Didine and introduced her briefly in several lithographs, although there is no known portrait that Daumier may have made of his wife. In a print in the *Matrimonial Customs* series (L.D. 679) the man, perhaps a self-portrait of Daumier, says, "Well, my Didine, have you had enough dancing?" and she replies, "Oh, don't talk to me any more, my legs feel as though they have left my body. . . . " She appears in a few other prints and watercolors, her character only slightly suggested. Biographers of Daumier have been fascinated with the anonymity of his wife. Jean Cherpin notes that she appears vaguely, like a will-o'-the-wisp. She is slender, demure, dignified, and never portrayed in positions of action. In some scenes she is wearing a poke bonnet and a shawl; in a snow scene she is shown front view with her hands in a muff. Daumier seems to have made her an extra in the background in some prints, very often in back view, standing straight and slim, a foil to the other women he portrayed as decrepit and ugly old hags. The marriage must have been a happy one, although their only child died. Their home was modest, and Marie-Alexandrine was a thrifty housewife.

From his studio-home in the heart of Paris, Daumier had not far to wander to observe most of the types he would memorize for his lithographs and wood engravings, the laundresses beating clothes on the river banks, the people in shops, restaurants, theaters, courts. At that time, before the great remodeling of the city by Baron Haussmann during the Second Empire, much of Paris was still a medieval city, with a labyrinth of crowded tenements and filthy streets.

Along with his observations among the people, Daumier returned often to the Louvre to see again works by his favorite artists in the Dutch and Flemish galleries. It is reported that he frequently met his friend Delacroix in front of the works of Rubens and that Baudelaire one day found him studying the El Greco canvases in the Spanish gallery. Doubtless Daumier's frequent visits to the Louvre greatly influenced his work.

There are few great artists who have been able to suggest the natural freedom of moving figures as has Daumier. From his acute observations of people, he learned to streamline their motions. The simple and economical construction in his figures parallels good journalism; he was the journalist-caricaturist, who used what today would be termed the "candid camera" approach with an odd-angle point of view. None of Daumier's drawing, in prints or in paintings, had the fashionable elegance that Gavarni incorporated so well in his drawings on the lithograph stones. Daumier could not have produced the floating ease seen in the watercolors of prostitutes and elegant mistresses that Constantin Guys so easily dashed off. He could never have conceived fantasies like those by Grandville. He was simply Daumier, the genial interpreter of commonplace subjects and commonplace people.

The latter years of the July Monarchy, overburdened with unbalanced budgets, disclosed the internal weakness of the regime and a growing dissatisfaction with the old King. The continued corruption was attacked at a number of political banquets, this agitation coinciding with an economic upheaval—a bad harvest in 1846, followed by an industrial crisis, stock-market declines and widespread unemployment. With mobs of protestors in the streets, and growing opposition to Guizot, the King, too late, dismissed his Minister of Foreign Affairs, appointing Louis-Mathieu Molé, who was replaced the next day with Thiers, but the mob had captured the Hôtel de Ville (City Hall) and advanced on the Tuileries. On the afternoon of February 24, the Revolution of 1848 was accomplished, with Louis-Philippe abdicating in favor of his grandson, the little Comte de Paris. The English historian Alfred Cobban describes the fall of the French constitutional monarchy thus: "It was the end of a regime that had been so lacking in principle that it could only be known by the name of the month of its founding, as the July Monarchy."

After the insurrection and the bloody days of June 1848, there followed the short-lived provisional government and the election of Louis-Napoléon as president, with his quick change to emperor in 1852. During this period Daumier produced two more series of the political leaders, 57 drawings of *The Representatives Represented* and 37 with the added title *Legislative Assembly*. The portraits are realistic and only slightly caricatured, with large heads attached to miniature bodies. This popular group of portraits is a cross section of the chosen representatives of the people, including the famous, the nonentities, the political hacks—the usual trouble-makers surfacing at a time of change. None of these portraits, however, is as powerful in drawing or values as Daumier's earlier portrayals of the Improstituted Deputies of the Juste-Milieu.

The Provisional Assembly, following Louis-Philippe's abdication, gave encouragement to art. It ordered a competition for a painting or a sculpture of the Republic to replace the portrait of the old King at the Hôtel de Ville. Of some 900 entries, 20 sketches were accepted in April 1848, with Daumier's canvas awarded eleventh place. Although only a preliminary sketch, "The Republic Nourishes and Instructs Her Children" poses a powerful and dignified woman seated as she nurses two small boys, while a third sits at her feet reading a book. Two commissions came to Daumier from the Ministry of the Interior, but he was dilatory in filling these orders and in 1850 was still promising to deliver his painting *The Republic*, which he never finished. It has been suggested that Daumier may have had difficulty in adjusting his eyes to such large dimensions as 14 square feet of canvas, when he had been accustomed for decades to working with the few inches of *Le Charivari*. At the same period he worked on bas-reliefs of *The Fugitives*, but this large sculpture, like many of his paintings, seemed never to reach a finished state.

In 1850 the detestable figure of Ratapoil (Hairy Rat) resembling Louis-Napoléon with his pointed beard and drooping mustache, began to appear in Daumier's lithographs as a personification of militarism (Plate 76). Ratapoil, as Daumier conceived him, was the agent-supporter of Louis-Napoléon—the propagandist, outshouting the people in his mad endeavor to engineer Louis' confirmation as President of France and, eventually, his assumption of the title of Emperor. In drawing Ratapoil, Daumier was striving to undermine the insidious popularity and "Caesarism" of Louis-Napoléon Bonaparte.

By a decree of February 17, 1852, the press was brought under a more severe control than it had known since the First Empire. No journal dealing with political or social questions was to be issued without the permission of the government; the list of press offenses was enlarged and penalties increased; those accused were to be tried without a jury; after three warnings a journal might be suspended or even suppressed. Under this strict censorship of political caricature, Daumier once again turned to the streets of Paris for the daily happenings and fads of the times, the hoopskirt craze (Plates 83, 84, 93 and 97), the Chinese vase mania, music halls (Plate 78), amateur actors (Plates 95 and 96), the new omnibuses (Plates 88 and 89), the stock exchange (Plates 87 and 92), the great excitement over the appearance of several comets (Plate 94). Daumier was filling his weekly quota of lithos with many sketches of Parisians, in winter (Plates 81 and 97), in summer (Plates 90 and 91), at the yearly art Salons (Plate 80), at the 1855 World's Fair (Plates 85 and 86).

With a temporary relaxation of the censorship, sanctioned by Louis-Napoléon, some political caricature was allowed during the Crimean War (Plate 82) in the mid-1850s, and again in 1859, when Daumier produced the album *The Good Austrians* concerning a short, bungling war in northern Italy (L.D. 3158–3185).

Also in 1859, Daumier introduced his first personal adaptation of Monnier's character Joseph Prudhomme, the typical representative of the middle class. This consummate example of bourgeois taste and manners was to reappear intermittently over several years in more than 40 Daumier drawings (Plate 105).

In February 1860, Daumier was dismissed by *Le Charivari*, "in the middle of the month," as his friend Baudelaire wrote in describing his sinking fortunes. In a March issue, *Le Charivari* thanked Daumier for the lithographs he had drawn for more than 30 years, work which, in reality, had brought much fame to the paper. While he was now free at last from "hauling his cart," as he described his journalistic labors, free to paint and create sculpture, he was to know wretched poverty for nearly two years, with his income so low that he was forced to seek odd jobs. When Etienne Carjat founded *Le Boulevard* late in 1861, he announced that Daumier was to produce a group of lithographs for the new paper. The first appeared in March 1862. There were ten drawings in all, among the best compositions Daumier had ever lithographed (Plates 99–103). While he had lost his *Charivari* income, he had gained immeasurably in his breadth of vision, his more subtle composition, his humanism and understanding of character. When Carjat's commission ended, Daumier probably was paid much less than he had been receiving from *Le Charivari*, while some of his finest watercolors produced during this period failed to sell even at the very low price of 50 francs. It was reported that toward the end of 1862 Daumier was suffering from "cruel penury" and that he was forced to sell some of his furniture, possibly to pay moving expenses from the Ile Saint-Louis to Montmartre, where a number of artists had established a new colony.

It was in the 1860s that the photographer Nadar made a number of portraits of Daumier that are the best likenesses known, although many of his artist friends had made drawings, sketches and caricatures from time to time. Most of these show that Daumier wore his dark, curly hair long (in Nadar's photographs it was beginning to gray). A fringe of beard appears under his jaws and chin, while his cheeks are clean-shaven. His high forehead, deep-set eyes, humorous mouth and determined chin contribute to the strength and intelligence of his face. His rather large nose, slightly retroussé, seems more rounded and not so pointed as in the wood-engraved caricatures Daumier drew of himself for the masthead of *Le Charivari.*

In his anthology of Daumier's medical prints, Jean Adhémar describes Daumier as being of medium height, with a strong constitution, seldom ill except for a period of exhaustion in 1858. He was known to talk very little on account of a stutter; he kept his famous short clay pipe in his mouth almost constantly to conceal this impediment. Failing eyesight and a drooping eyelid were eventually to force his retirement in 1872.

A last large series of wood engravings, drawn for the newspaper *Le Monde illustré*, ran from January 1862 to April 1869. These were reprinted several times from the original blocks for *Le Journal illustré* and for *La Presse illustrée.* The cataloguer of Daumier's wood engravings, Eugène Bouvy, credits him with a total of 991 works in this medium.

The editors of *Le Charivari*, becoming aware of how much their subscribers were missing Daumier's works and how much inferior in drawing and interpretation were the lithographs by Charles Beaumont, Cham (Amédée de Noé), Charles Jacque, Charles Vernier and others appearing in the paper, invited Daumier to return and gave a banquet in his honor. Along with his first new lithograph, on December 18, 1863, appeared the notice: "We announce with a satisfaction that will be shared by all our subscribers that our old collaborator Daumier, who for three years had left lithography in order to devote himself entirely to painting, has decided to take up again the crayon which has merited him so much success."

Among the new lithographs were four in a series *At the Brasserie*, which alternated with a series of eight pieces called *Sketches Made at the Theater.* One of the most masterful illustrations of the theater that Daumier ever drew is his "Literary Discussion in the Second Balcony" (Plate 104), which sums up all his technical skill in rendering atmosphere, the action of muscles moving under clothing and an unlimited variety of facial expressions. This is a tour de force in the best meaning of that phrase.

By 1864, Daumier began his long series warning France of war. The agitation for hostilities, aroused by national and international disturbances throughout Europe, was continuing with the Civil War in the United States and the rush of European powers for control in Mexico, South America and the Orient.

The *Current Events* Daumier produced from this time on show his last change in style. His figures and groups become more monumental, large in concept yet classically simple, stripped of all minute details, often appearing as stark silhouettes against bare backgrounds. His political lithos appeared about once a week, as he kept abreast of local elections and foreign campaigns, with continued prophetic warnings of the ever increasing danger to France from the Prussian war machine. Yet most Frenchmen ignored these graphic predictions of approaching disaster (Plates 108–114).

The relentless figure of Father Time appears often in Daumier's works during this turbulent period, while War is unmistakably depicted again and again in a helmet embellished with a large, curled plume. In one telling litho (L.D. 3656), the dogs of war represent the five nations Russia, France, England, Turkey and Prussia, each identified by typical headgear, with Prussia, as always, indicated by the spiked helmet. Russia appears a few times as a great white bear, England as John Bull or occasionally a lion. The figure of Peace, often an angel or a classical feminine figure, at last appears as the skeleton of Death in the ironic close and aftermath of the devastating Franco-Prussian War (Plate 120).

Upon the defeat of Napoléon III at Sedan in 1870, Daumier drew a huge and formidable German spiked helmet covering the entire French fort, with the caption "The Crowning of the Edifice" (L.D. 3811). Prussian King Wilhelm I is shown in January 1871 mounting the steps to his new throne at Versailles to be proclaimed Kaiser; the labeled "steps" are the prone bodies of the various small kings and rulers that Prussia had deposed (L.D. 3840).

Among the many symbolic characters Daumier bequeathed to caricaturists in future ages was his personification of France as a beautiful young woman, a majestic figure in classical attire, appearing first in *Le Charivari* in 1834, and continuing on to 1872, at times symbolizing Liberty, the Republic, the National Assembly, Universal Suffrage and the Free Press. The same statuesque figure, with a small crown, represents Europe, while in other variations she may be Justice or Peace. Opposed to this ideal figure, young and pleasing, is the old hag Diplomacy, ugly and wrinkled, who sometimes is labeled Conference, Monarchy, the Reactionary Press, or at other times represents the enemies of the moment: England, Austria or Prussia.

The remainder of Daumier's lithographs up to his retirement in 1872 chiefly cover current events: an armless Republic, commentaries on the government, taxes and reaction; Bismarck pumping gold reparations out of the soil of France; the ambitious little Thiers again rebounding into public life to become President of the new Third Republic. In one of Daumier's last prints he lays to rest two of the characters he had created, showing Basile the Jesuit, symbol of perversity and hypocrisy, supported by a crutch and holding onto the arm of Ratapoil, the embodiment of militarism, who is leaning on a club. One more print shows a French peasant, weary of wars, thumbing his nose at Ratapoil, who seemingly refuses to remain dead. Daumier's last lithograph appeared in *Le Charivari* on September 24, 1872.

Many biographers of Daumier have reported that he died in poverty, having been forced after his retirement to exist on a small government pension. Jean Cherpin, however, has made an extensive study in recent years of the five known account notebooks of Daumier, preserved in the Bibliothèque Nationale. These show his receipts from his lithographic production, the sales of pictures and drawings, and also his expenses. Since Daumier wrote but few letters, it is interesting to study his handwritten account books.

The first notebook, running from November 1837 to September 1840, lists the lithographs for that period, with the standard price received of 40 francs each, except that no payment was made when a stone was rejected by the censors. Wood engravings were sold at 50 to 100 francs each, according to their size.

The second notebook, covering September 1852 to November 1862, and the third for the period 1864 to 1872, list more lithos and expenses. The fourth, for the same period 1864 to 1872, begins to note the sale of paintings and drawings, while the fifth continues this record for the years 1875 to 1877. The notebooks are invaluable for the listings of amounts of purchases and particularly for the names of Daumier's friends, as well as those of connoisseurs and art dealers, indicating his rising fame as a painter. Some 56 works were sold between 1864 and 1868, while Daumier gave away many paintings and watercolors to his friends.

The prices of paintings sold ranged at first from 200 to 300 francs, rising by 1875 to 1000 to 1200 francs. The famous canvas *Don Quixote Chasing the Sheep* brought a record 1500 francs when acquired by Madame Bureau, the fifth account book noting this sale in October 1876. The total sales in this fifth notebook amount to 9930 francs, while there are many gaps in the listings. With his receipts from various journals for the many lithographs, Daumier's income, with his pension, may have reached 600 francs a month during his last five years. The total may have been even higher, considering that the entries in the account books were made irregularly and that some inscriptions have faded and become illegible. At the time, the average wage for a French workman was about 125 francs a month. Cherpin also points out that, without this income, Daumier could scarcely have maintained both his apartment in Paris and a summer home at Valmondois.

In October 1877, a committee of 30 important people in the world of arts and letters, with Victor Hugo as chairman, arranged an exhibition of Daumier's works. This first showing, the only one in Daumier's lifetime, opened the following spring, running from April 17 to June 15, 1878, at the Galeries Durand-Ruel. In the first room 112 lithographs were shown, with the exhibit changing weekly, while in other rooms were drawings and paintings and ten of the 1832 busts, loaned by the Philipon family. The catalogue of the exhibition listed 94 paintings and 139 drawings and watercolors. Thirteen of Daumier's friends loaned works to the show, and 66 art collectors contributed works they had acquired.

During this notable exhibition, another World's Fair was in progress in Paris, a Spanish dancer was drawing crowds, and, as Daumier's biographer Alexandre suggested, the death of Pope Pius IX earlier in the year may have kept many people away from an art exhibition. Cherpin, on the other hand, feels that Catholics may have avoided the showing because of Daumier's long association with the republican cause. At any rate, the attendance was less than expected, and a deficit of some 4000 francs remained, but the exhibition gained Daumier many favorable reviews and increased the sales of his paintings. Through the efforts of his friend Burty, the art critic, Daumier's pension of 1200 francs was raised by the Ministry of Fine Arts to 2400 francs beginning in July 1878.

It was reported that Daumier himself was unable to attend the exhibition, as he was at home recovering from surgery for cataract. Shortly after the opening, Carjat sent Daumier a letter "from your enthusiastic admirer and devoted friend," with a copy of an article he had written for his paper *La petite République*. His title for this tribute to Daumier was "the Michelangelo of the People."

Over a period of 50 years, Daumier's monumental production totaled at least 3958 lithographs (the number listed in Delteil's catalogue). In addition, nearly a thousand wood engravings are catalogued by Bouvy. Gobin credits Daumier with 65 sculptures including busts, figures and reliefs, while K. E. Maison has documented more than 300 paintings and about 858 watercolors and drawings.

Daumier had not long to enjoy his increased income and fame. In the winter of 1878–1879, he and Madame Daumier gave up the apartment in the city and moved to Valmondois. It was there that he suffered a severe attack of apoplexy and died on February 11, 1879. He was buried at Valmondois on February 14. Since Daumier had expressed a desire to rest near his friend Corot, who had died in February 1875, his remains were transferred to the Père Lachaise cemetery in Paris on April 16, 1880. His wife was also buried there upon her death in 1895. The translation of the epitaph on the tomb reads:

PEOPLE
Here lies DAUMIER, Man of good,
The great artist, the great citizen.

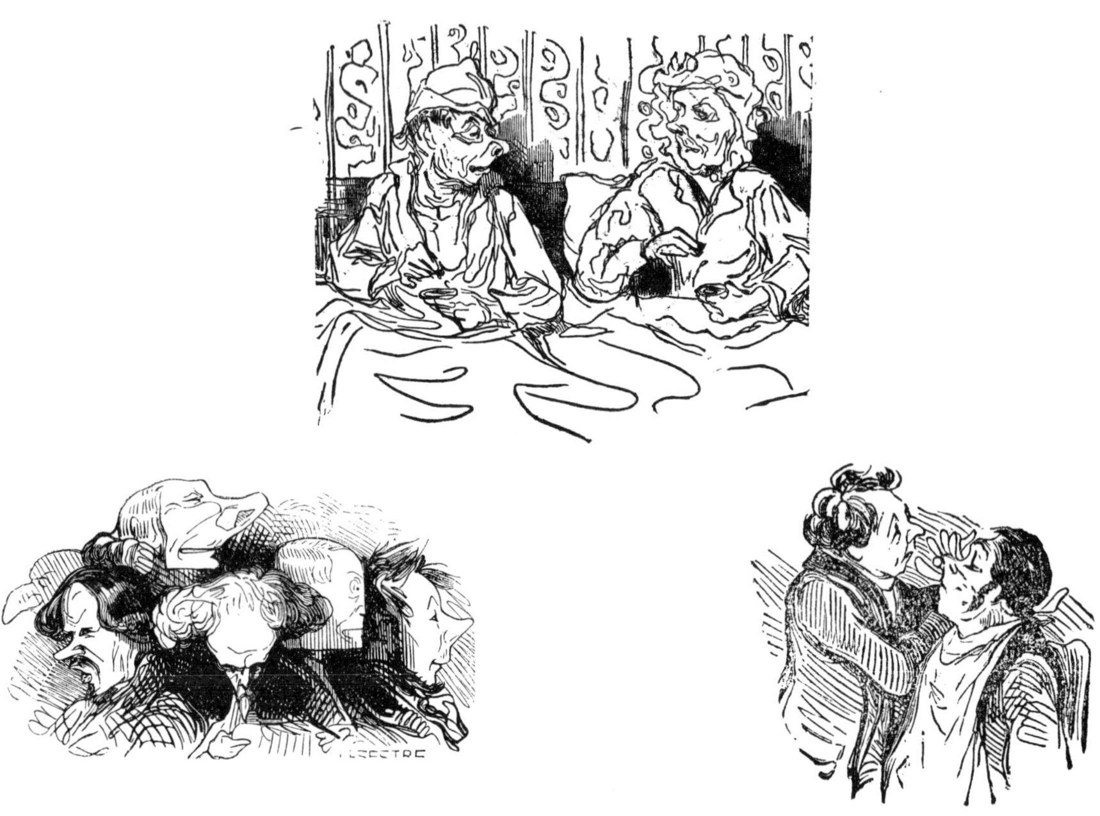

ABOVE: "Married Couple in Bed Taking Snuff and Chatting." B.268. From *Le Charivari*, Sept. 26, 1839. BELOW, LEFT: "A Spry, Spruce and Snappy Set of Strappers" (caricature of the *Charivari* artists Monnier, Philipon, Traviès, Grandville, Desperrets and Daumier). B.128. From *Le Siècle*, Dec. 26, 1838. BELOW, RIGHT: "Barber Shaving a Customer." B.177. From *Le Charivari*, Mar. 11, 1843.

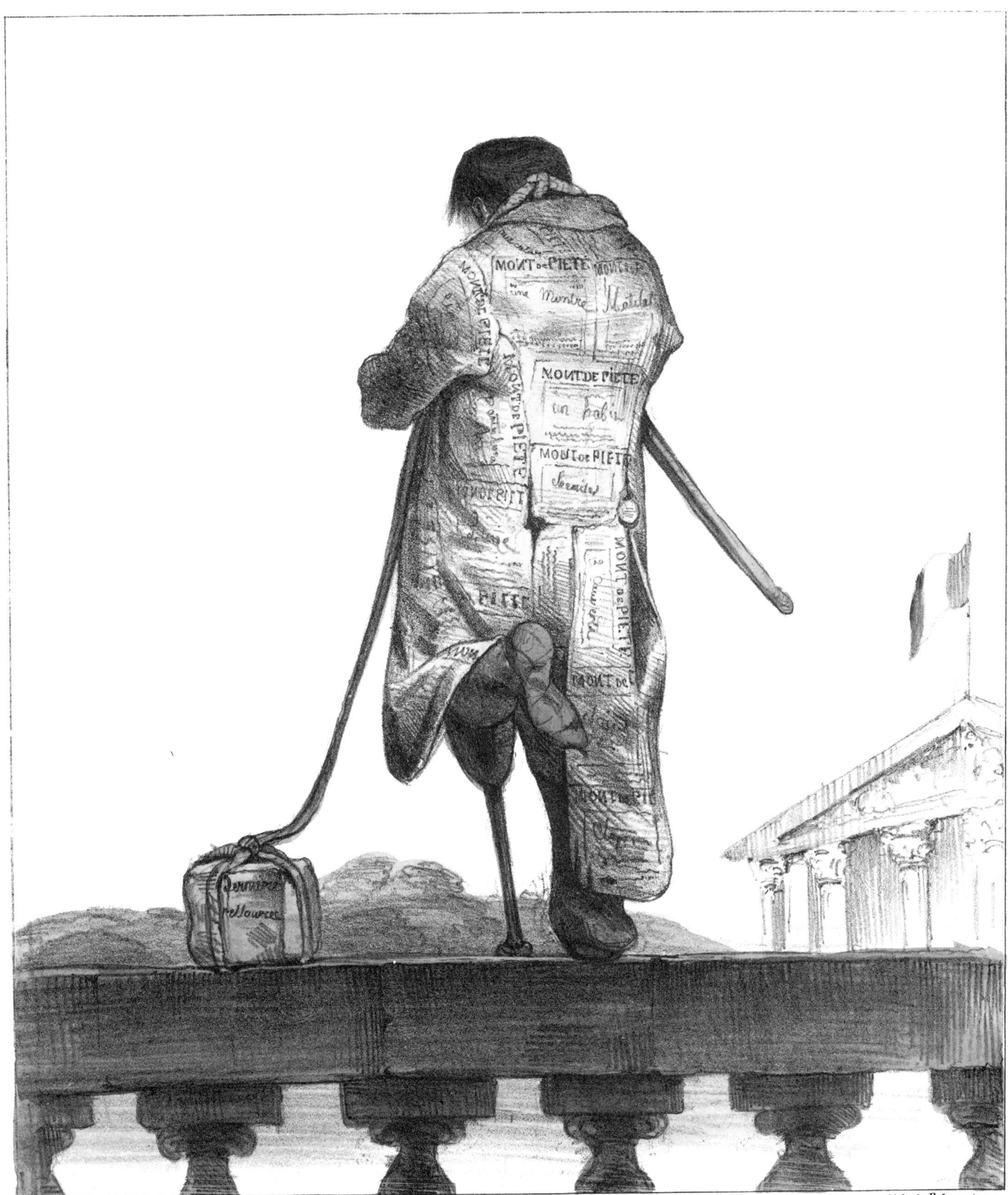

UN HÉROS DE JUILLET,
Mai 1831.

1 Less than a year after the July Revolution of 1830, an impoverished veteran of the fighting is ready to end his life in despair. [June 1, 1831]

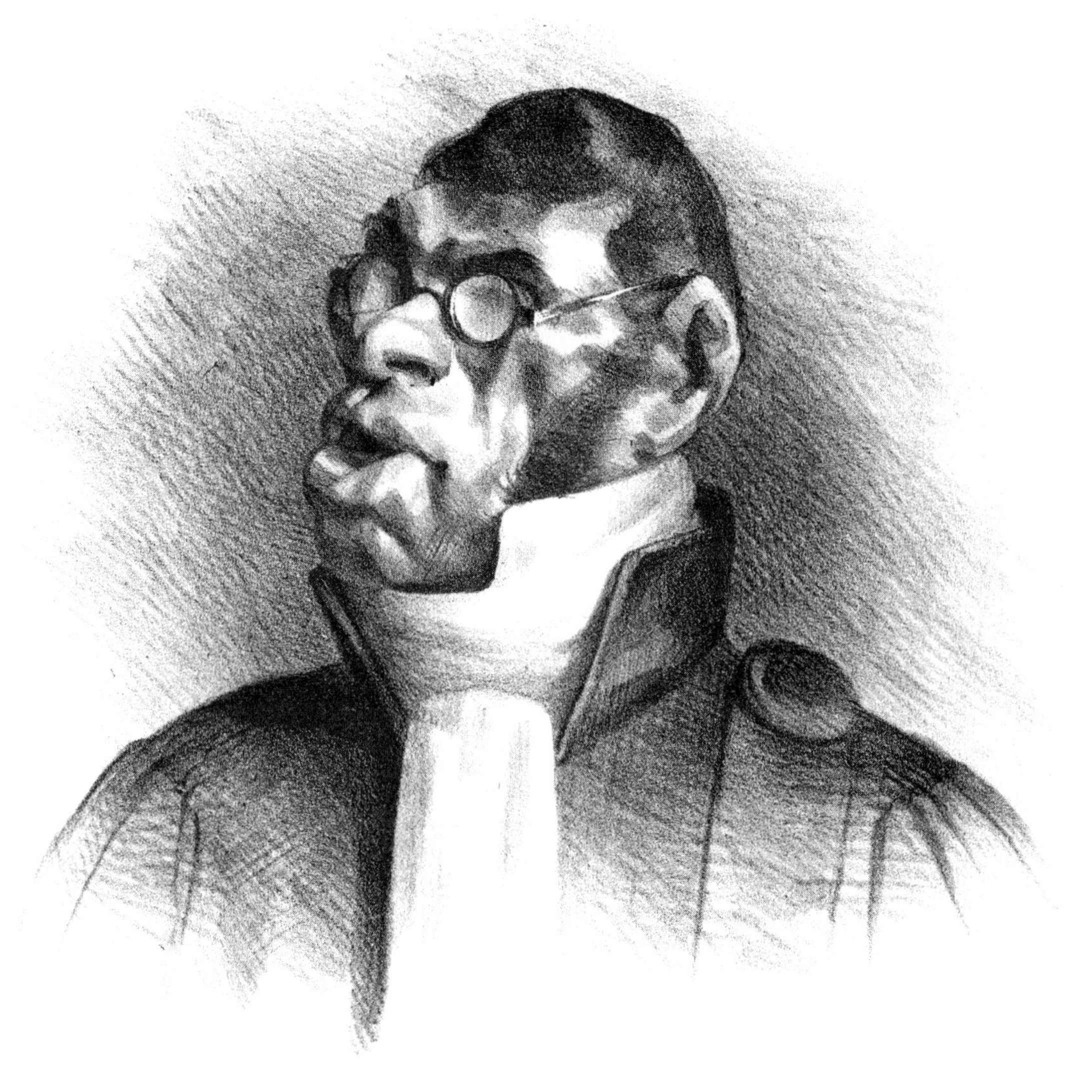

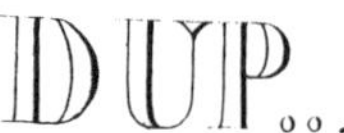

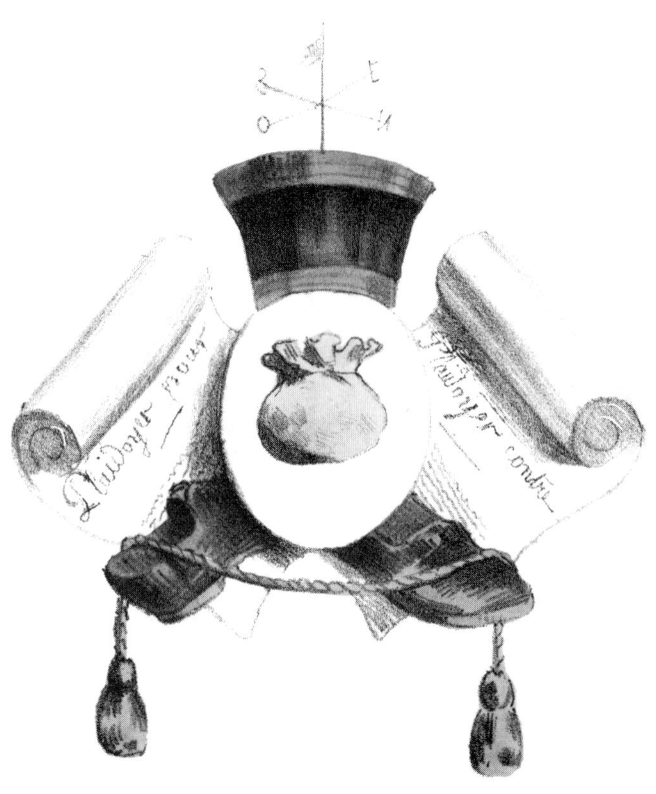

2 Caricature and humorous coat-of-arms of the politician Dupin. [June 14, 1832]

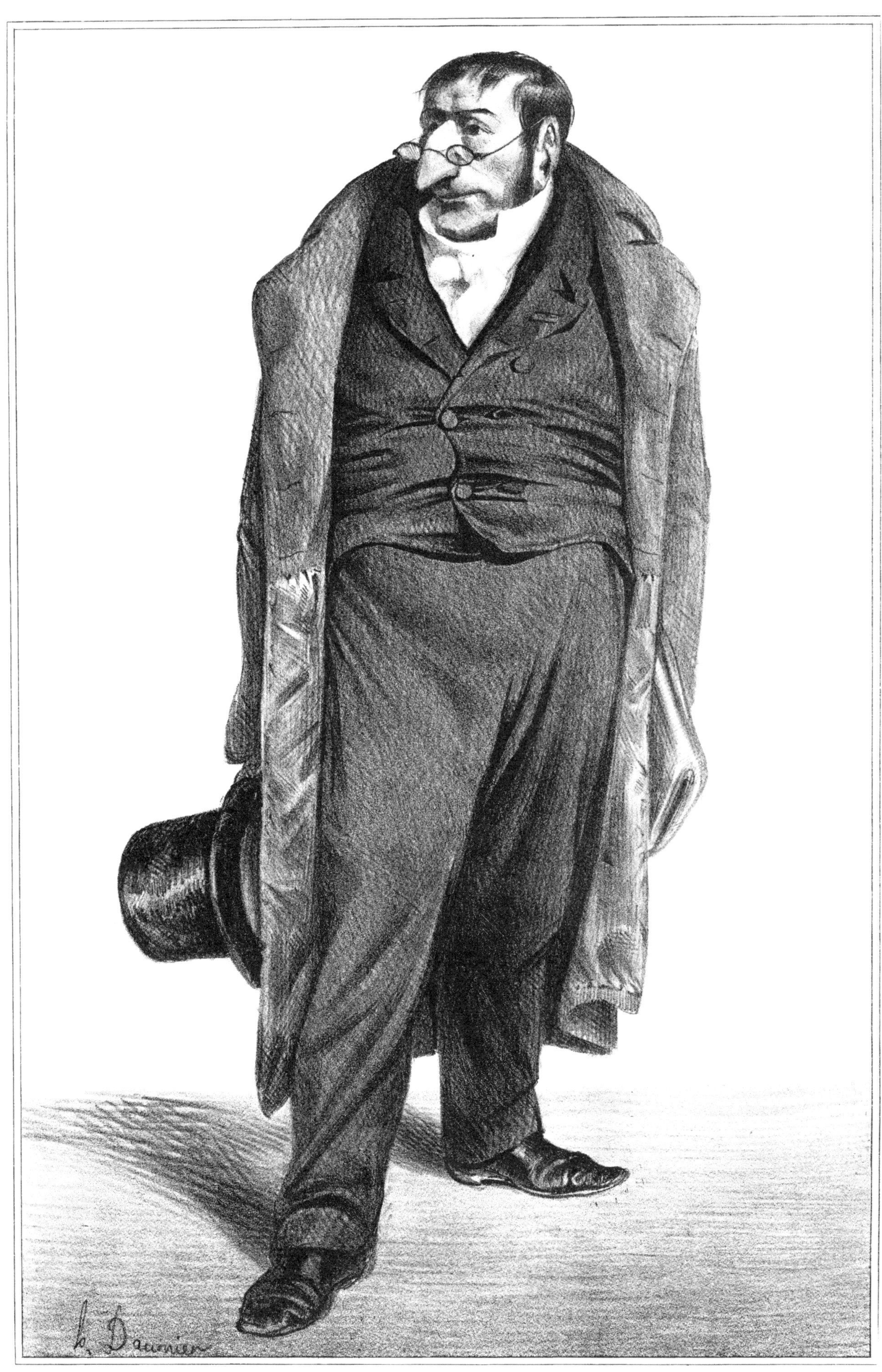

3 Caricature of the government minister d'Argout. [July 11, 1833]

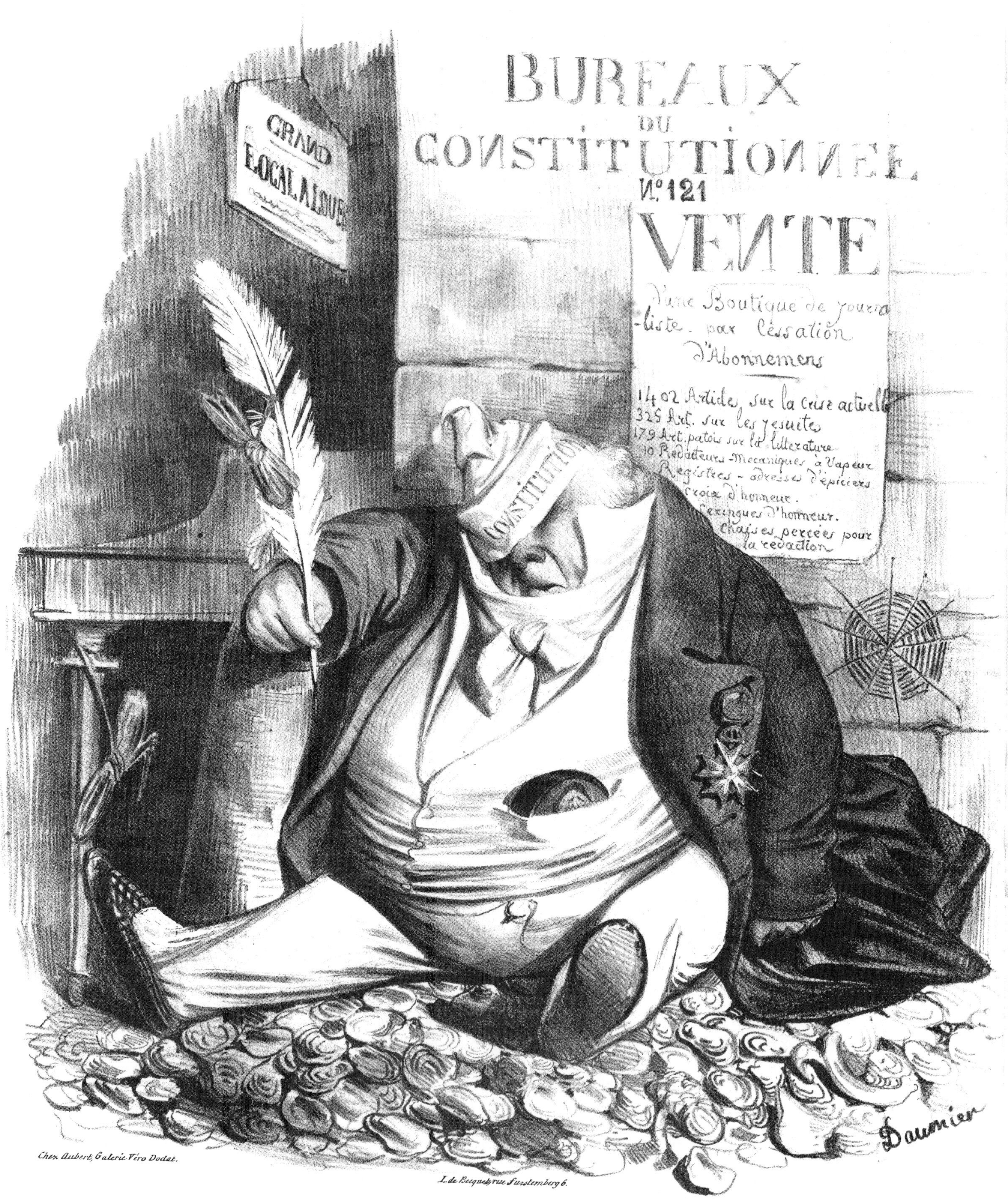

4 Satire on the reactionary paper *Le Constitutionnel* and its editor Etienne. [Oct. 22, 1833]

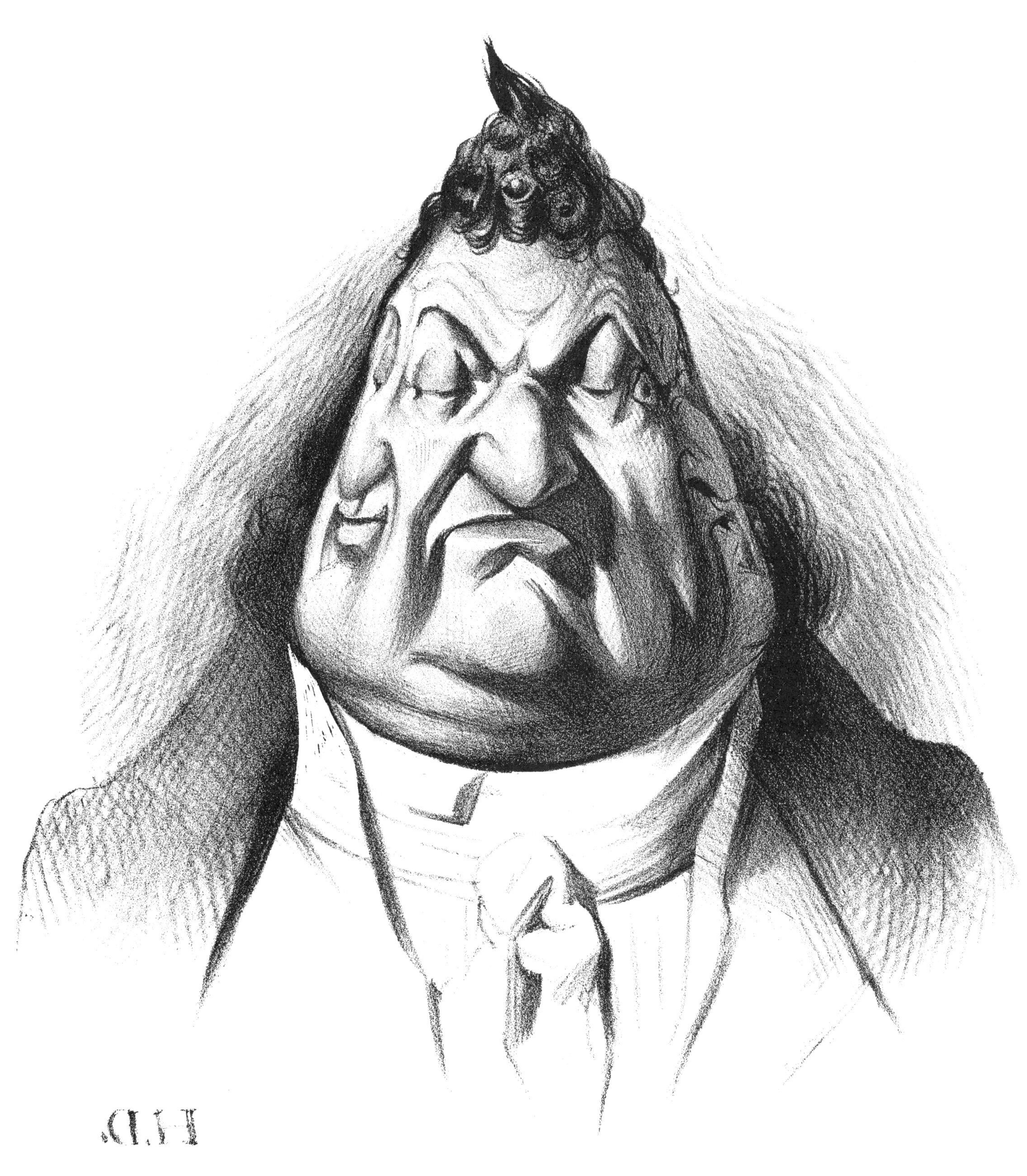

5 Variation on the depiction of Louis-Philippe as a pear (*poire* = fool). [Jan. 9, 1834]

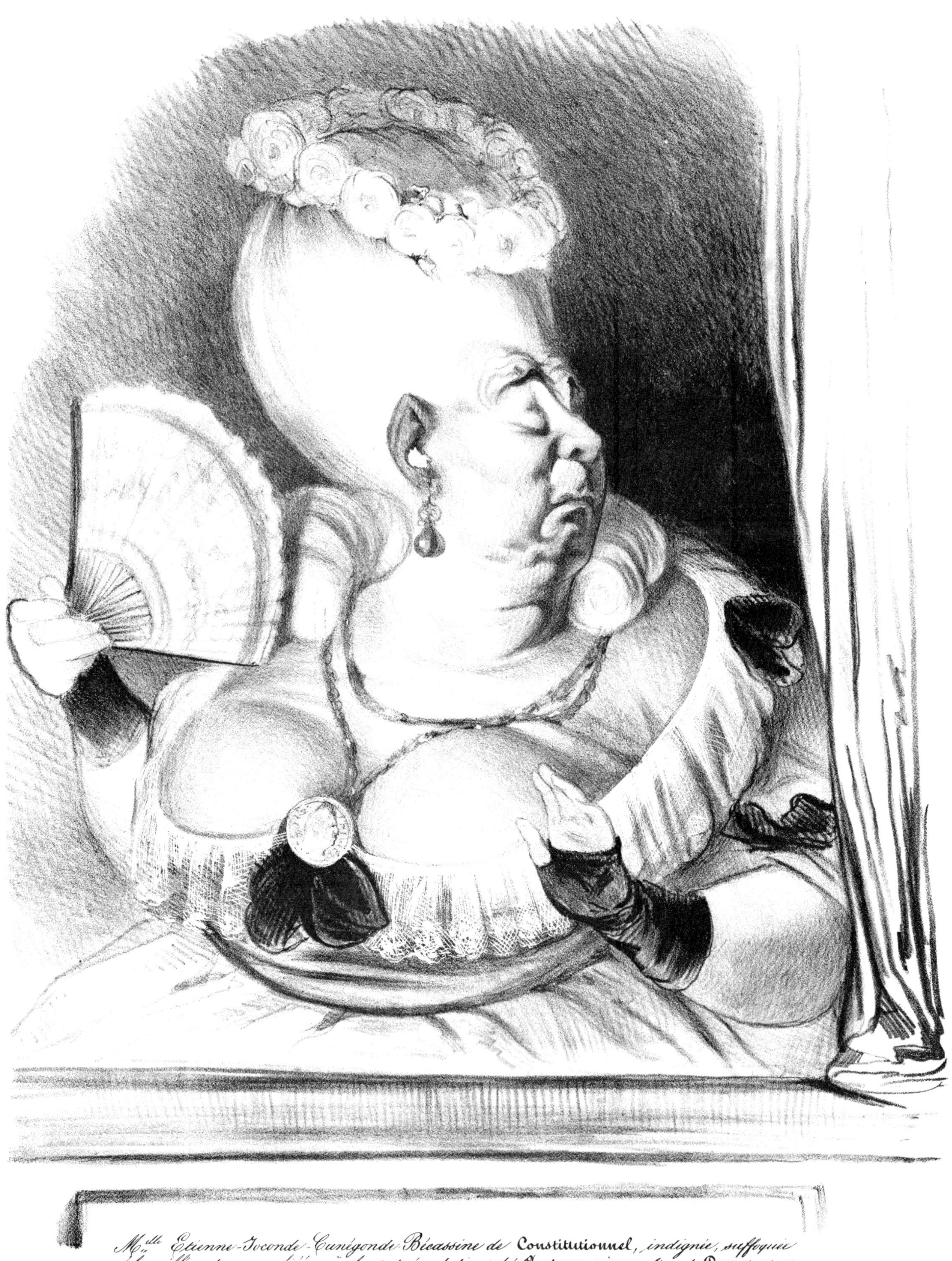

6 Etienne, editor of *Le Constitutionnel*, as an old-fashioned beldame shocked at modern plays. [May 8, 1834]

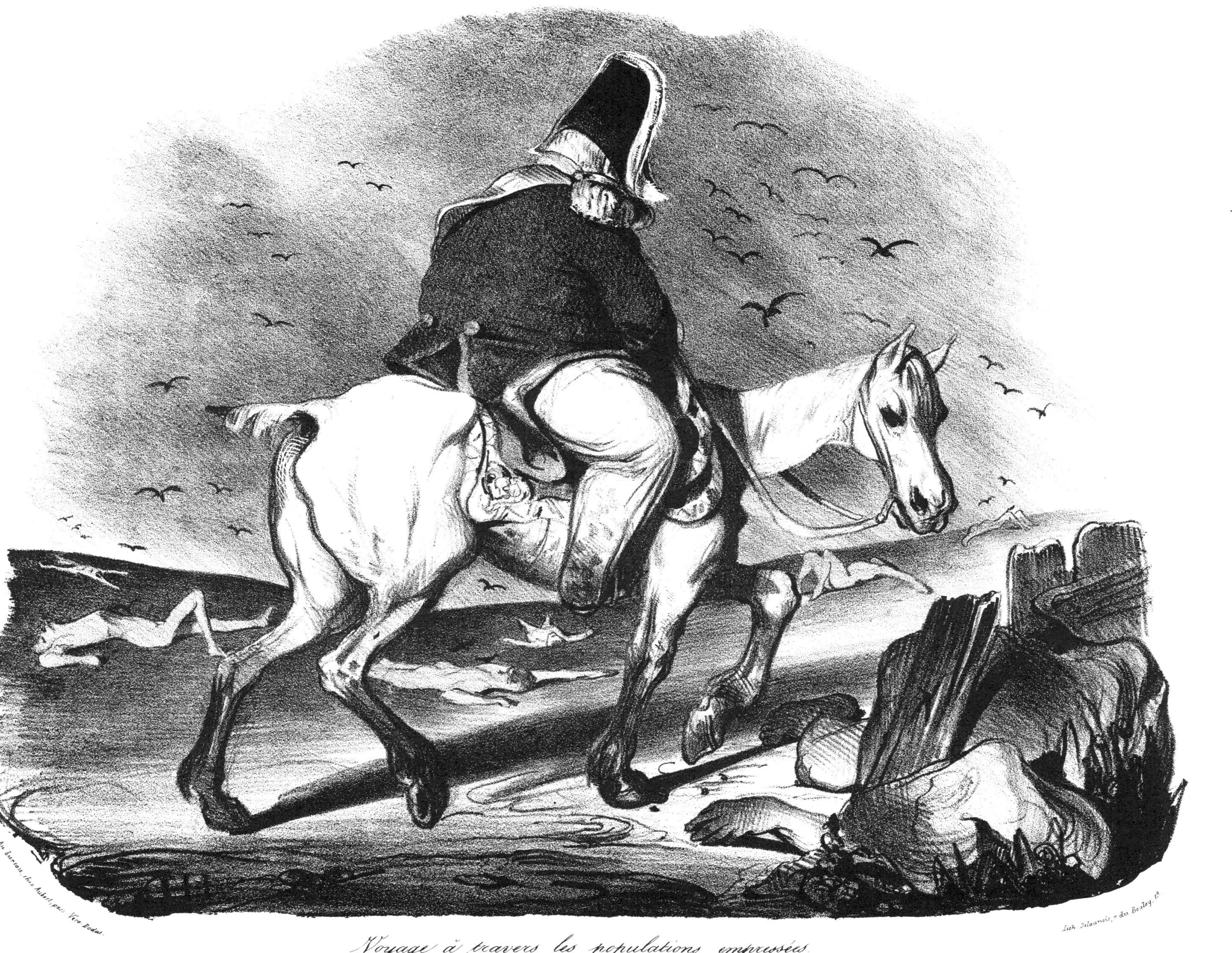

7 Louis-Philippe visits the French provinces, oblivious to their wants. [Aug. 14, 1834]

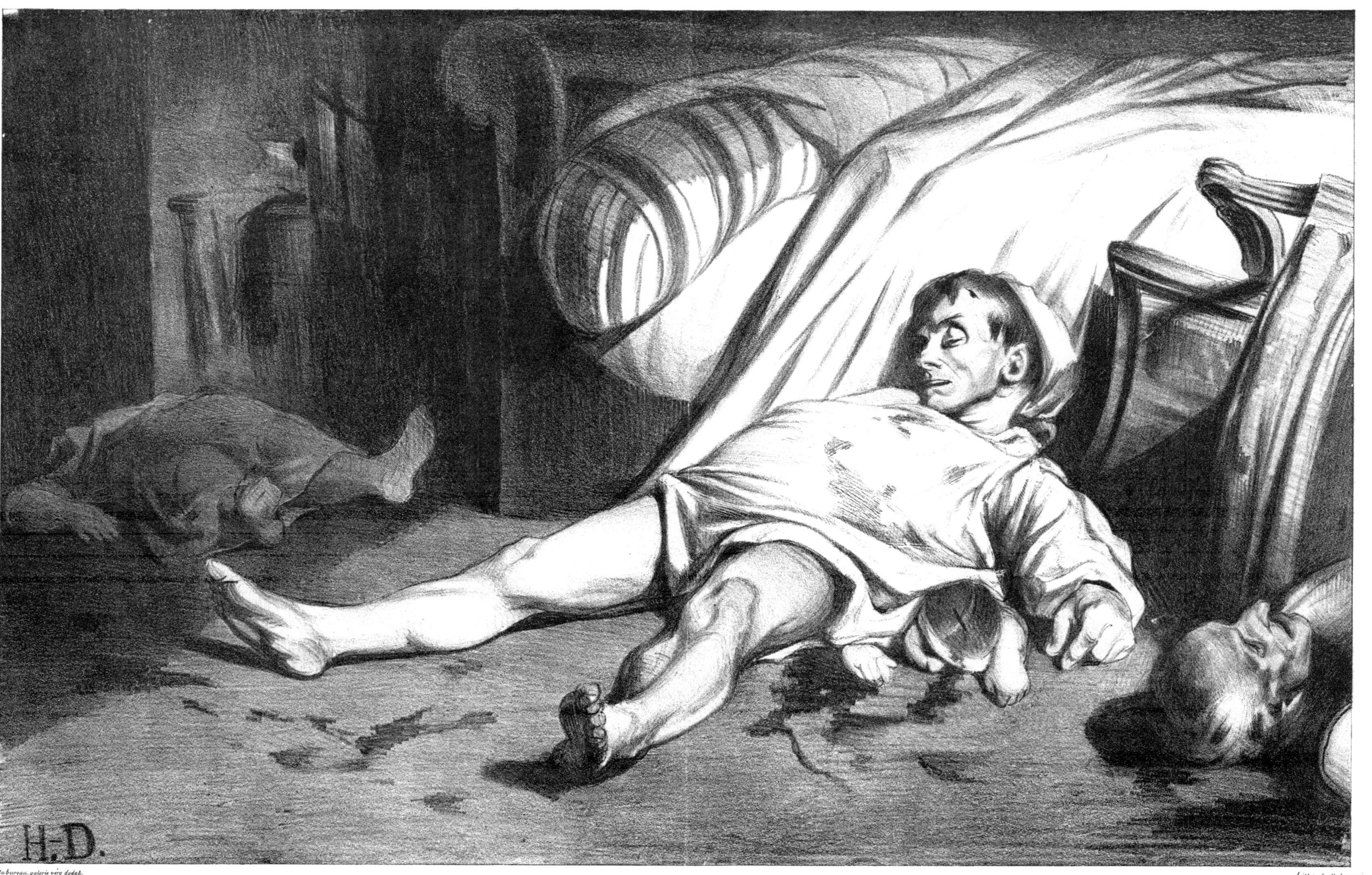

RUE TRANSNONAIN, LE 15 AVRIL 1834

8 Innocent civilian victims of a reprisal by government troops. [Aug.–Sept. 1834]

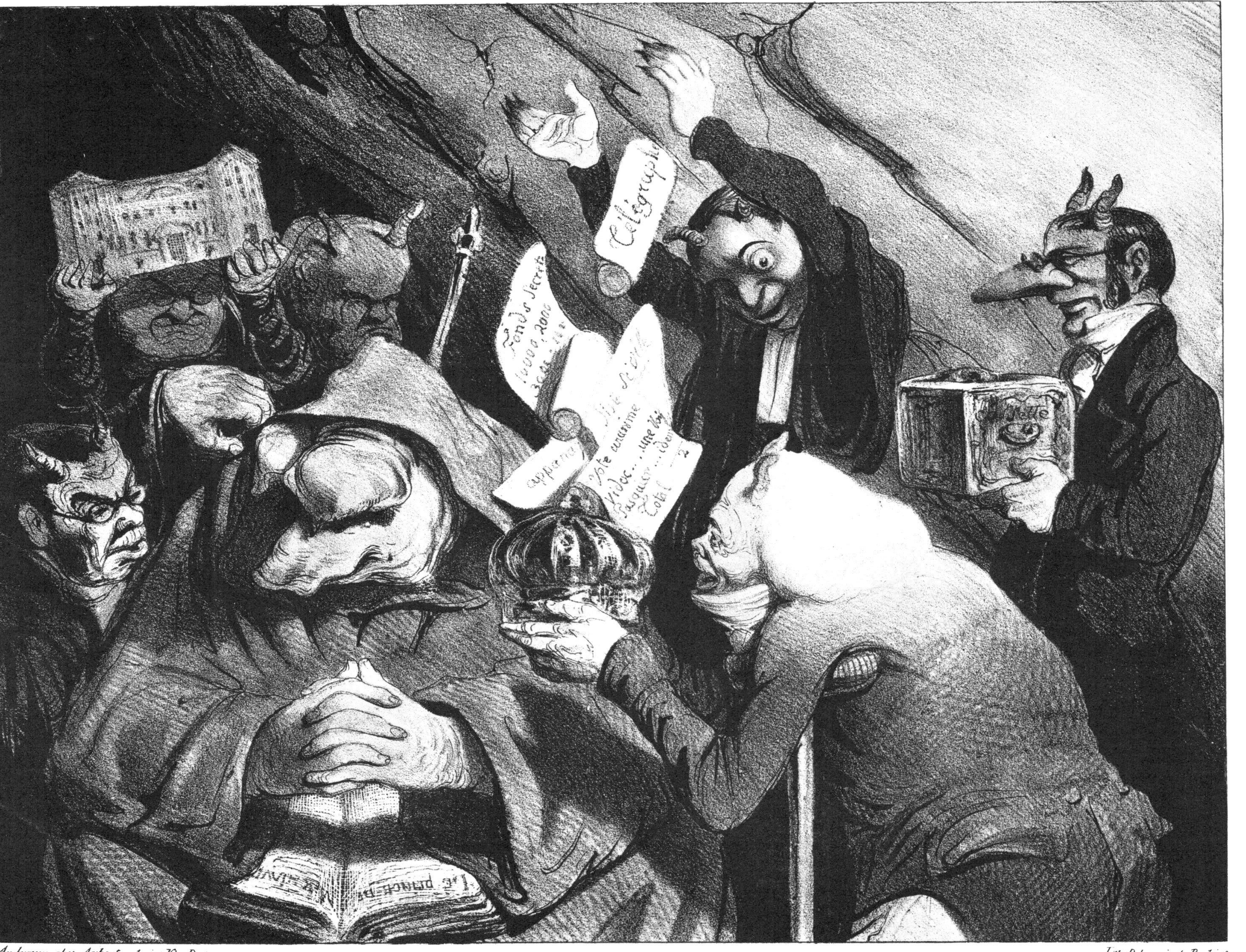

La Tentation

9 Parody of an old-master "Temptation of St. Anthony," in which Louis-Philippe is tempted by his ministers. [Jan. 1, 1835]

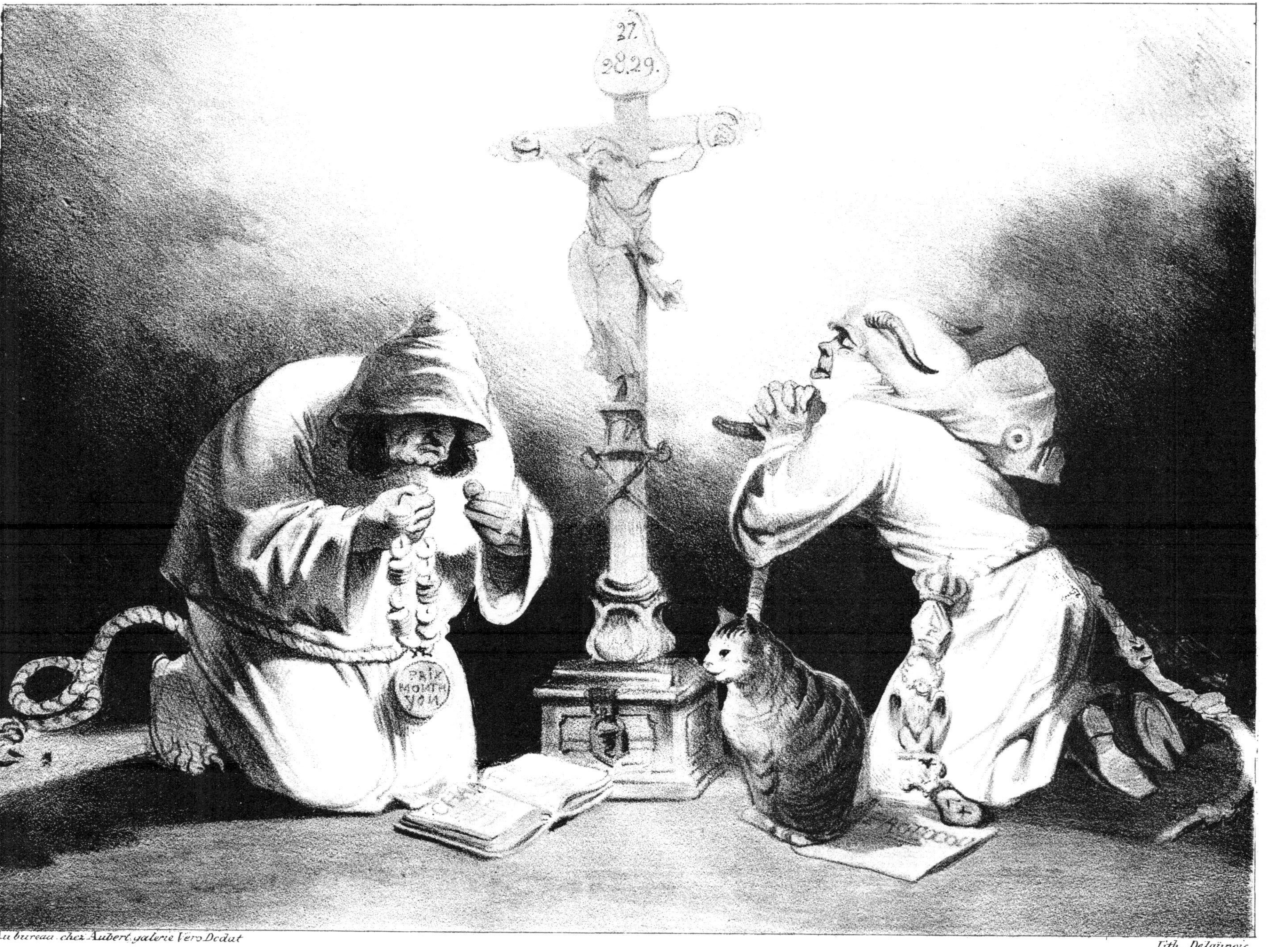

Quand le Diable devint vieux, il se fit Ermite.

10 Louis-Philippe and Talleyrand as diabolical monks, with crucified France between them. [Mar. 26, 1835]

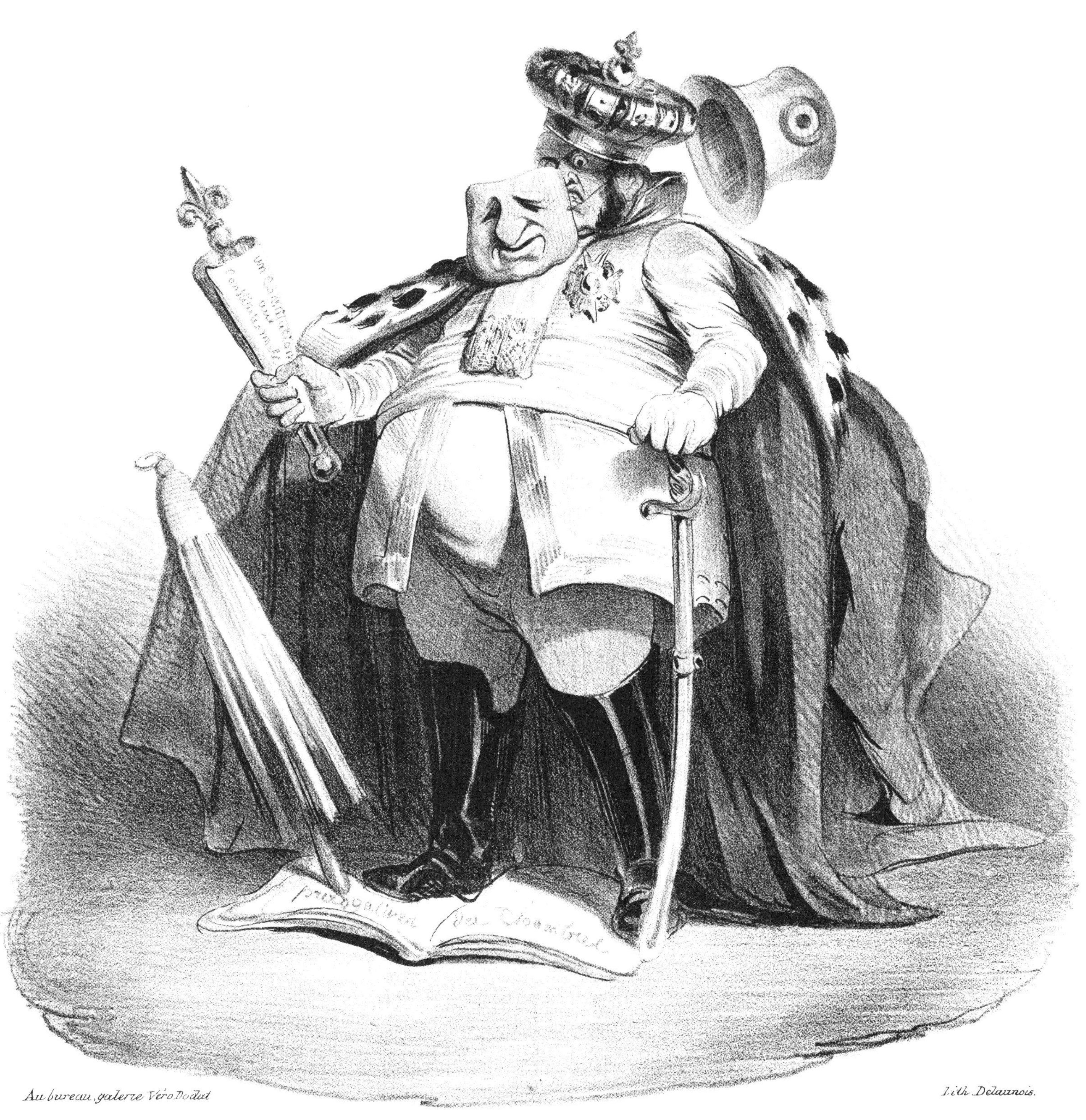

Principal acteur d'un Imbroglio-tragi-comique.

11 The King's friendly mask and citizen's hat fall away to reveal a vicious autocrat who tramples on legislative rights. [Mar. 29, 1835]

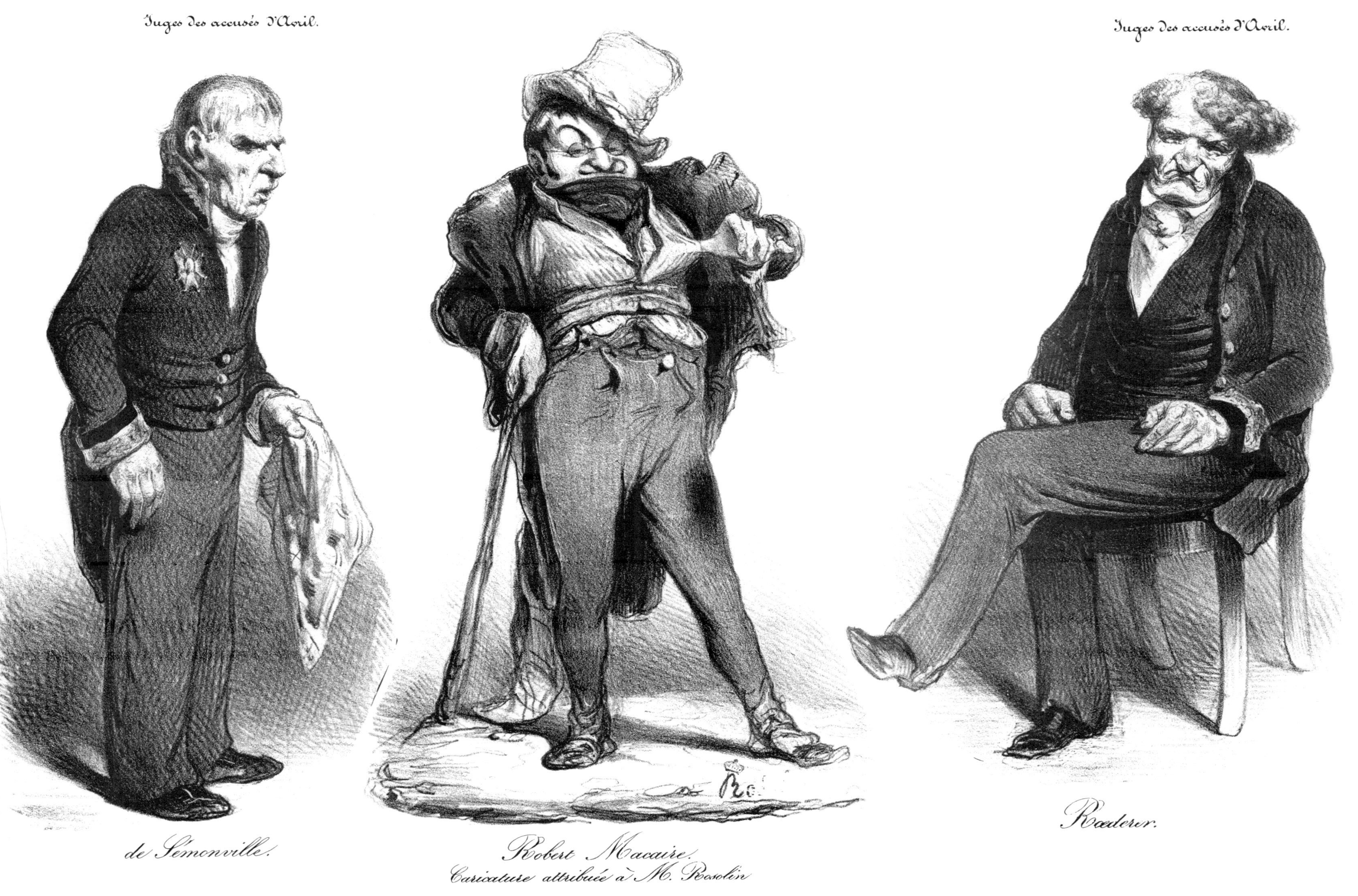

12 Three of the judges in a monster trial of anti-government rioters; in the center, Thiers as the robber and con man Robert Macaire. [July 30, 1835]

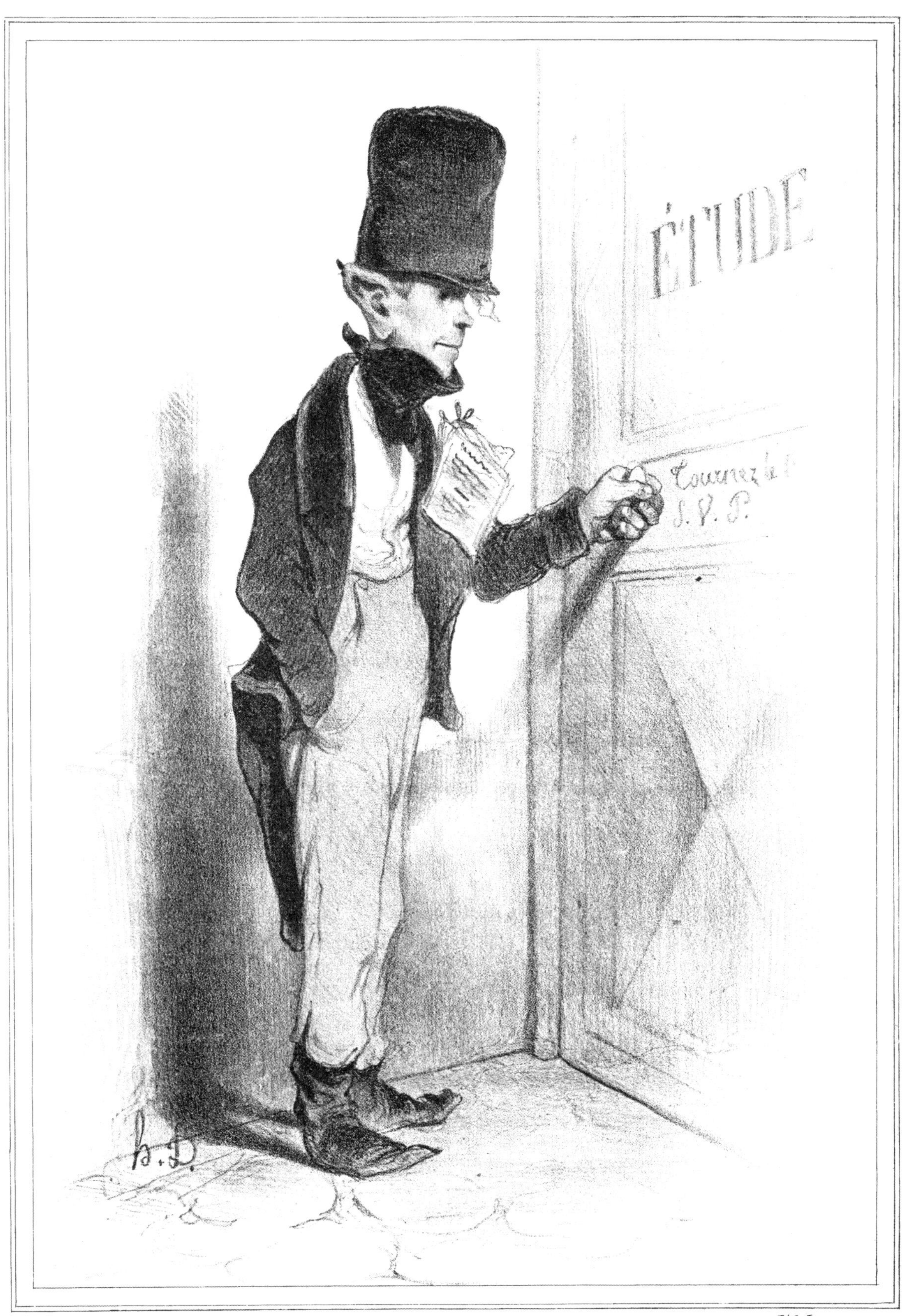

Au bureau chez Aubert gal. Véro-Dodat. Lith. Junca.

Le Petit Clerc,

(dit: Saute-Ruisseau.)

Le petit clerc mange peu, court beaucoup, flâne davantage et revient le plus tard possible à l'étude où il est le souffre-douleur. Il s'appelle ordinairement Pitou, Godard ou Galuchet.

13 Apprentice to a law firm. [Sept. 23, 1835]

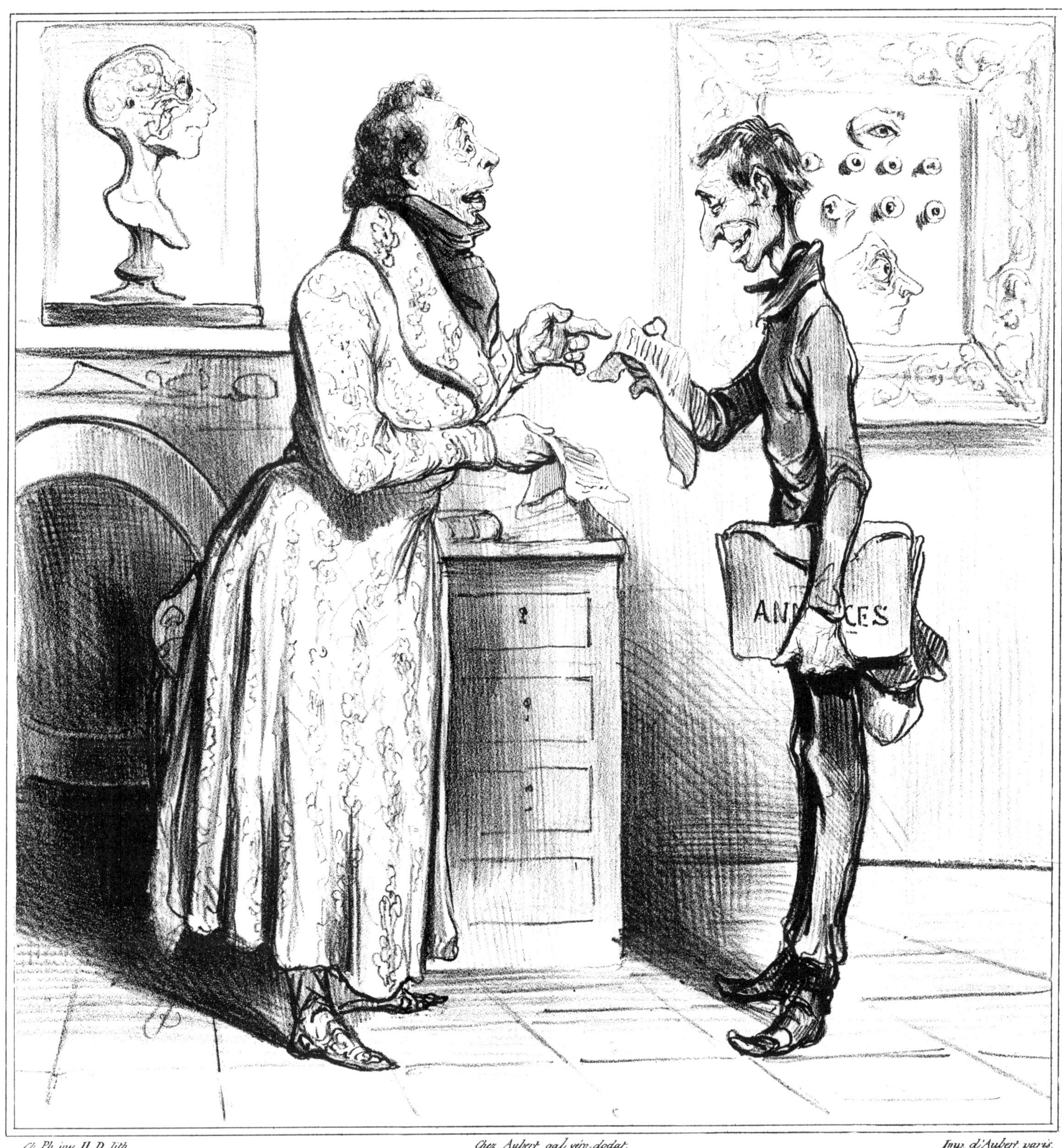

Ch. Ph. inv. H. D. lith. *Chez Aubert gal. véro-dodat.* *Imp. d'Aubert, paris.*

Tu vas porter cette note aux journaux.

Un provincial ayant par mégarde avalé une blague, devint subitement chauve et insolvable, le célèbre Docteur **Robert-Macaire** *en conclut que les blagues ruinant les uns doivent, d'après le système homéopathique, enrichir les autres. le traitement médical lui a complètement réussi. Avis aux perruques.*

Et comme je suis nommé, dans cet article, demain, en vertu de la loi du 9 7bre 1835,
je réclamerai l'insertion de la lettre que voici:

Monsieur le Rédacteur,
Je vous prie de déclarer que vous ne tenez pas de moi l'article dans lequel vous m'avez nommé hier, je m'occupe il est vrai de guérir la calvitie (rue Belle charge N.°1) mais je la traite par un autre moyen que celui dont vous parlez.
J'ai l'honneur etc.
Robert-Macaire (rue Belle-charge, N.°1)

14 The swindler Robert Macaire as a publicity-seeking quack doctor. [Nov. 5, 1837]

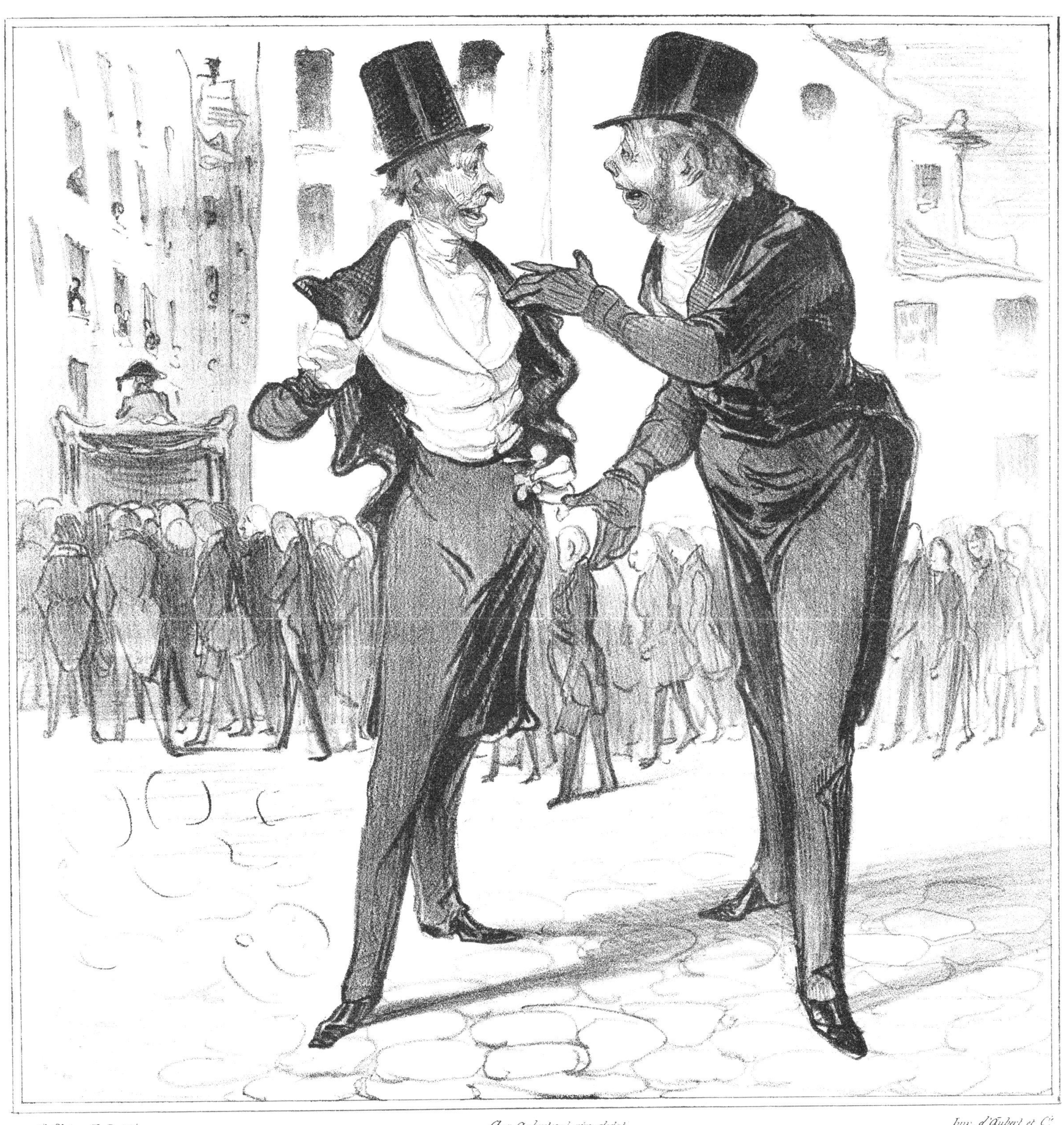

15 Robert Macaire planning a fraudulent new career as a homeopathic doctor. [Dec. 24, 1837]

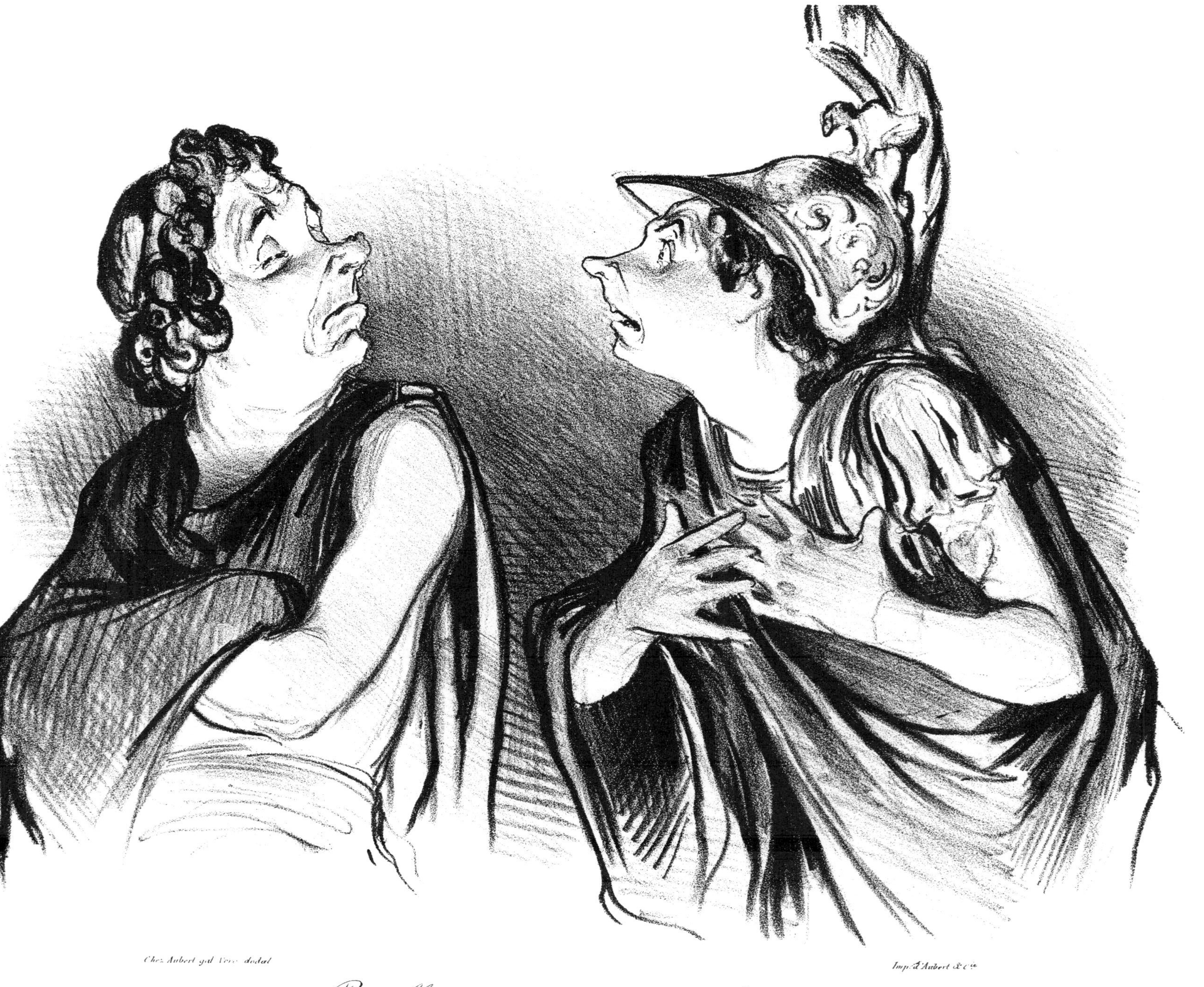

Pour aller jusqu'au cœur que vous voulez percer,
Voila par quel chemin vos coups doivent passer.

16 Lampoon of an old classical tragedy. [Mar. 28, 1839]

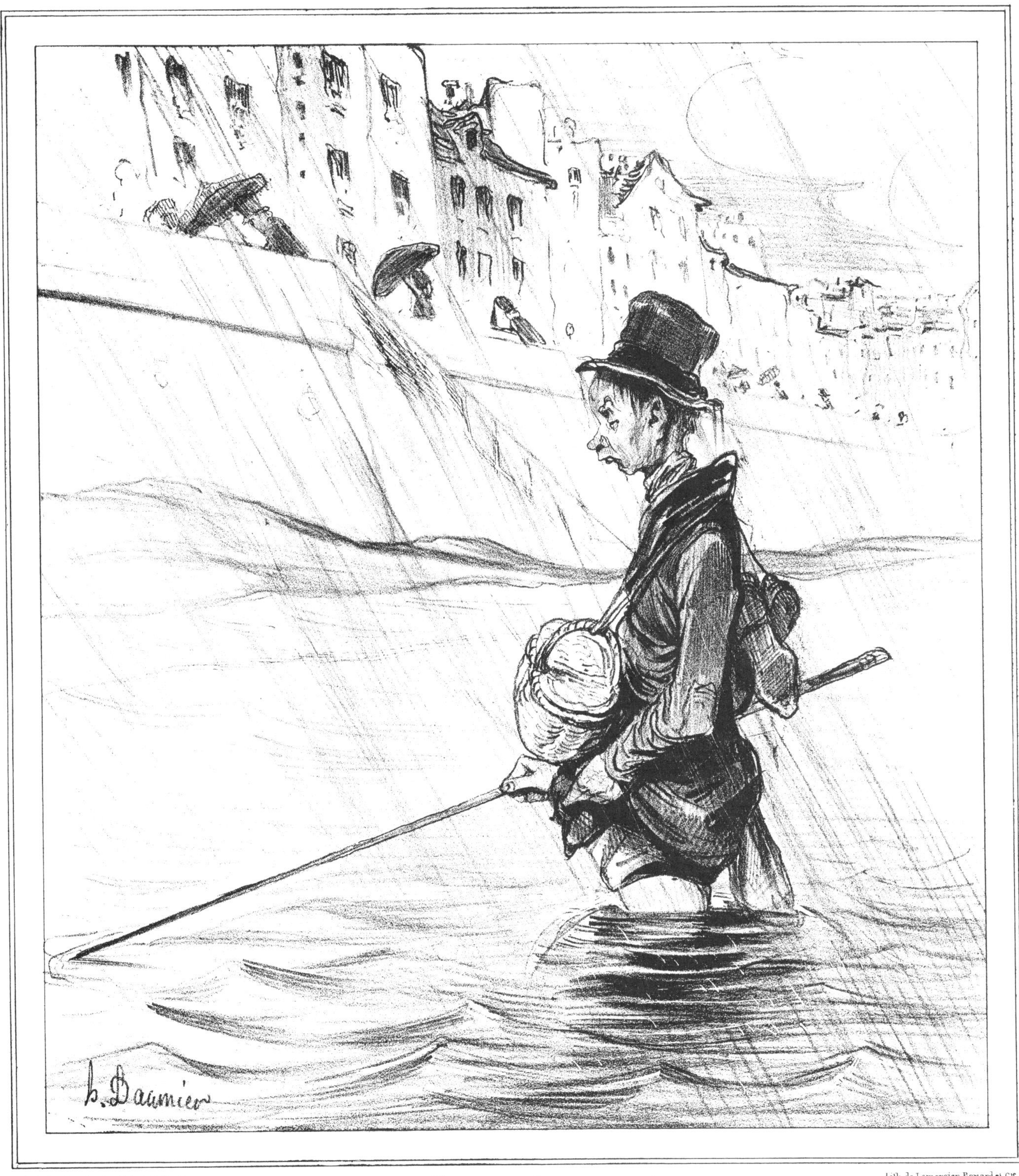

à Paris, chez Dupin Galerie Colbert. Lith. de Lemercier, Benard et Cie

. . . . Ayez pitié du pauvre pêcheur !

Le Martin-pêcheur (sur Seine)

Cette espèce de Martin-pêcheur ne pêche rien du tout. Au lieu de se plaire à voltiger et à poursuivre sa proie en zig-zag, le Martin-pêcheur bipède reste immobile comme une borne aquatique les bruits qui l'environnent, la pluie, la grêle, le tonnerre, les éclairs, les quolibets des passans, rien ne l'émeut rien ne saurait le détourner de sa ligne. Quelquefois, après une journée entière d'attente il finit par sentir l'extrémité du roseau fléchir sous un poids inacoutumé, son œil s'anime, son cœur bondit d'espoir et de bonheur, il tire avec précaution et ramène . . . un vieux chausson ou une vieille savatte, mais, à défaut de poissons il est toujours certain d'attraper des rhumatismes ou des fluxions de poitrine. Le Martin-pêcheur stationne d'ordinaire le long des quais par le froid, le vent et la pluie, enfoncé dans l'eau jusqu'à mi-corps; c'est ainsi qu'il descend gaîment le fleuve de la vie. Et, lors qu'enfin la mort vient le saisir, il se prend à douter de l'existence du goujon.

17 A dedicated angler described as a kingfisher in a mock course in "natural history." [Mar. 15, 1838]

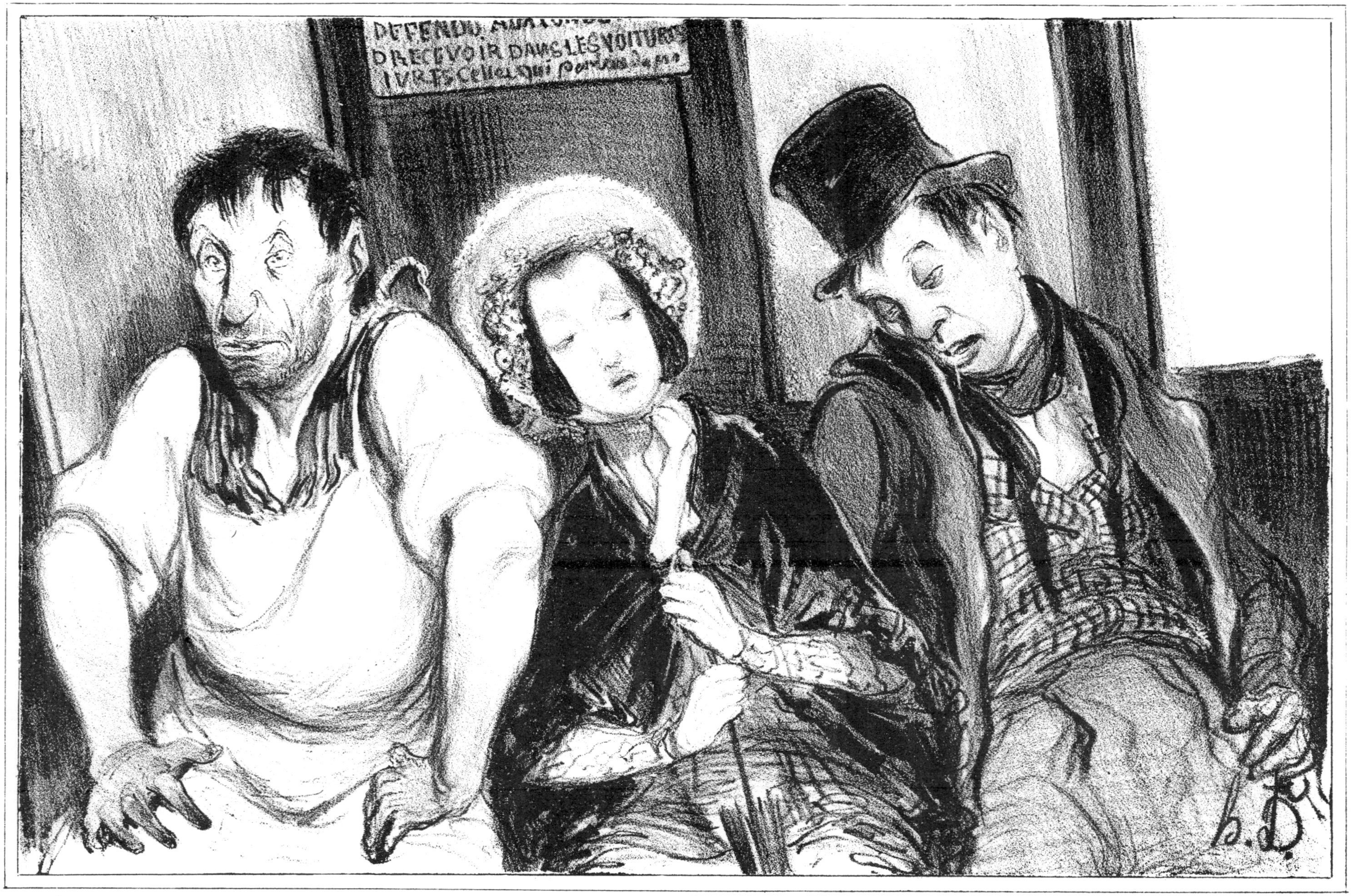

Chez Bauger R. du Croissant 16. Imp. d'Aubert & Cie

INTERIEUR D'UN OMNIBUS

Entre un homme ivre et un Charcutier

18 Riding on a bus between a butcher and a drunk. [Nov. 13, 1841]

Chez Bauger R. du Croissant 16. Imp. d'Aubert & Cie.

Oh !.. absolument comme si on y était ; la grande ôte son corset, et la petite cherche une puce.

19 Watching women undress. [Dec. 1, 1841]

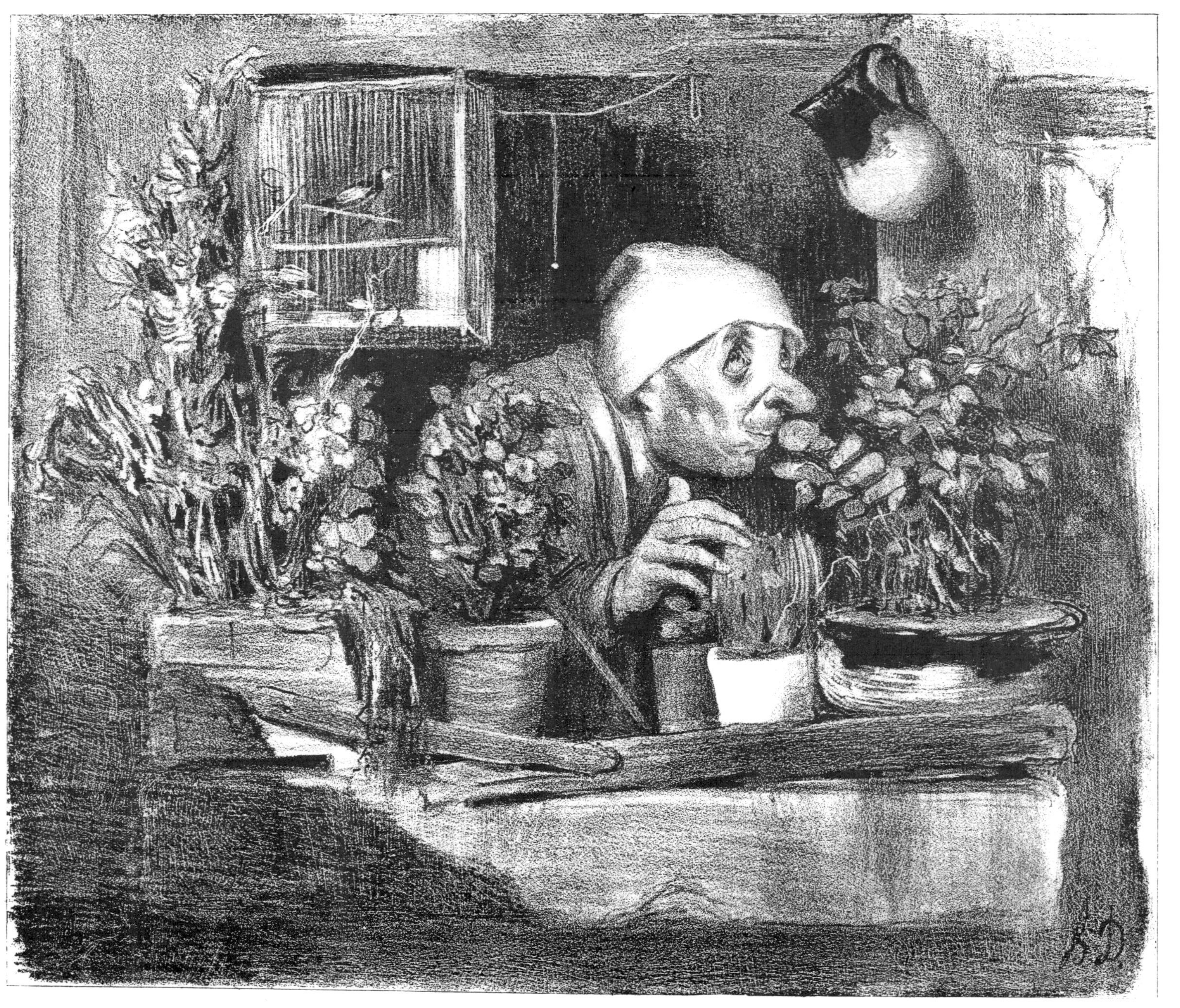

L'ODORAT.

20 A window garden symbolizing the sense of smell. [Jan. 18, 1843]

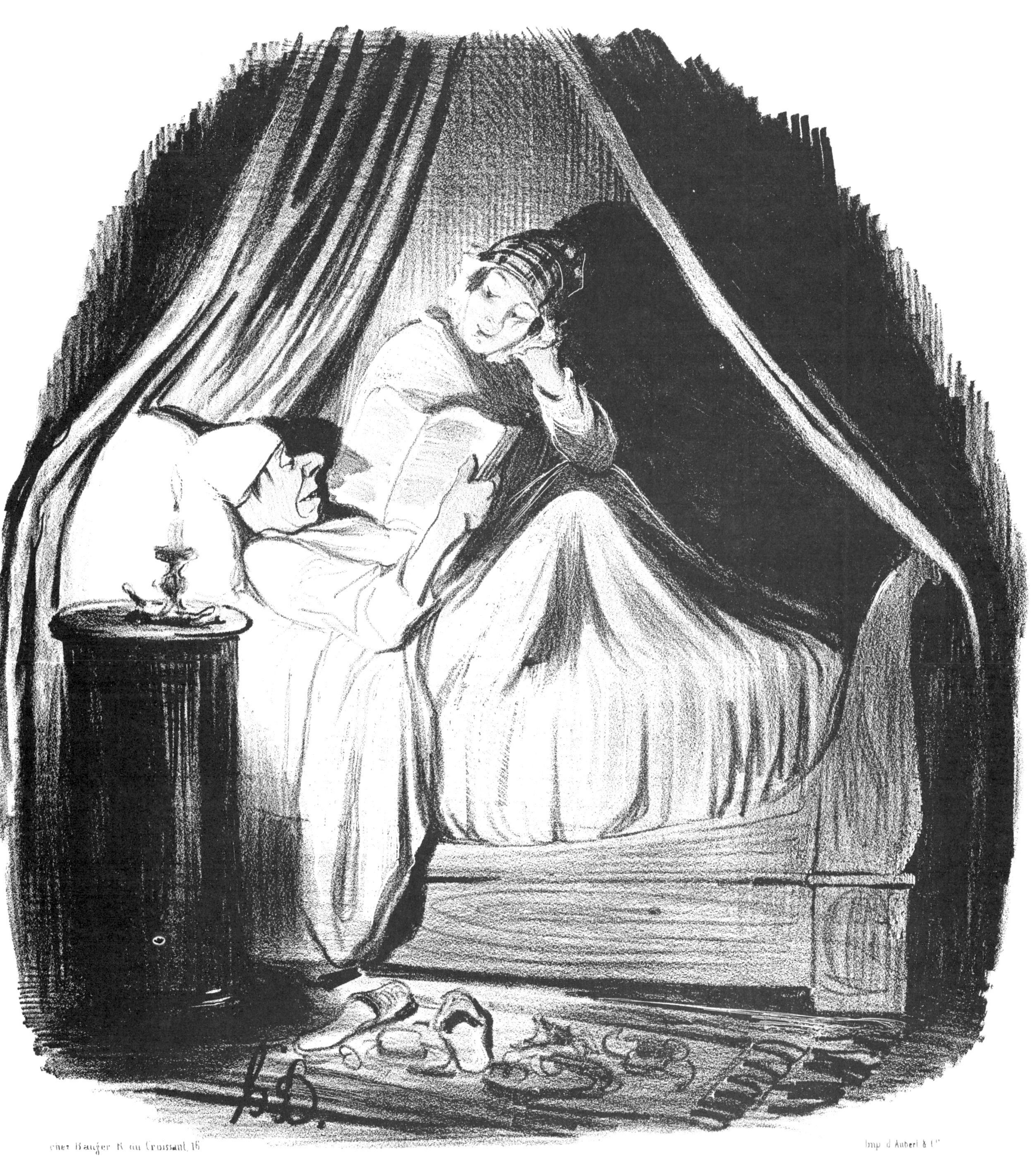

LE MARI (*lisant*) : « nous étions mollement étendus sur la mousse odorante ; les rayons de la lune perçaient les branches du Saule agité par la Brise du soir. Enivrés d'amour nous lancions au Ciel des Sermens qui retombaient dans nos cœurs. »
LA FEMME (*à part*) : Peut-on lire ces choses avec un bonnet de coton, et une boule comme la sienne !.....

21 The homely husband reads aloud a passionately romantic story. [Oct. 29, 1839]

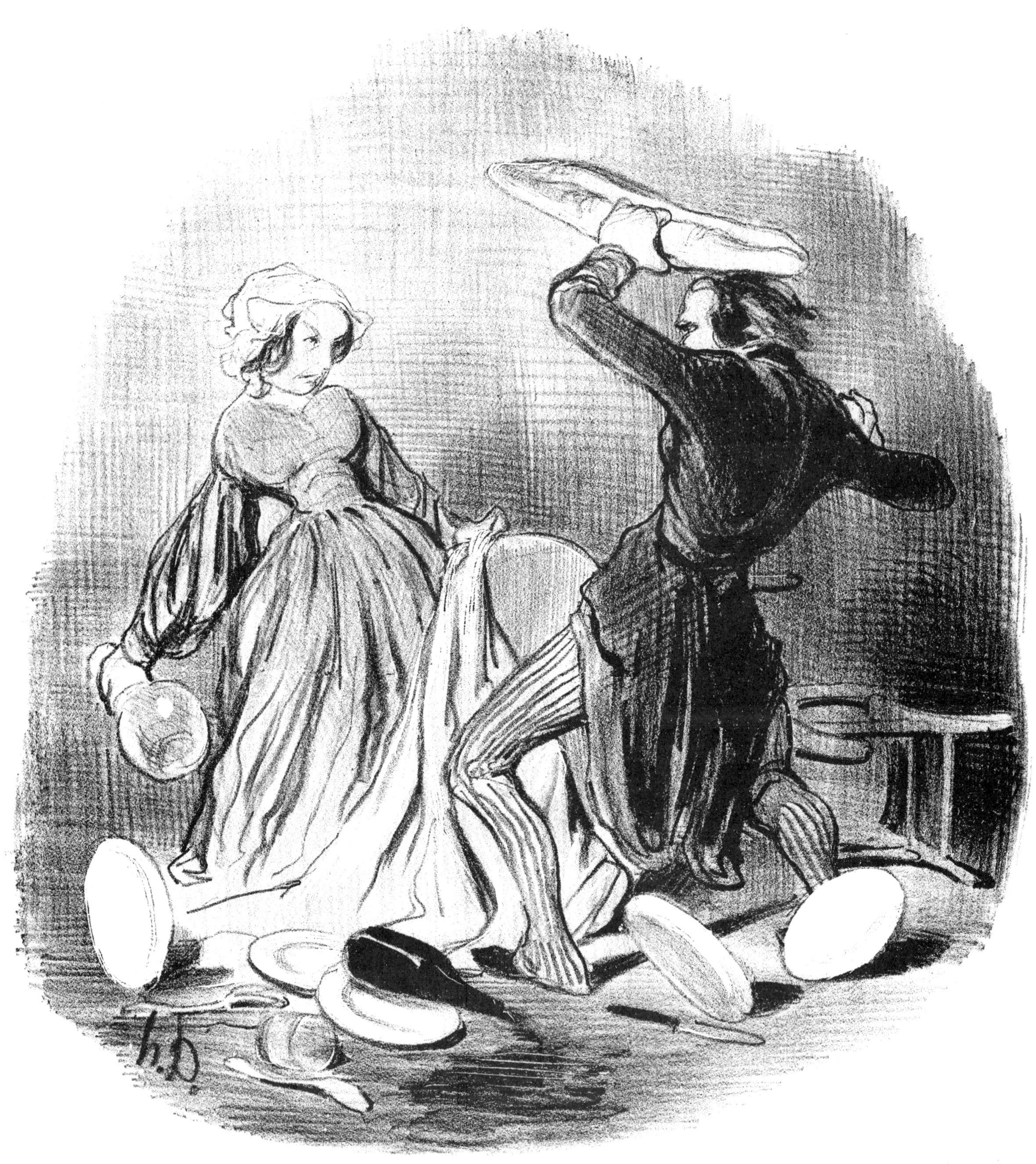

– Ah ! tu trouves que ta femme ne te soigne pas assez, brigand ; quand tu dépenses tout, canaille !... Eh bien je m'en ferai des accroche-cœur, polisson !..... et je m'acheterai des bonnets.... et je te ferai manger des bouchons de liège, gredin.......

– Mon ange j'ai tort, tu es une bonne femme de ménage..... mais tu casses tout.

22 A wife enraged by her husband's mild complaints about her housekeeping. [June 6, 1841]

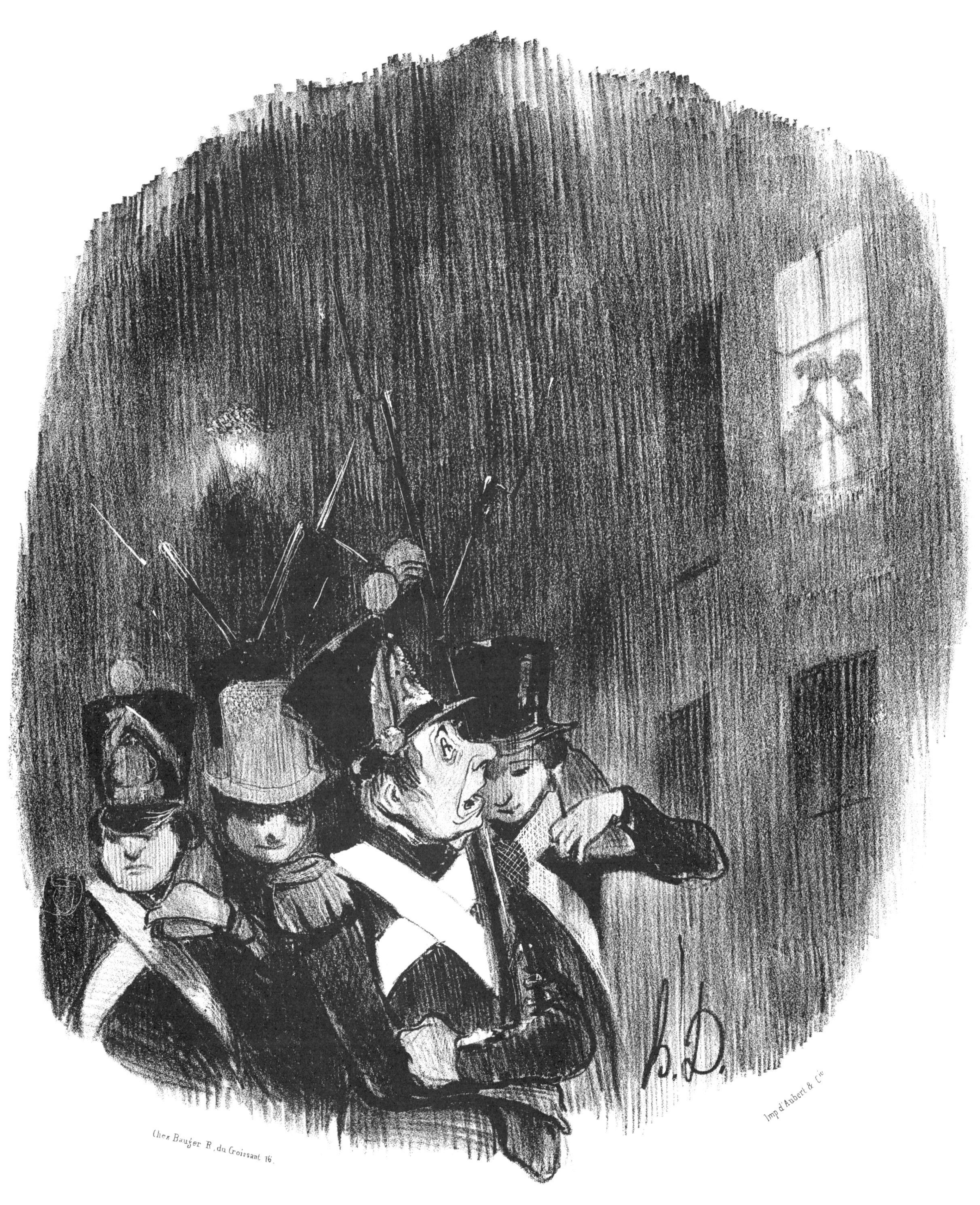

23 A member of the National Guard passing his own house while on duty.
[Oct. 24, 1839]

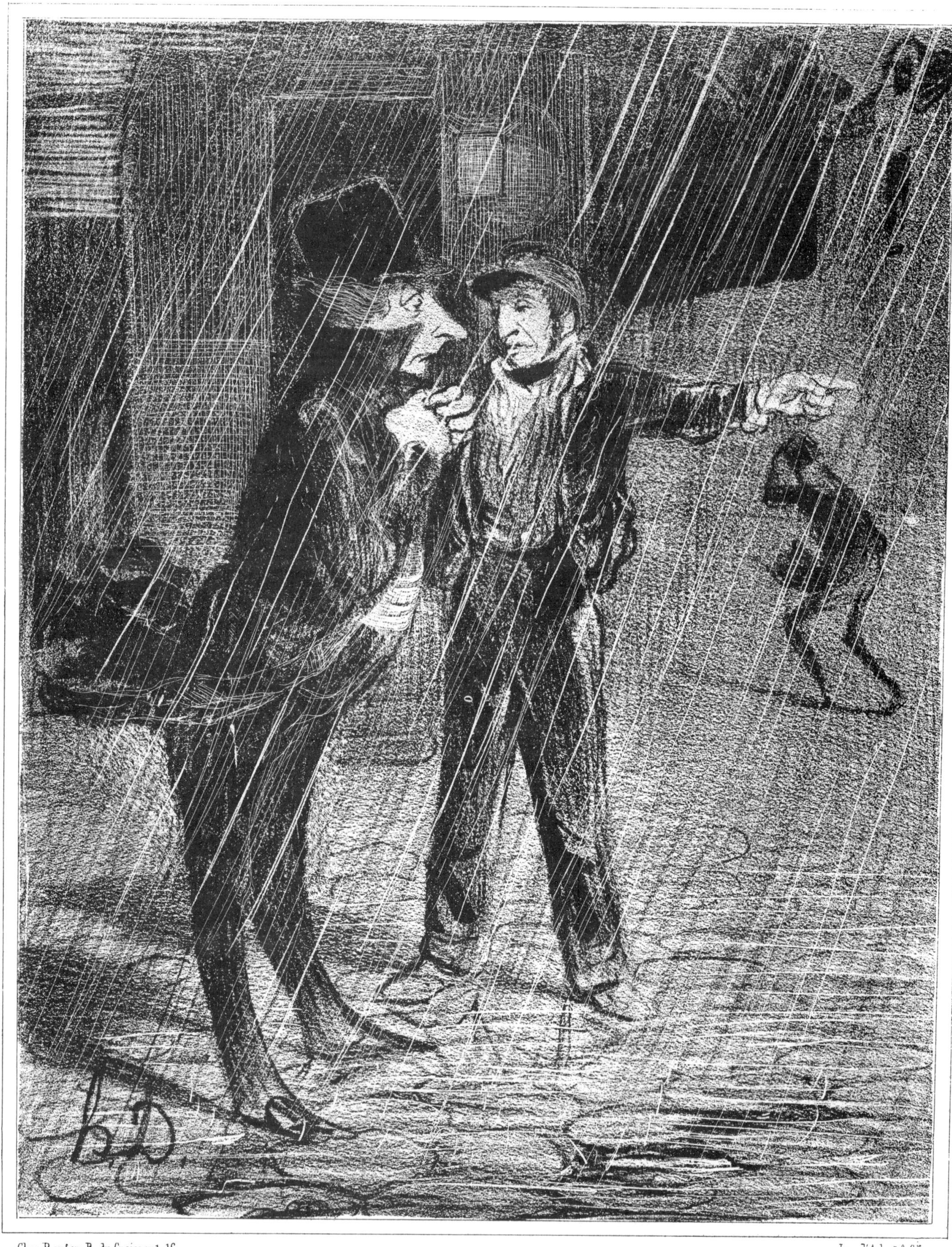

Chez Baufer R, du Croissant 16. Imp d'Aubert & Cie

Comment à Chaillot!.....Mais en montant vous m'avez dit Bercy — vous m'avez payé et je vous ai dit merci!.. — Cré nom de nom!.... allons reconduisez-moi ... — du tout il est minuit nous ne marchons plus. — Cré nom de nom!........

24 The coachman, who has deposited his passenger at the wrong end of Paris, informs him that service is over for the night. [Dec. 24, 1839]

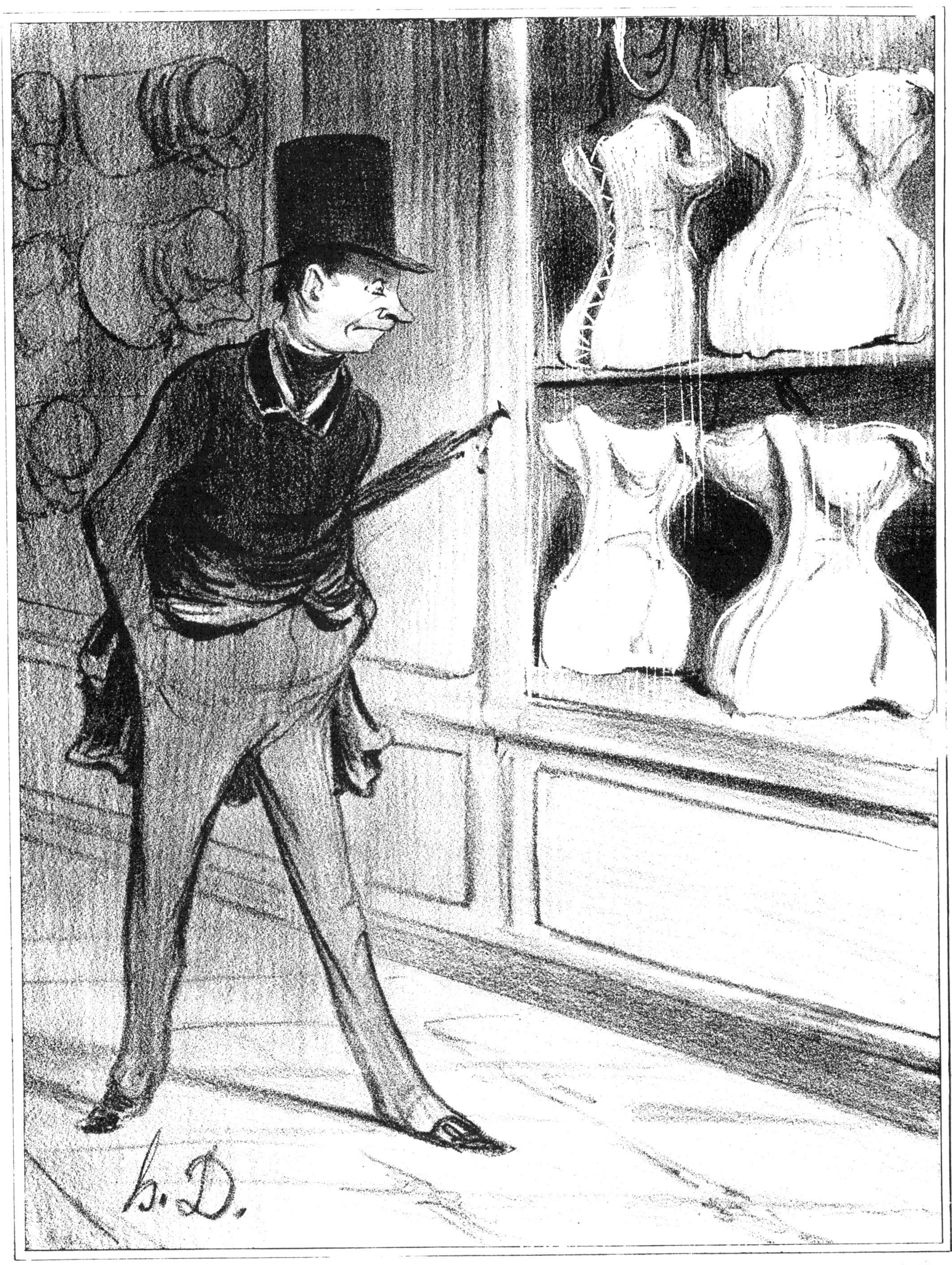

Chez Bauger, R. du Croissant 16. Imp. d'Aubert & Cie

C'est unique! j'ai pris quatre tailles, juste comme celles là dans ma vie; Filine ma première! Cocotte, cette gueuse de Cocotte! la grande Mimi, et mon épouse là haut dans le coin:

25 The four corsets remind him of the four women in his life. [Feb. 7, 1840]

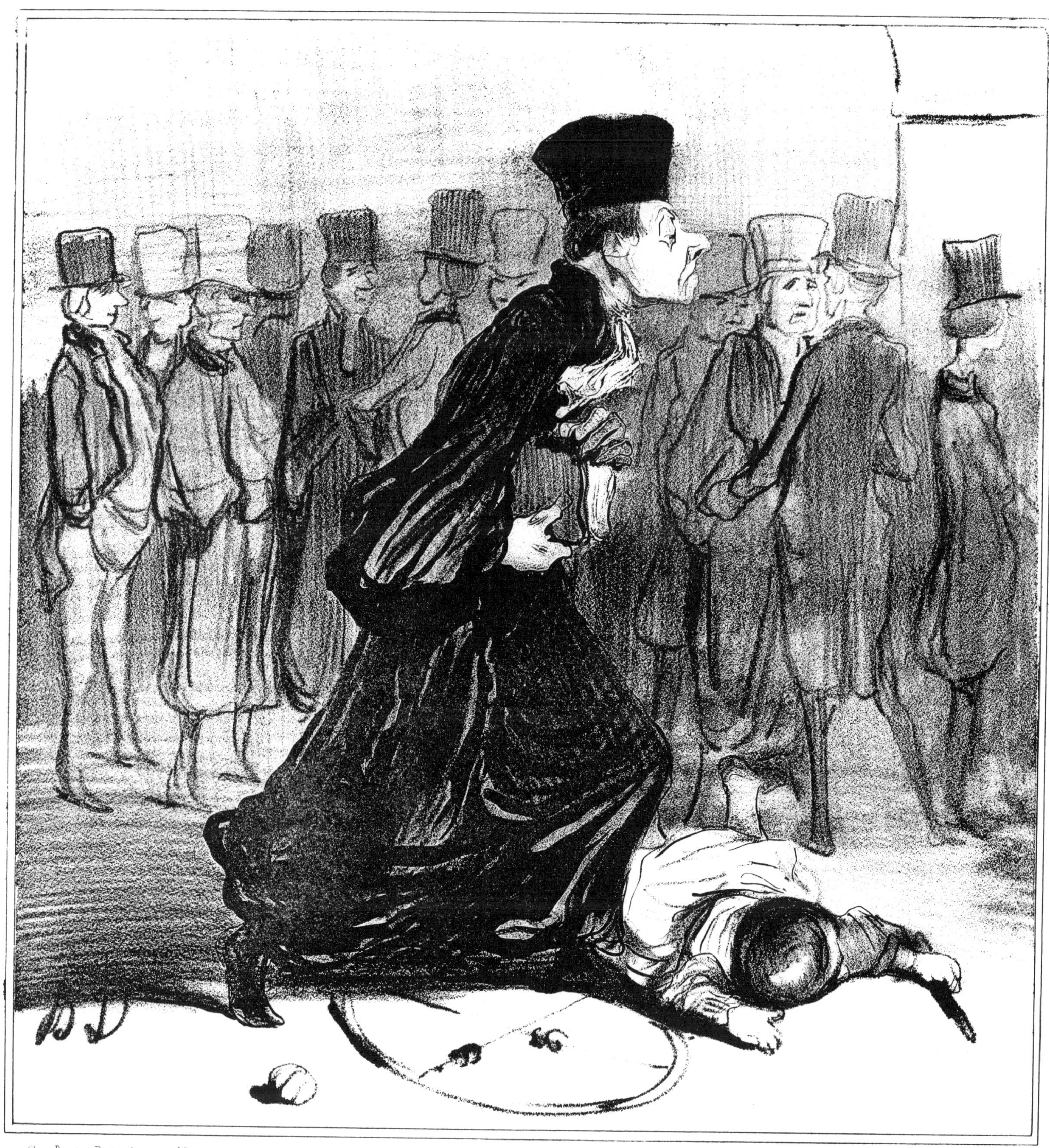

Chez Bauger R. du Croissant 16 — Imp. d'Aubert & Cie

Mr Tout affaires, avocat sans causes, se donne l'air empressé, et renverse, chaque jour, dans la salle des pas perdus, une douzaine de moutards, écrase cinq ou six carlins, et espère grâce à cette gymnastique, faire croire à ses nombreux clients.

26 A lawyer without cases who pretends to be tremendously busy. [June 30, 1840]

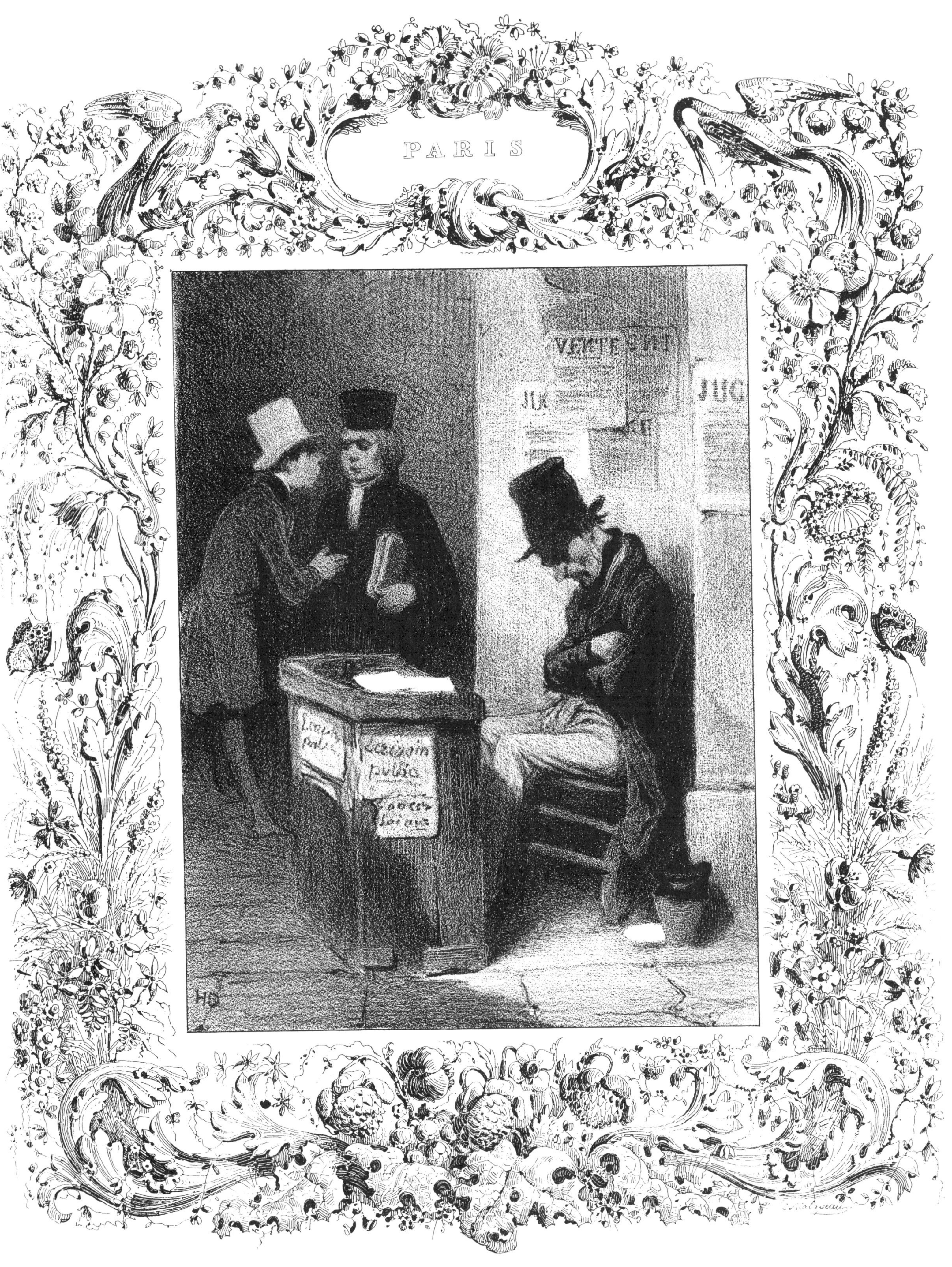

LA SALLE DES PAS PERDUS.

27 A public scribe drowses in the waiting hall of the main law courts. [Nov. 17, 1839]

h. D.

Imp. d'Aubert & Cie — Au Bureau du Charivari R. du Croissant 16

La Seine est une rivière qui prend sa source dans le département de la Côte d'Or, et va se perdre dans la Manche. Elle traverse Paris: les habitans de cette Cité, se dérobant aux feux de l'été viennent chercher la fraîcheur et la pureté de ses eaux.

28 Men's public baths in the Seine. [June 26, 1839]

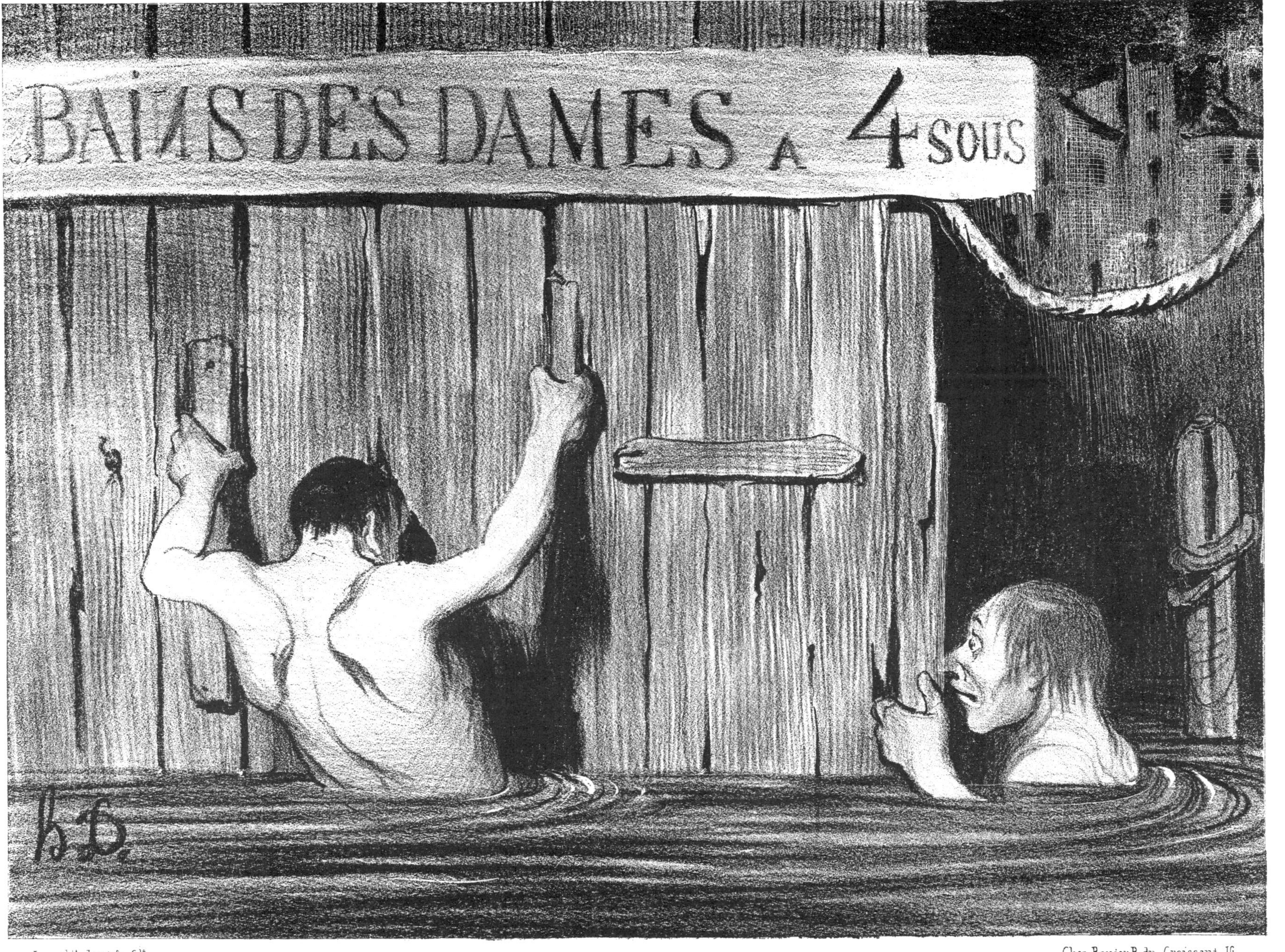

Imp. d'Aubert & Cie — Chez Bauger R. du Croissant 16.

Excusez; regard' donc la grosse Fifine qu'on aurait juré que c'était une Vénus. . . . ah ben en v'la un déchet!

29 Spying on the women's public baths. [Oct. 4, 1839]

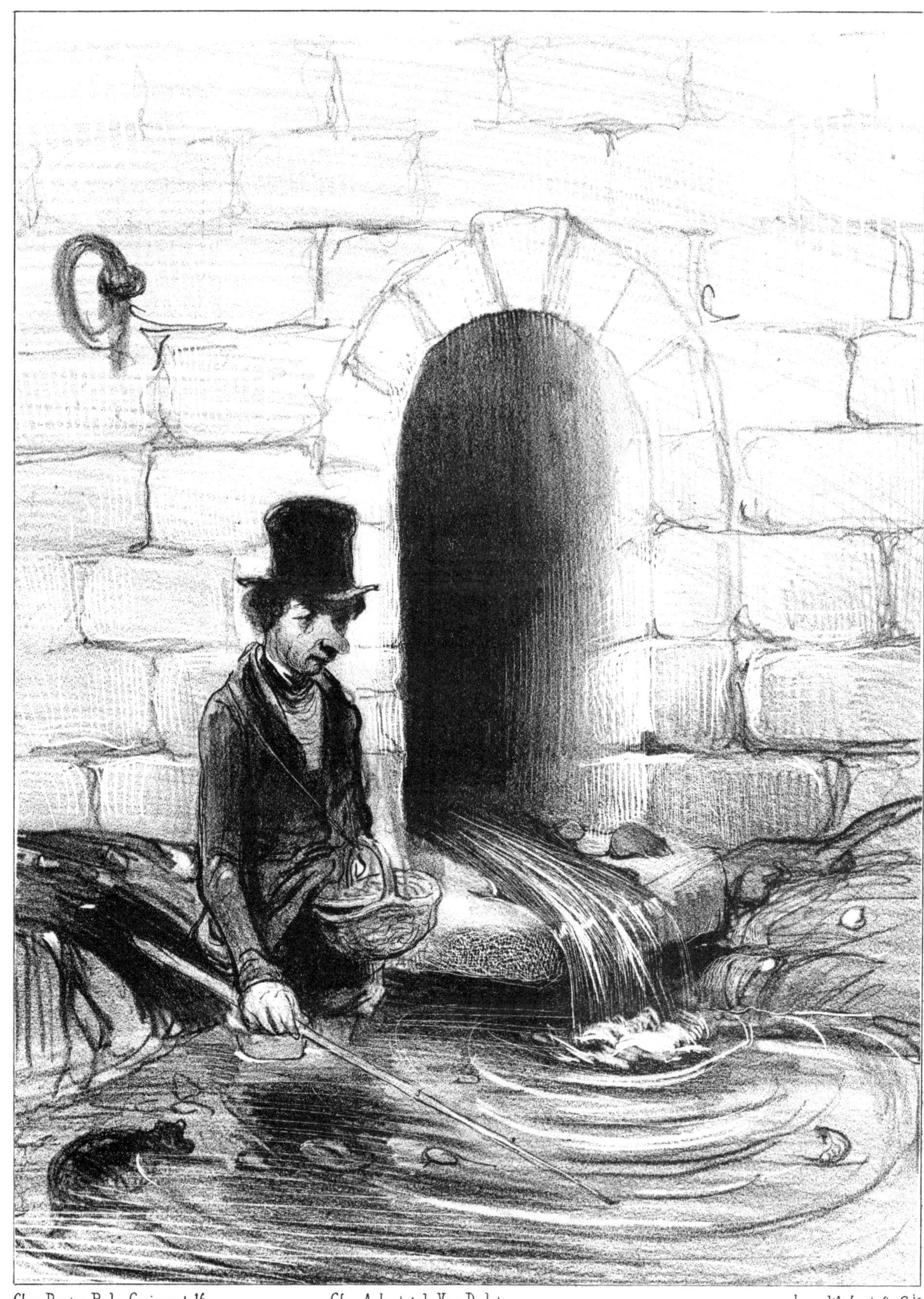

Chez Bauger R. du Croissant 16. Chez Aubert gal. Vero-Dodat. Imp. d'Aubert & Cie

LE PÊCHEUR ACHARNÉ

ou

il ne faut pas disputer des gouts.

30 An inveterate fisherman at a sewer mouth. [Aug. 16, 1840]

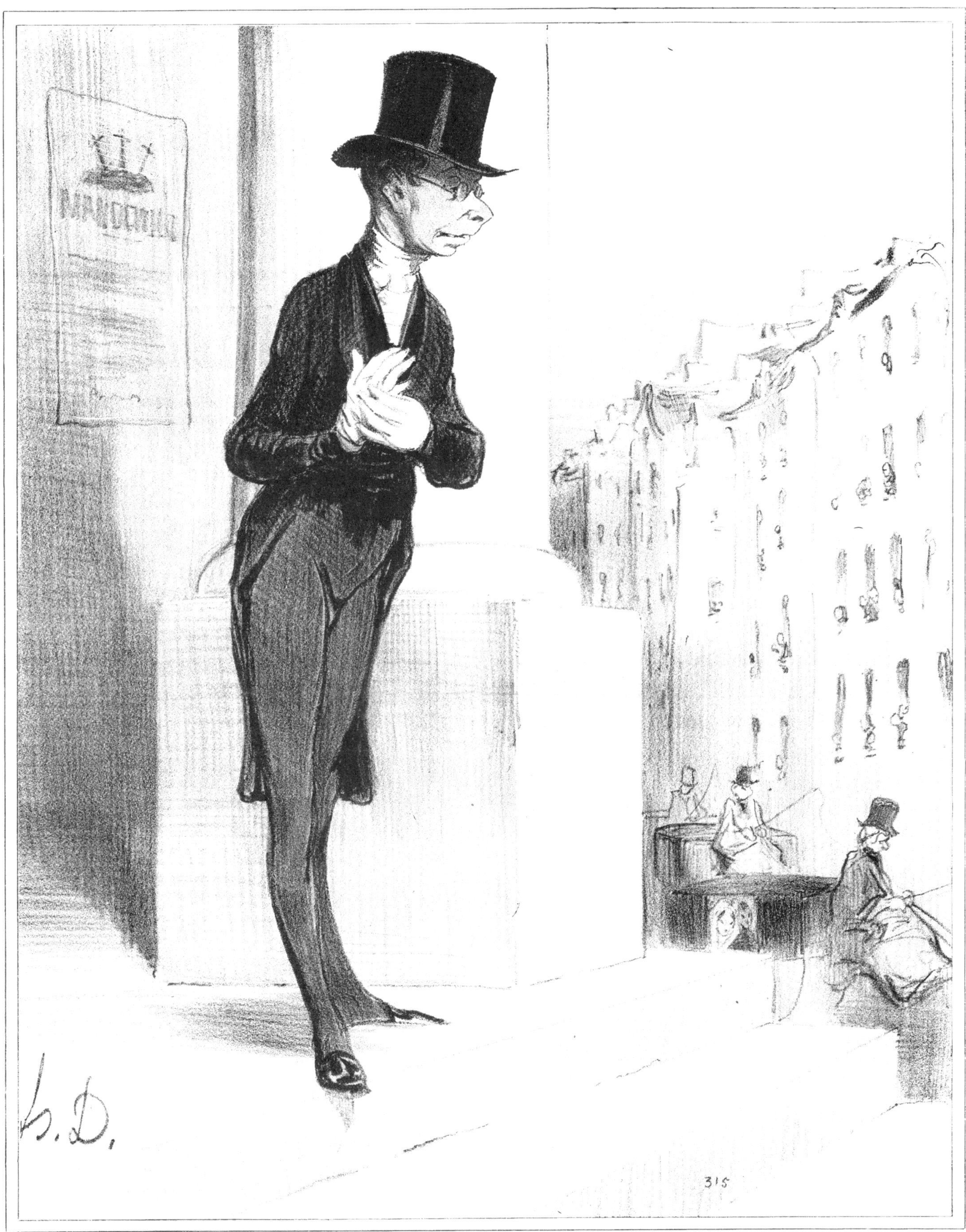

Chez Beauger. R du Croissant 16.

Imp. d'Aubert & Cie

PIQUE-ASSIETTE.

Voyons! une noce de première classe chez Very! en avant les gants blancs, je salue la mariée comme ami du mari .... et le mari ; comme connaissance de la mariée !

31 A professional sponger about to crash a fashionable wedding party. [Dec. 25, 1841]

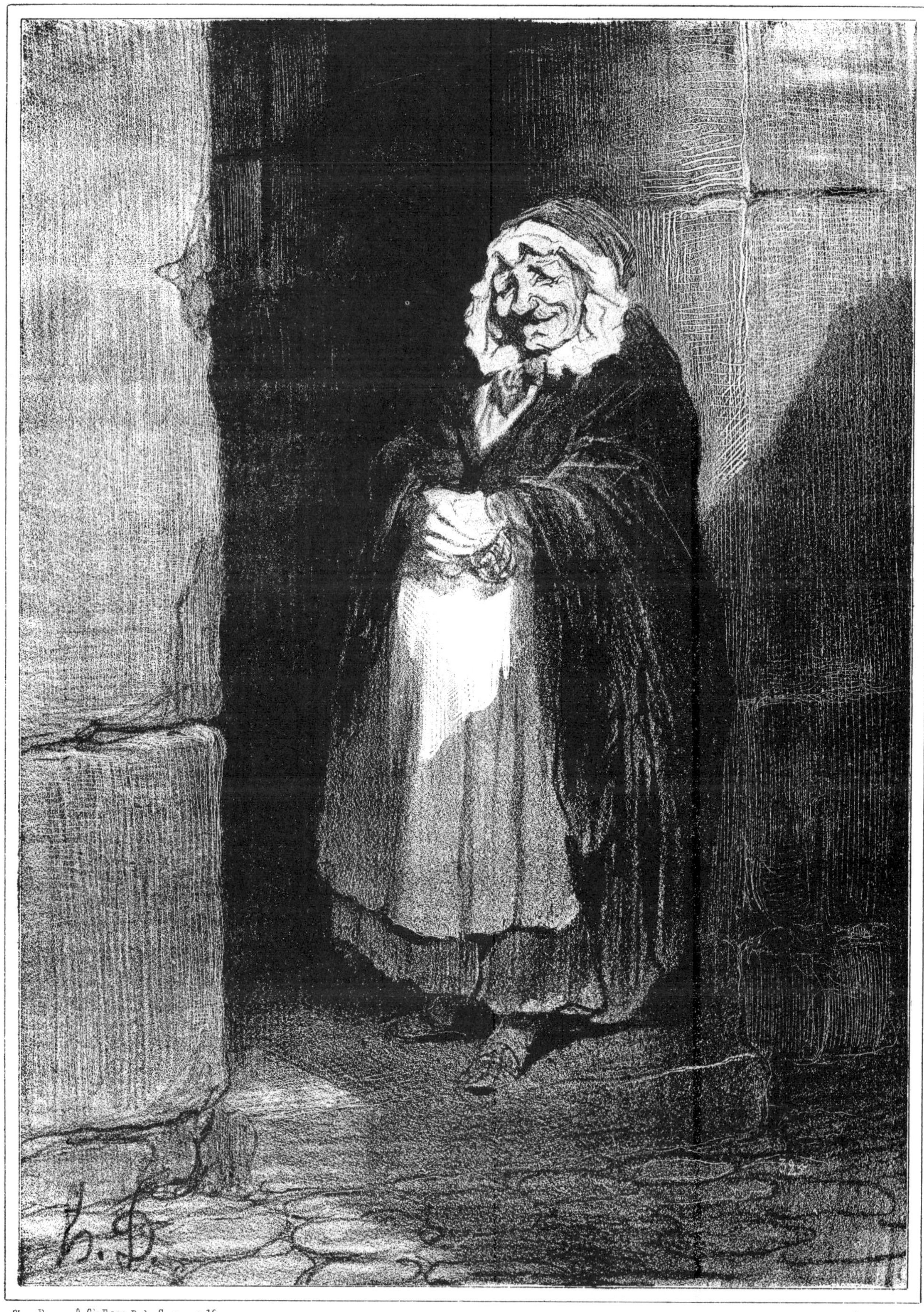

Chez Bauger & Cie Edrs R. du Croissant 16. Imp. d'Aubert & Cie.

LA GARDE-MALADE.

Décidément, il n'y a que les fruitières pour vous procurer de belles connaissances Un epileptique, un hydrophobe et une folle !...... Si l'epicier pouvait me faire avoir avec cà la maladie de poitrine qu'il m'a promise, c'est ça qui me ferait joliment du bien !

32 A sick-nurse, the French equivalent of Dickens' Sairey Gamp. [May 22, 1842]

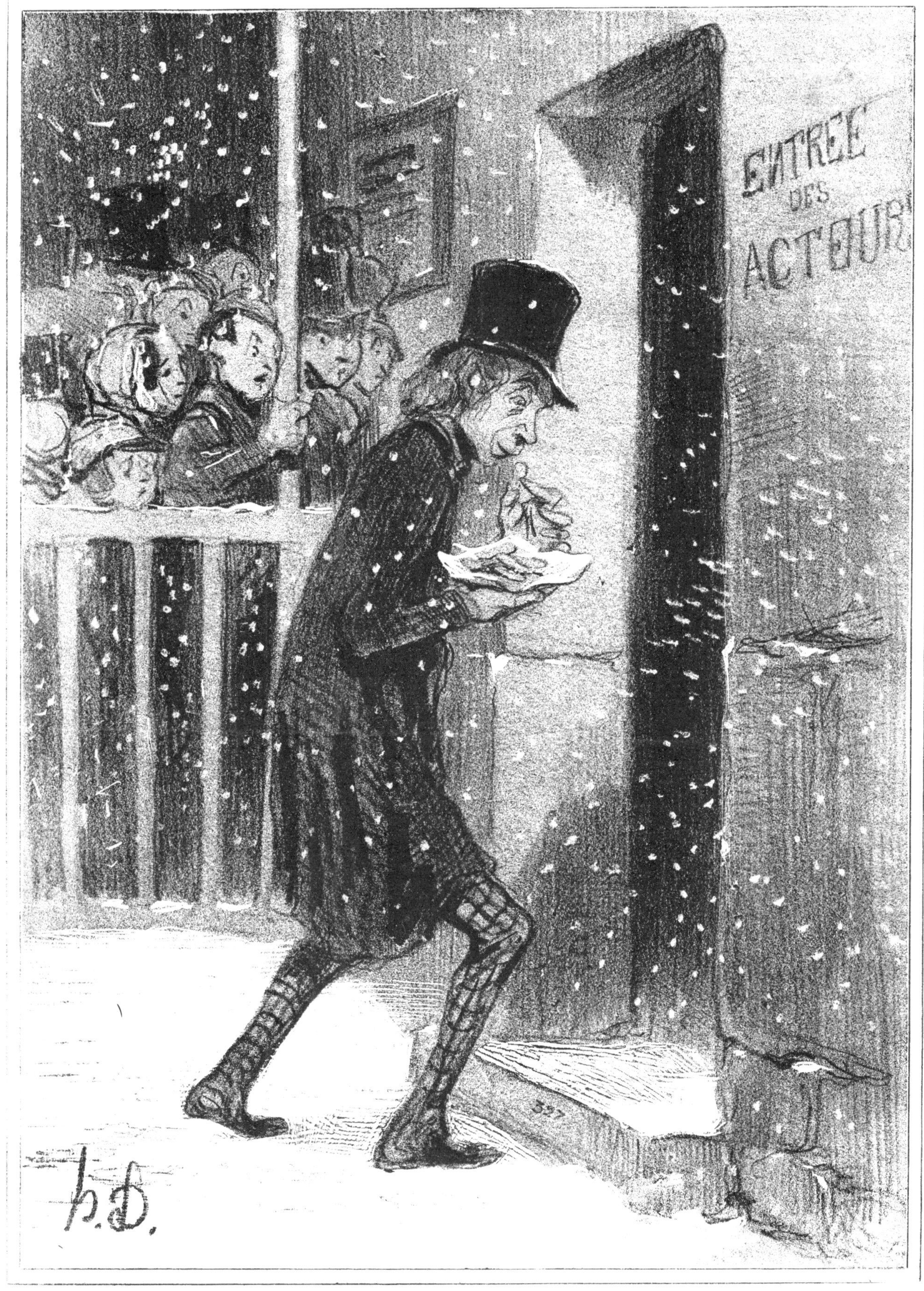

Chez Bauger & Cie R. du Croissant, 16.

L'ACTEUR DES FUNAMBULES.

En v'là un temps qui vous rend passionné! et tout à l'heure va falloir être brûlant d'amour en turc... et dire «ô Zuléma, partage mes trésors et mon trône... viens, viens t'enivrer dans les plaisirs et l'abondance!» avec un sou de pommes de terre frites dans le ventre!

33 A minor actor in a small theater who plays wealthy monarchs though actually starving. [Feb. 19, 1842]

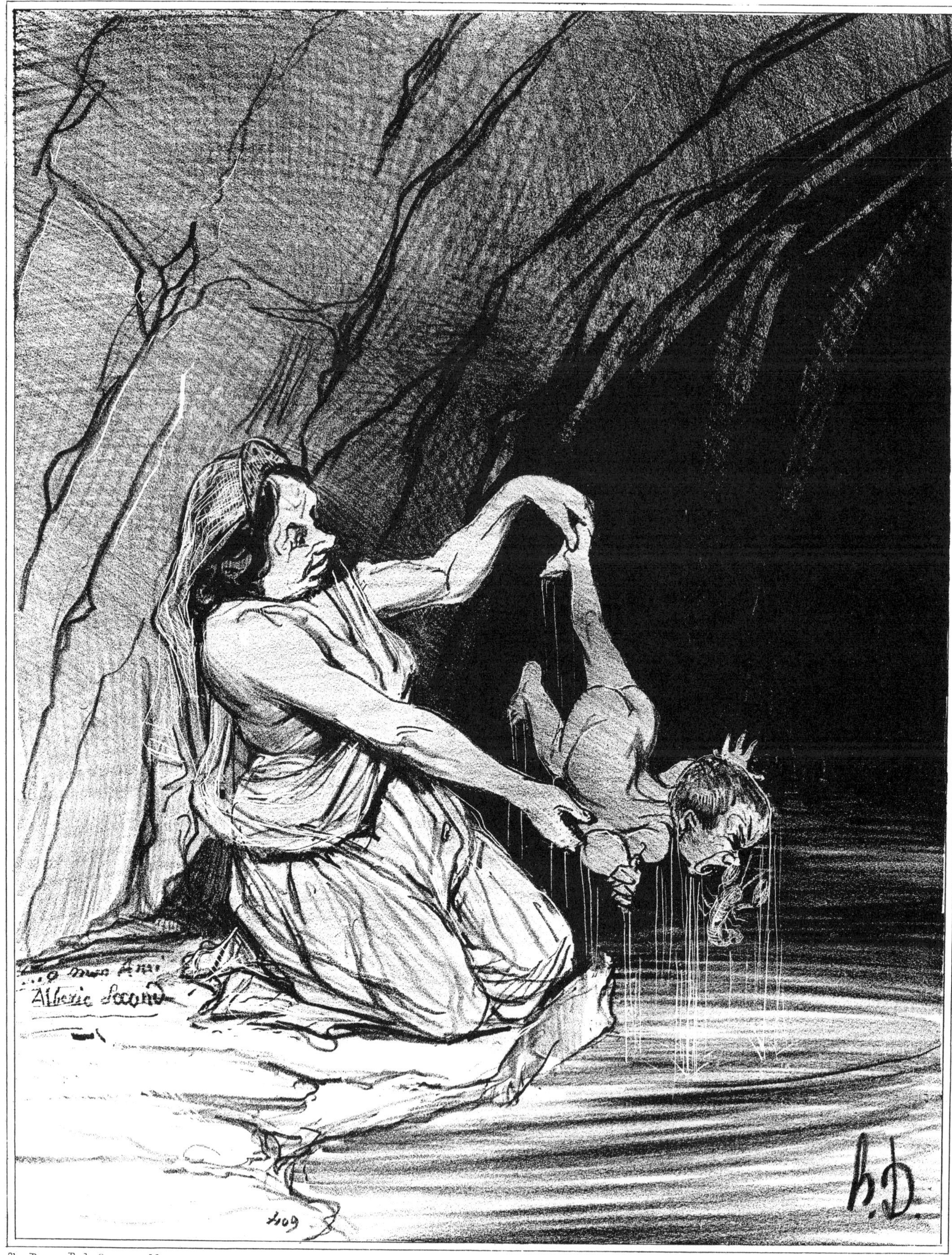

Chez Bauger, R. du Croissant, 16. Imp. d'Aubert & Cie.

LE BAPTÊME D'ACHILLE.

Comme on trempe une arme de guerre,
Thétis de son moutard voulant faire un héros,
Le trempa dans le Styx dès qu'il vit la lumière;
Ce qui prouve qu'un bain est bon à tout propos.

(De l'influence des bains, Poëme par Mr Vigier.)

34 Satire on the myth of Achilles dipped in the Styx by his mother Thetis.
[Aug. 28, 1842]

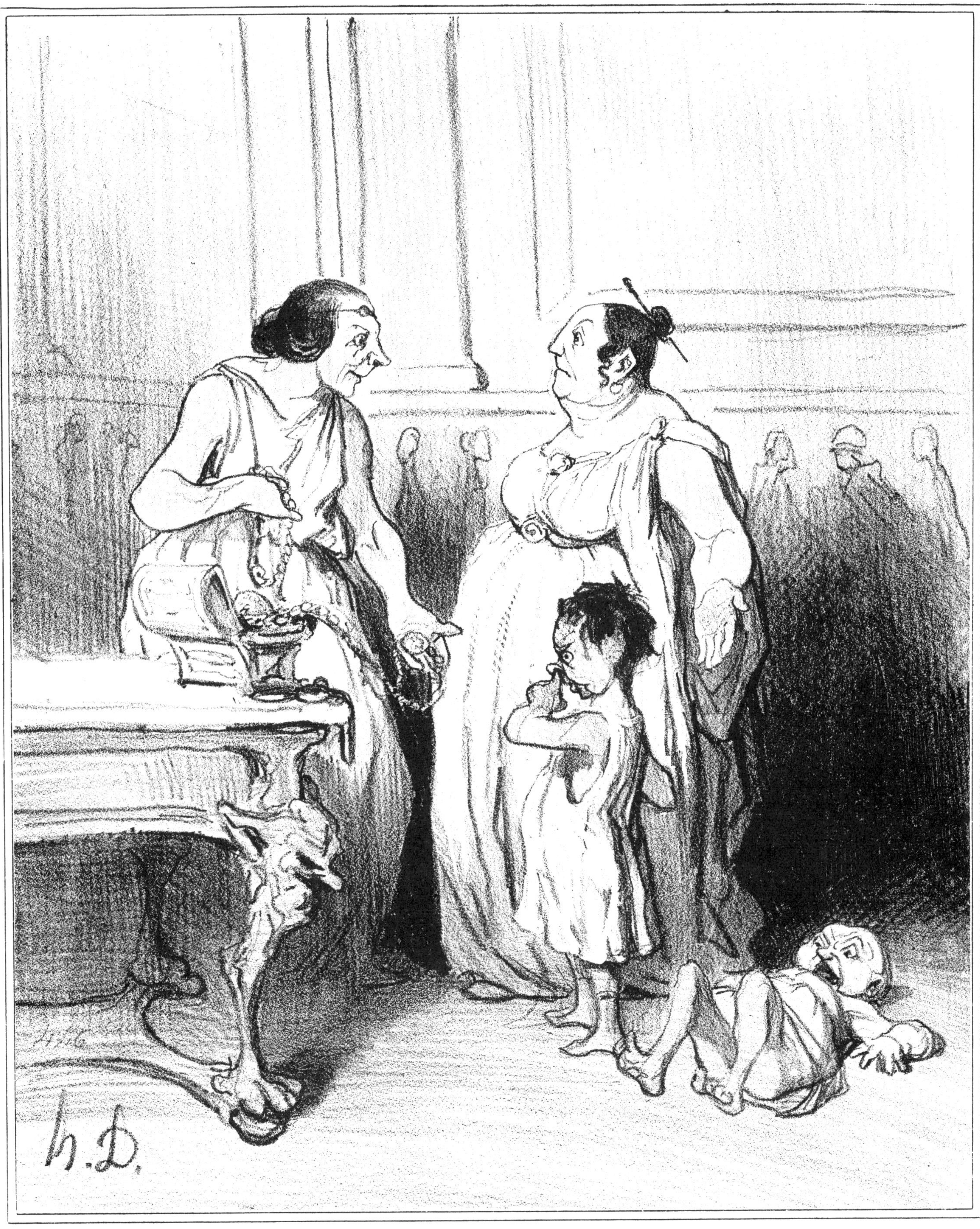

Chez Bauger R. du Croissant, 16.

Imp. d'Aubert & Cie.

LA MÈRE DES GRACQUES.

Un jour qu'une Lorette avec effronterie
Lui vantait des joyaux qui valaient quelques sous,
En montrant ses deux fils, l'espoir de la patrie,
Cette Romaine dit : Voilà mes seuls bijoux!!

(Plutarque.)

35 Satire on the Roman legend of the mother of the Gracchi, whose sons were "her jewels." [Dec. 23, 1842]

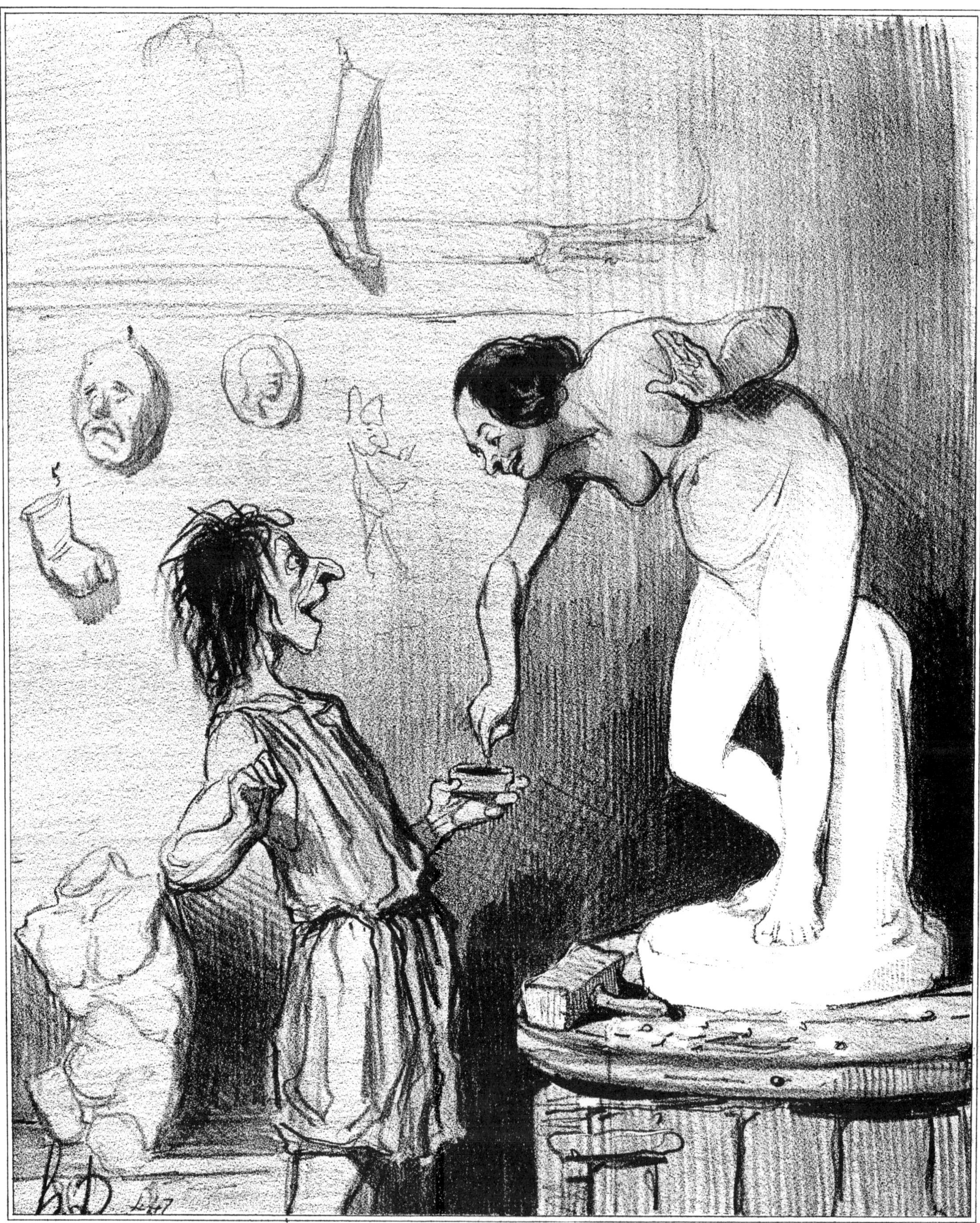

Chez Bauger, R. du Croissant, 16. Imp. d'Aubert & Cie.

PYGMALION.

O triomphe des arts! quelle fût ta surprise,
Grand sculpteur, quand tu vis ton marbre s'animer,
Et, d'un air chaste et doux, lentement se baisser
Pour te demander une prise.

(Comte Siméon.)

36 Satire on the classical legend of the sculptor Pygmalion whose statue of Galatea came to life. [Dec. 28, 1842]

Chez Paunier & Cie Edit. R. du Croissant 16.

Imp. d'Aubert & Cie

UN HOMME A LA MER

–Harponne-le donc plus vigoureusement... nous ne pourrons pas l'avoir sans ça! –Et toi, tiens lui bien les jambes en l'air, c'est l'important!.. il n'y a rien qui enrhume comme de se mouiller la plante des pieds!.....

37 Saving a rower who has fallen overboard. [June 11, 1843]

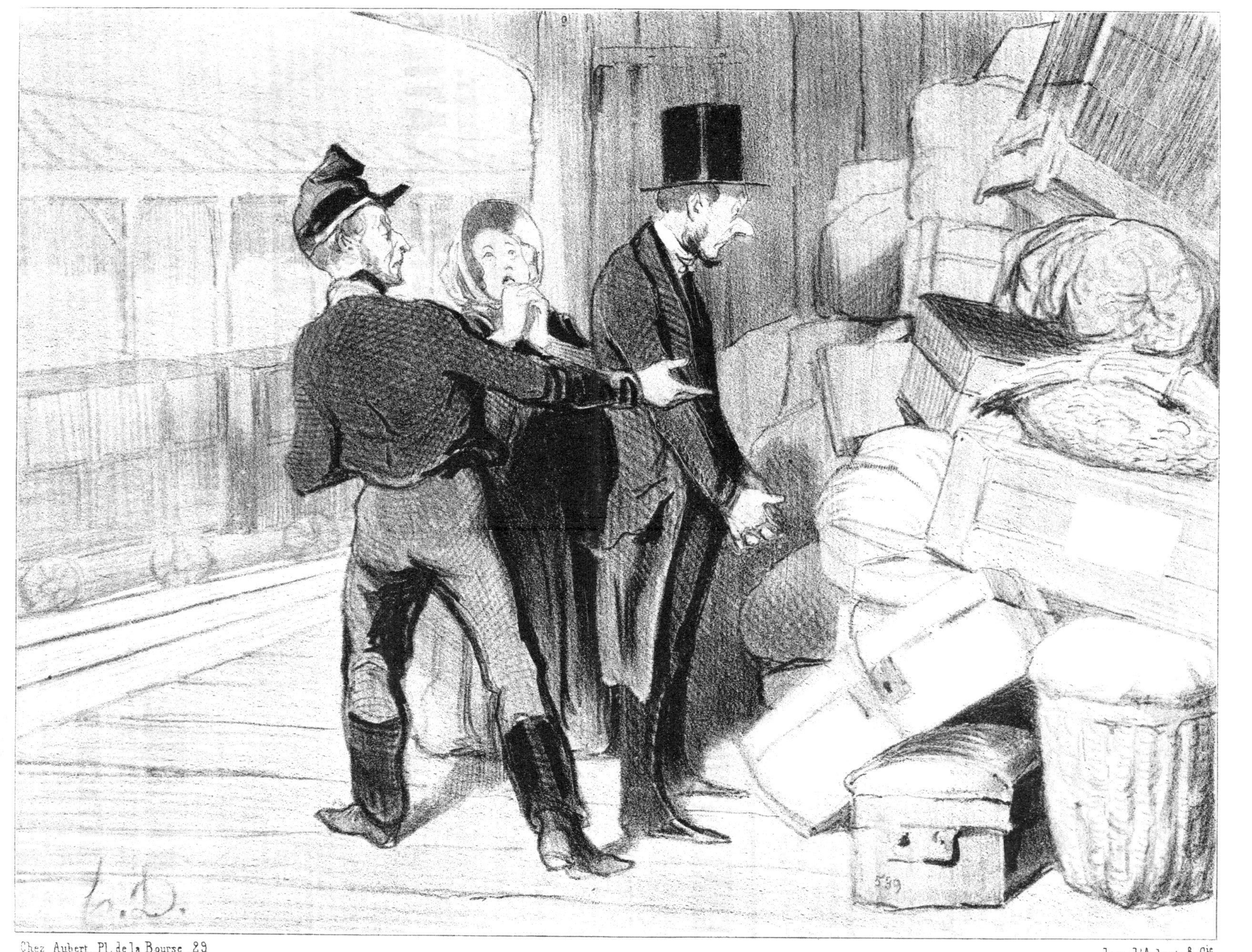

Chez Aubert, Pl. de la Bourse, 29 Imp. d'Aubert & Cie.

– Vous cherchez votre malle, monsieur, elle est là!... et le carton à chapeau de madame aussi....

38 Trunk buried and hatbox crushed by indifferent railroad employees. [Dec. 19, 1843]

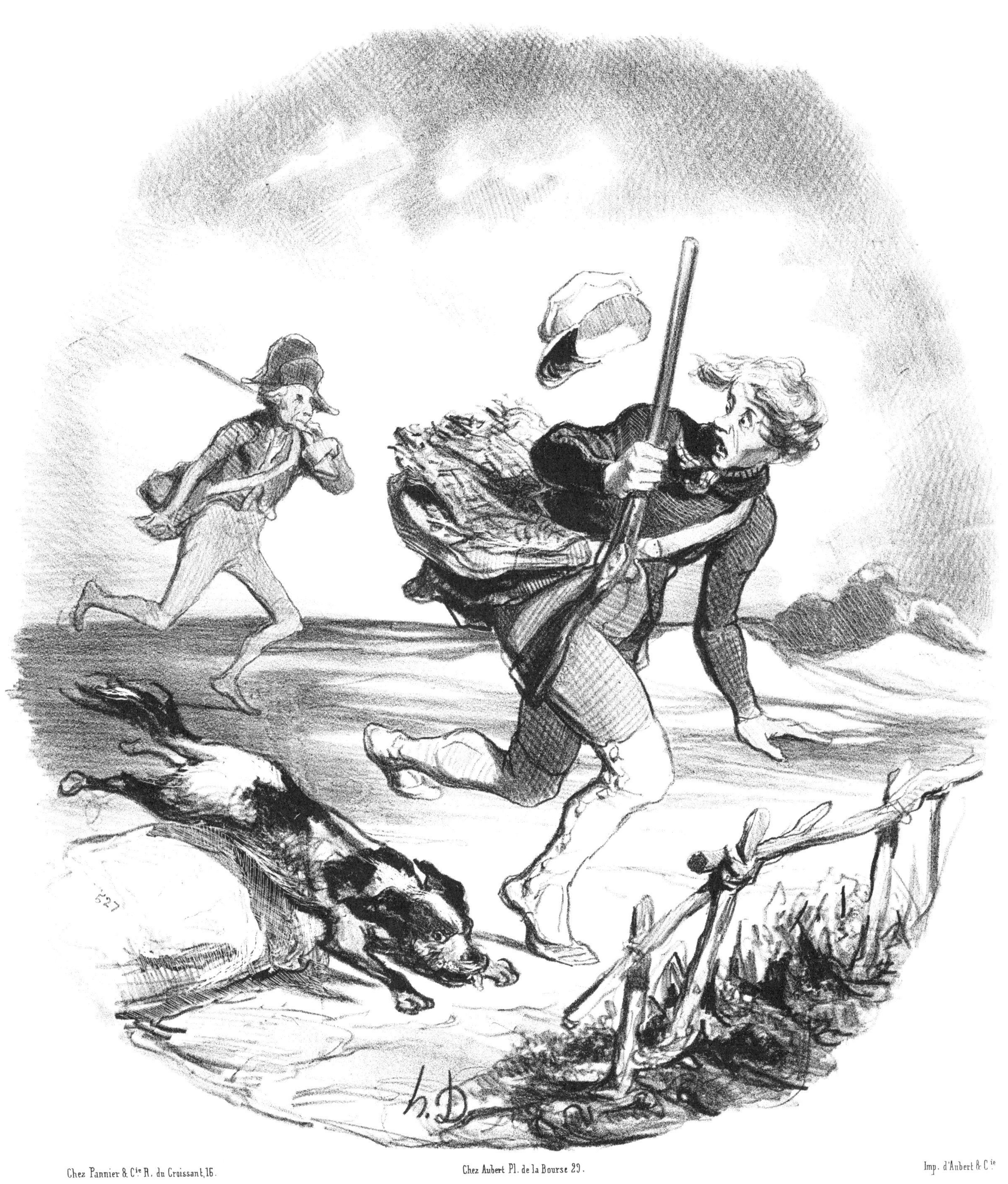

Le Chasseur chassé.

39 A country guard chasing a trespassing hunter. [Oct. 15, 1843]

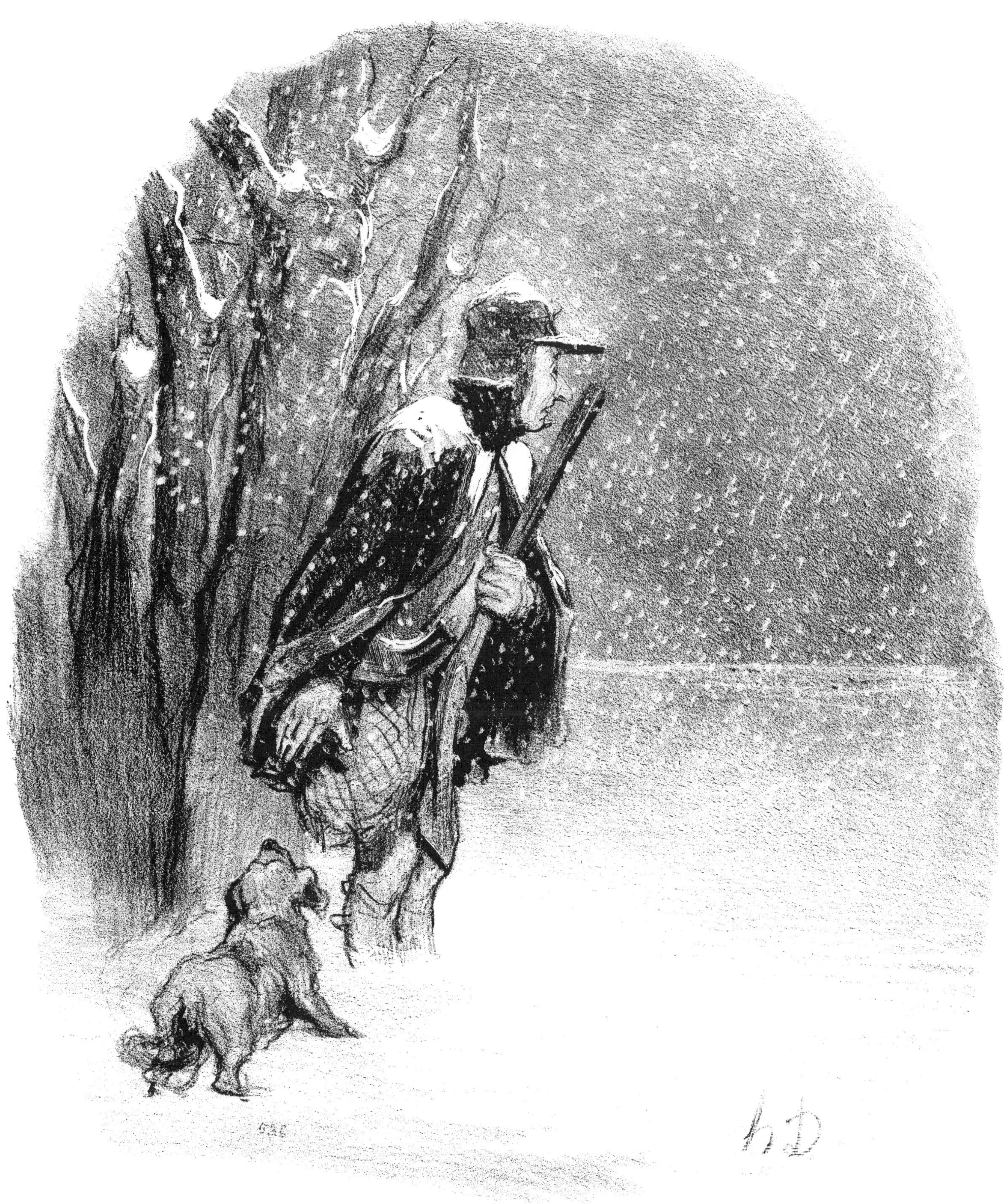

LA NEIGE.

Imp. d'Aubert & Cie.

Tais-toi, Phénix! comment veux-tu que je voye venir...... c'est drôle, j'ai pourtant là une fameuse place!

40 Waiting for game in an allegedly good spot. [Dec. 6, 1843]

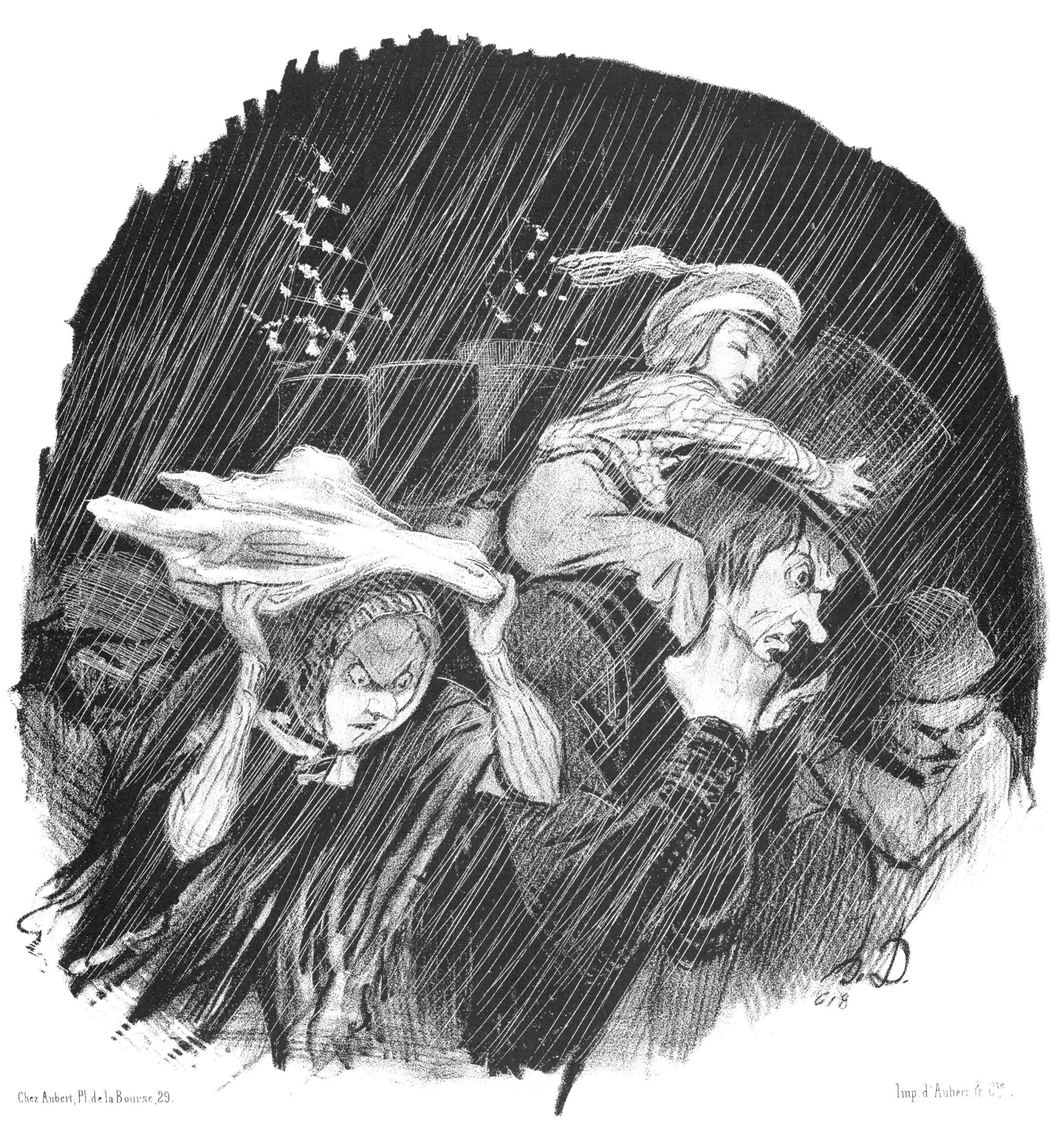

UN SOIR DE FÊTE NATIONALE.

Ça ne manque jamais..... on sort pour aller voir le feu, et on ne jouit que de l'eau!..

41 Fourteenth of July fireworks rained out. [Aug. 21, 1844]

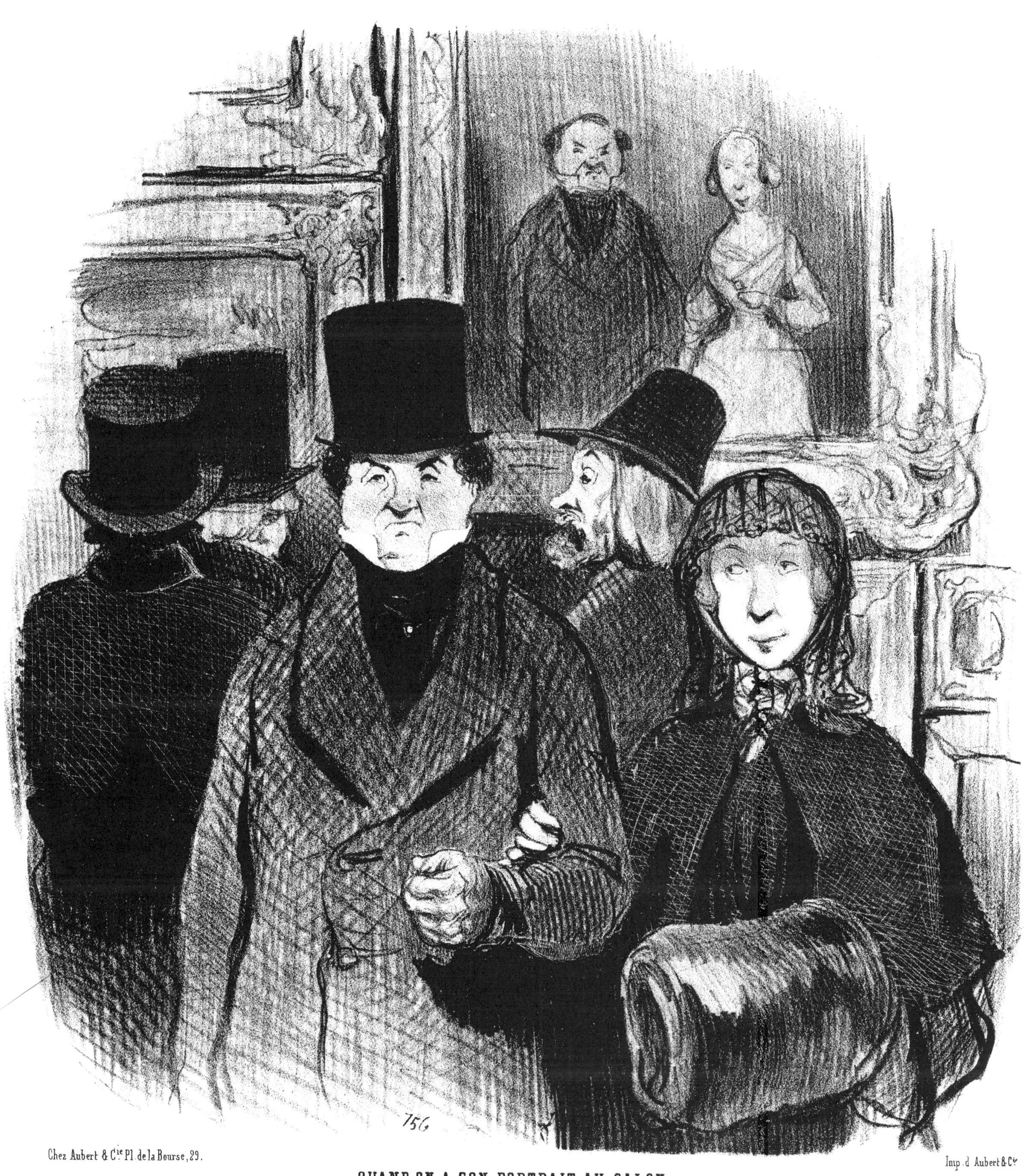

42 An art student derides the sitters of a Salon portrait in their presence. [Apr. 26, 1845]

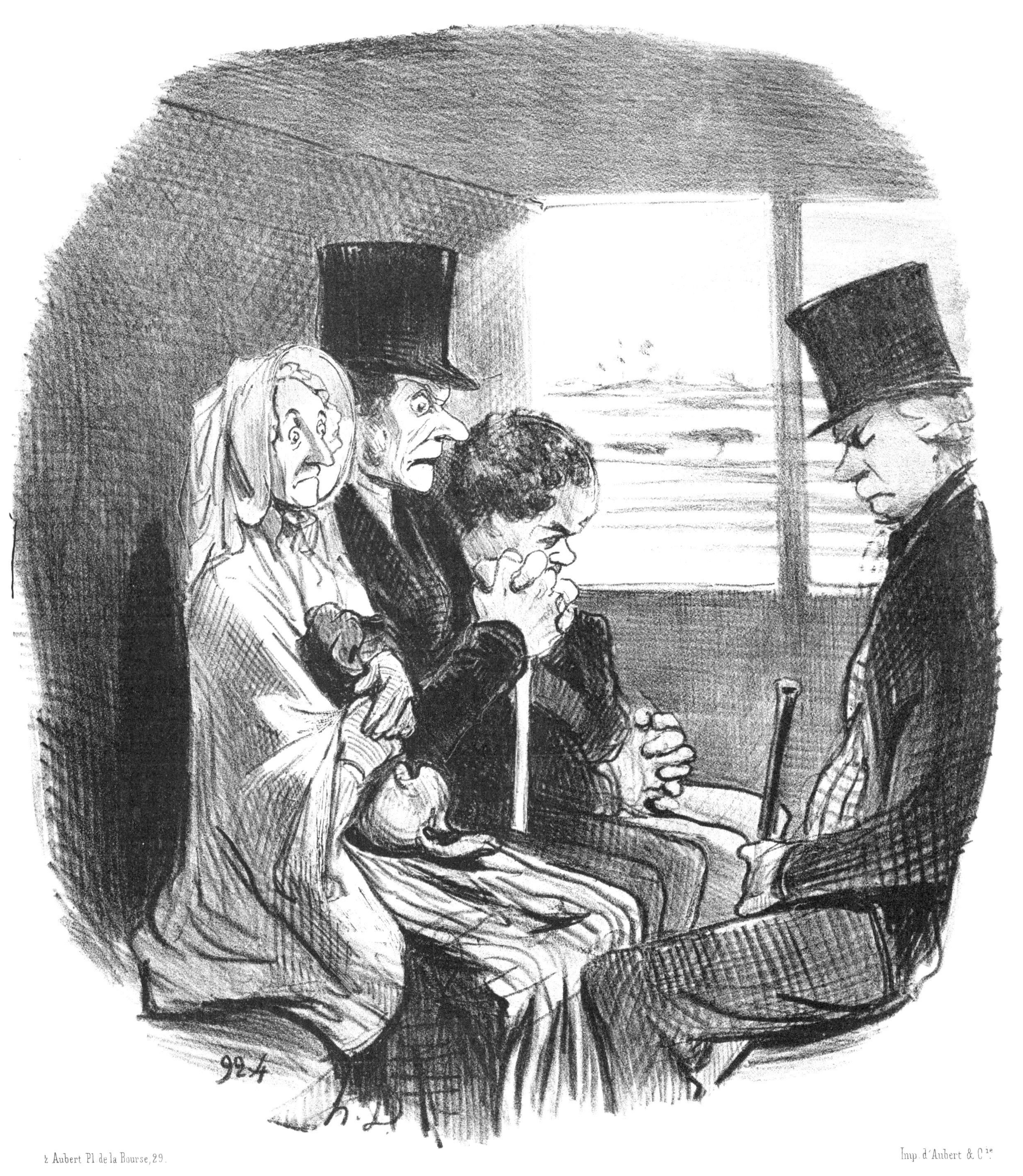

43 Frightened at their first train ride. [July 19, 1846]

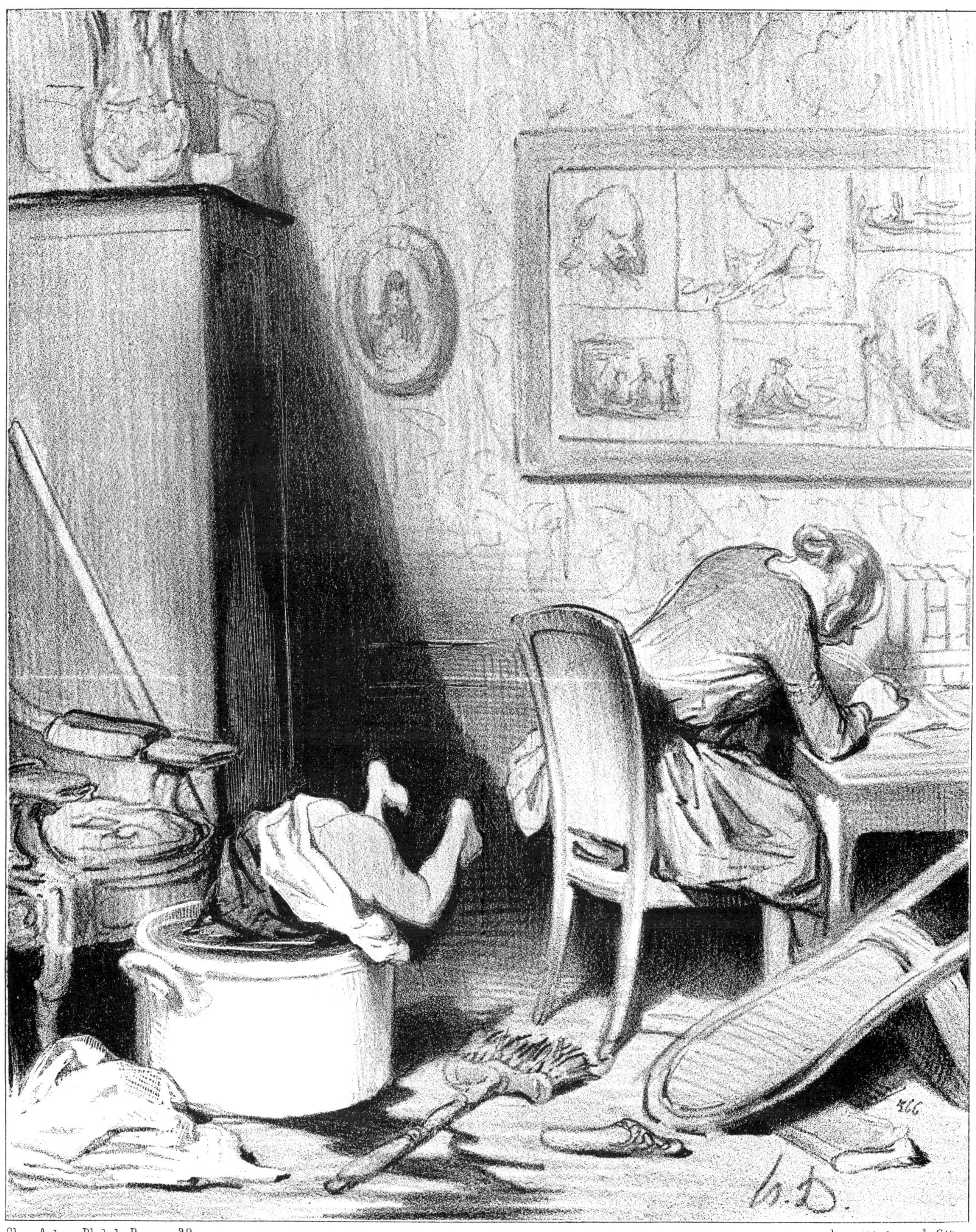

La mère est dans le feu de la composition, l'enfant est dans l'eau de la baignoire !

44 A female author neglecting her home and child. [Feb. 26, 1844]

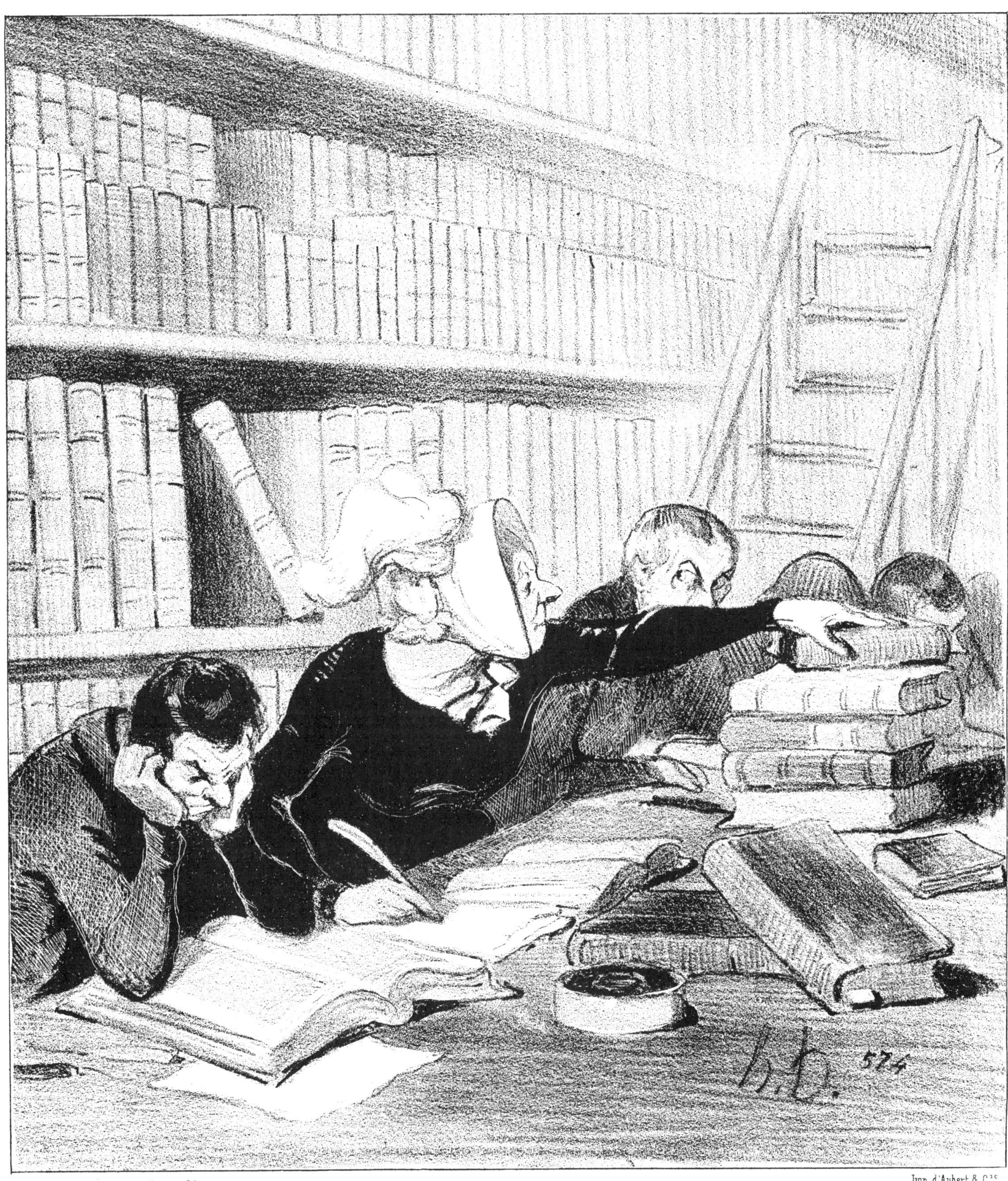

– Monsieur, pardon si je vous gène un peu.... mais vous comprenez qu'écrivant en ce moment un roman nouveau, je dois consulter une foule d'auteurs anciens !......

– (Le Monsieur à part.) Des auteurs anciens !... parbleu elle aurait bien dû les consulter de leur vivant, car elle a dû être leur contemporaine !....

45 A female author annoying researchers at the library. [Mar. 8, 1844]

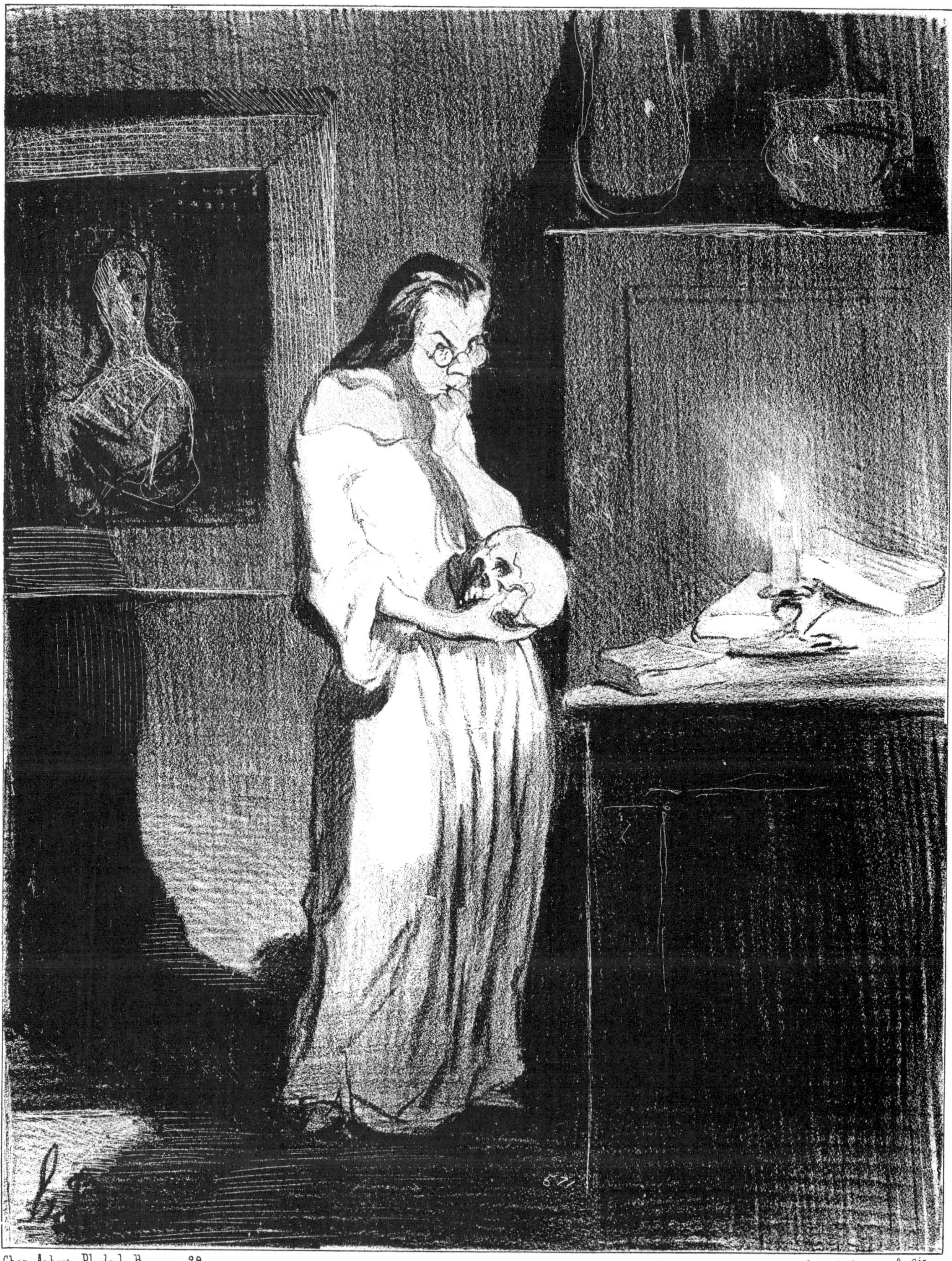

Femme de lettre humanitaire se livrant sur l'homme, à des réflexions **crânement** philosophiques !

46 A female author contemplating man. [Mar. 10, 1844]

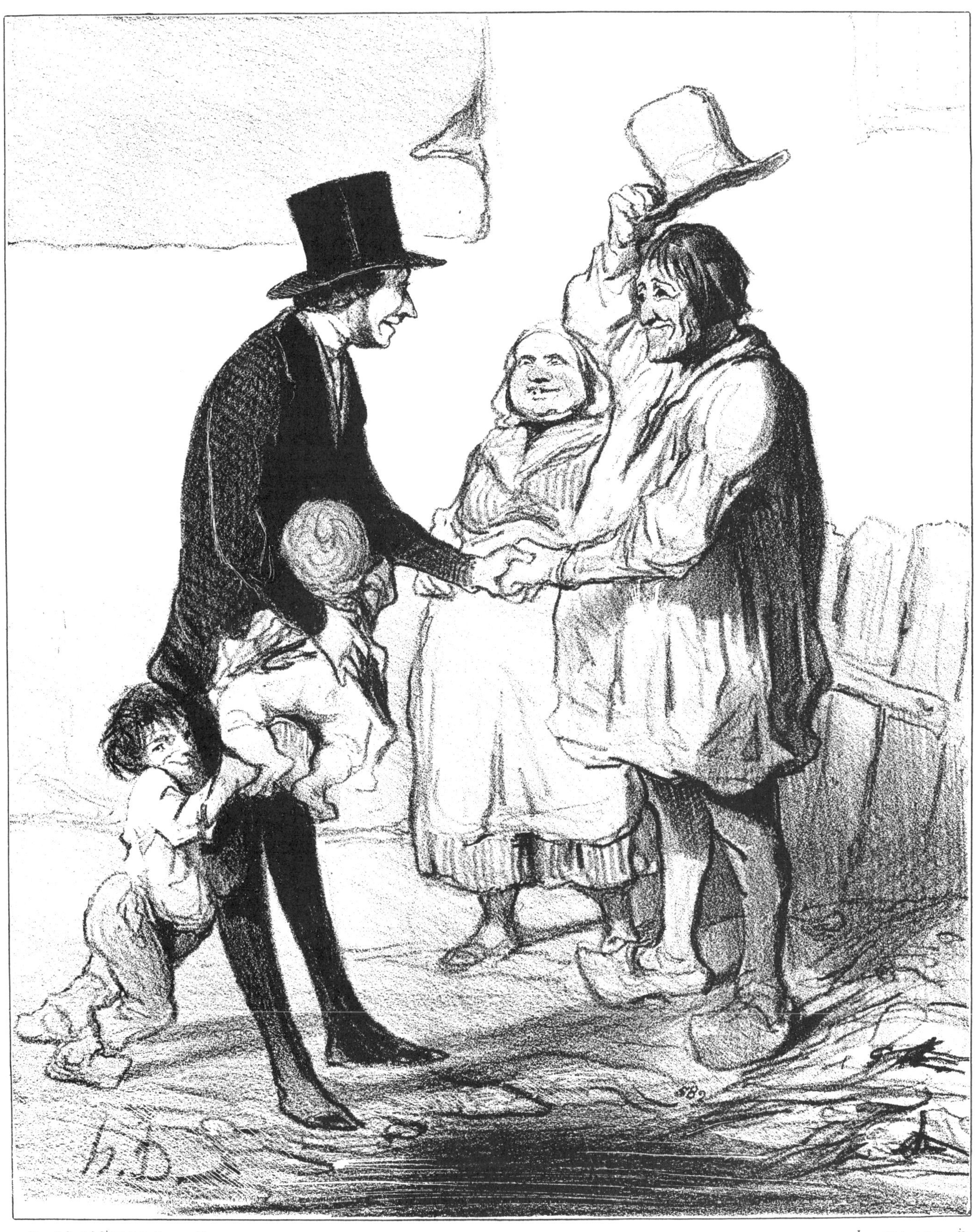

Mon cher ami, ne croyez pas que je vienne vous demander votre voix; je respecte trop l'indépendance des opinions; c'est madame la baronne qui m'a dit: Allez voir ce pauvre Galouzot. dites à sa petite femme qu'elle me néglige; que je lui en veux, informez-vous de leurs délicieux enfants et dites que je veux absolument les avoir à diner.

47 Canvassing for votes among the peasantry. [Mar. 21, 1844]

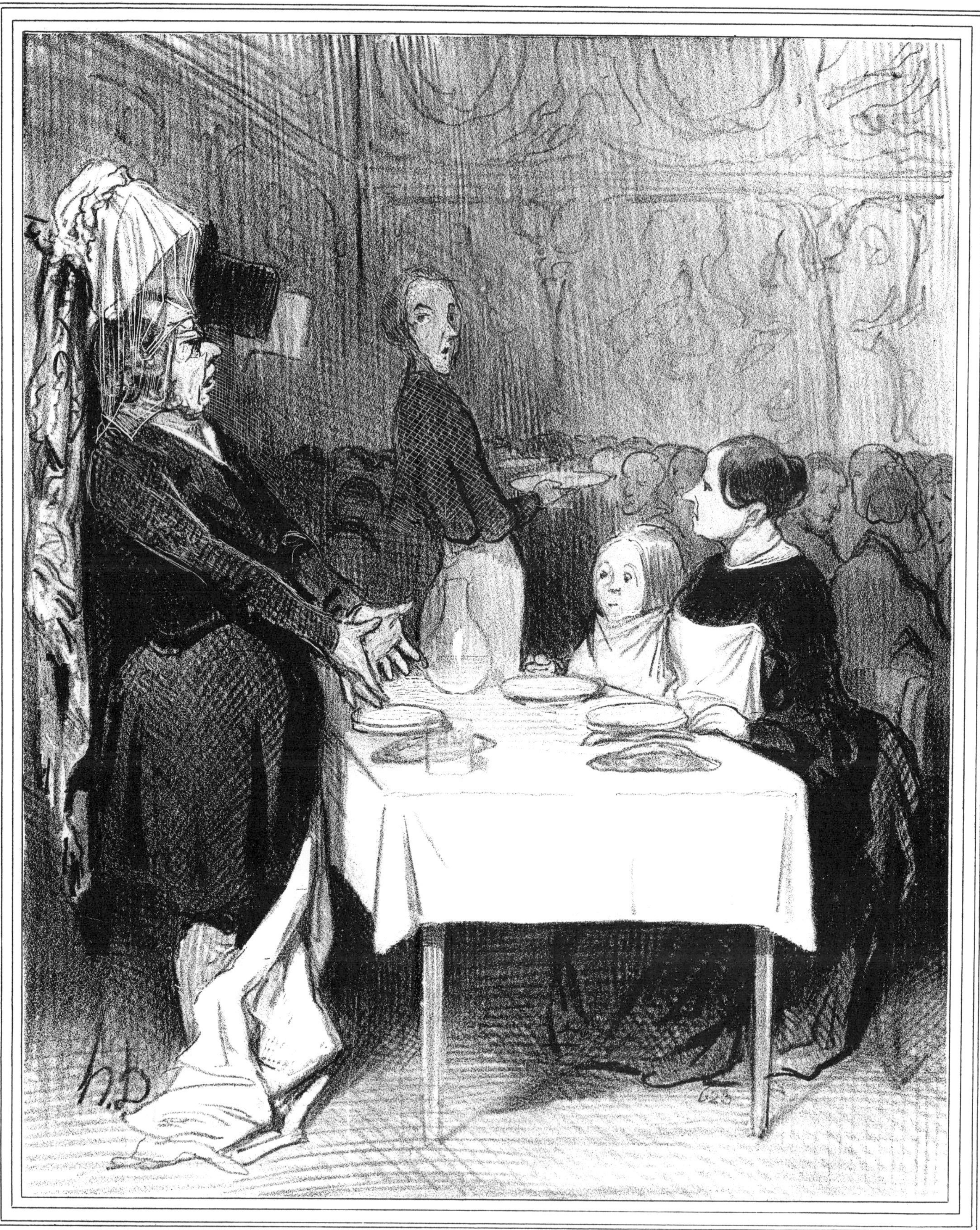

Chez Aubert & Cie Pl. de la Bourse, 29. Imp. d'Aubert & Cie.

CE QU'ON APPELLE **DINER** AU RESTAURANT.

— Garçon!.. voilà une heure et quart que je suis dans votre établissement sans chaise.... et vous n'avez encore servi que des cure-dents à mon épouse qui meurt de faim... vous me ferez sortir de mon assiette ordinaire, et je finirai par mettre les pieds dans le plat.... entendez-vous, garçon!
— Voilà, monsieur.... voilà, voilà, voilà!!!

48 A stranger in Paris complaining about restaurant service. [June 7, 1844]

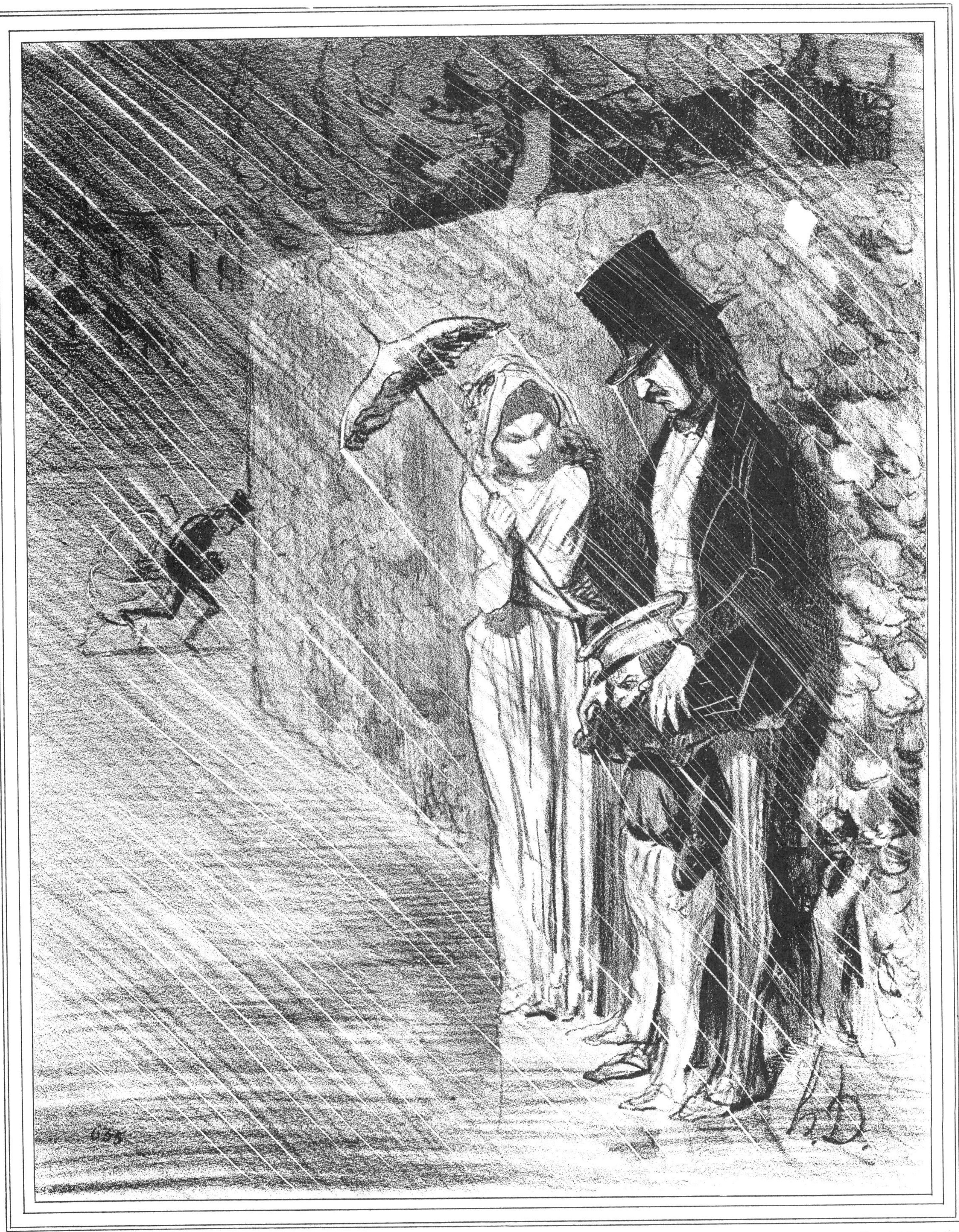

49 Tourists at Versailles disappointed in the weather. [July 28, 1844]

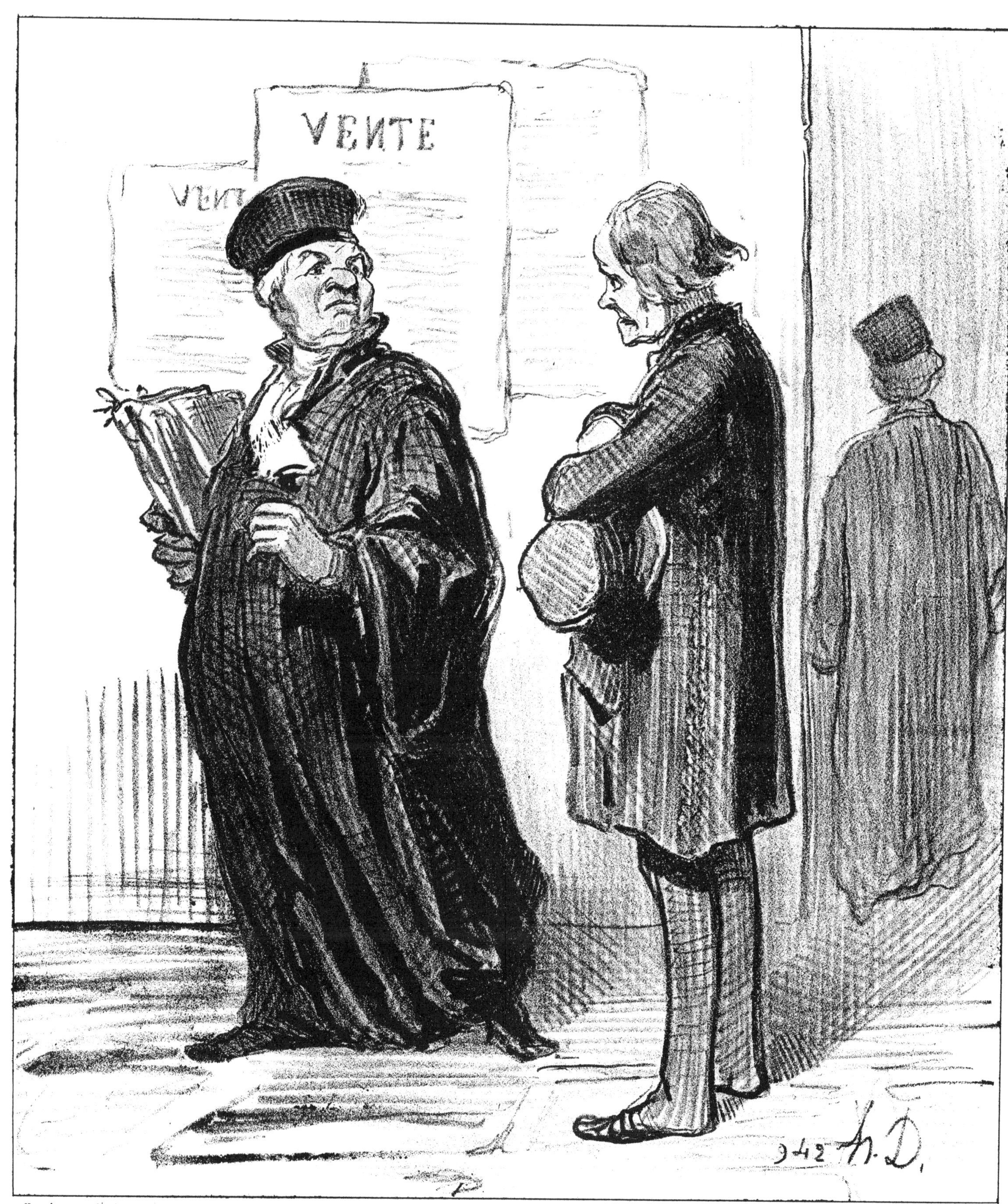

– Mon cher monsieur, il m'est absolument impossible de plaider votre affaire..... il vous manque les pièces les plus importantes....... *(à part)* les pièces de cent sous !.........

50 Lawyer refusing to take on an impecunious client. [Aug. 6, 1846]

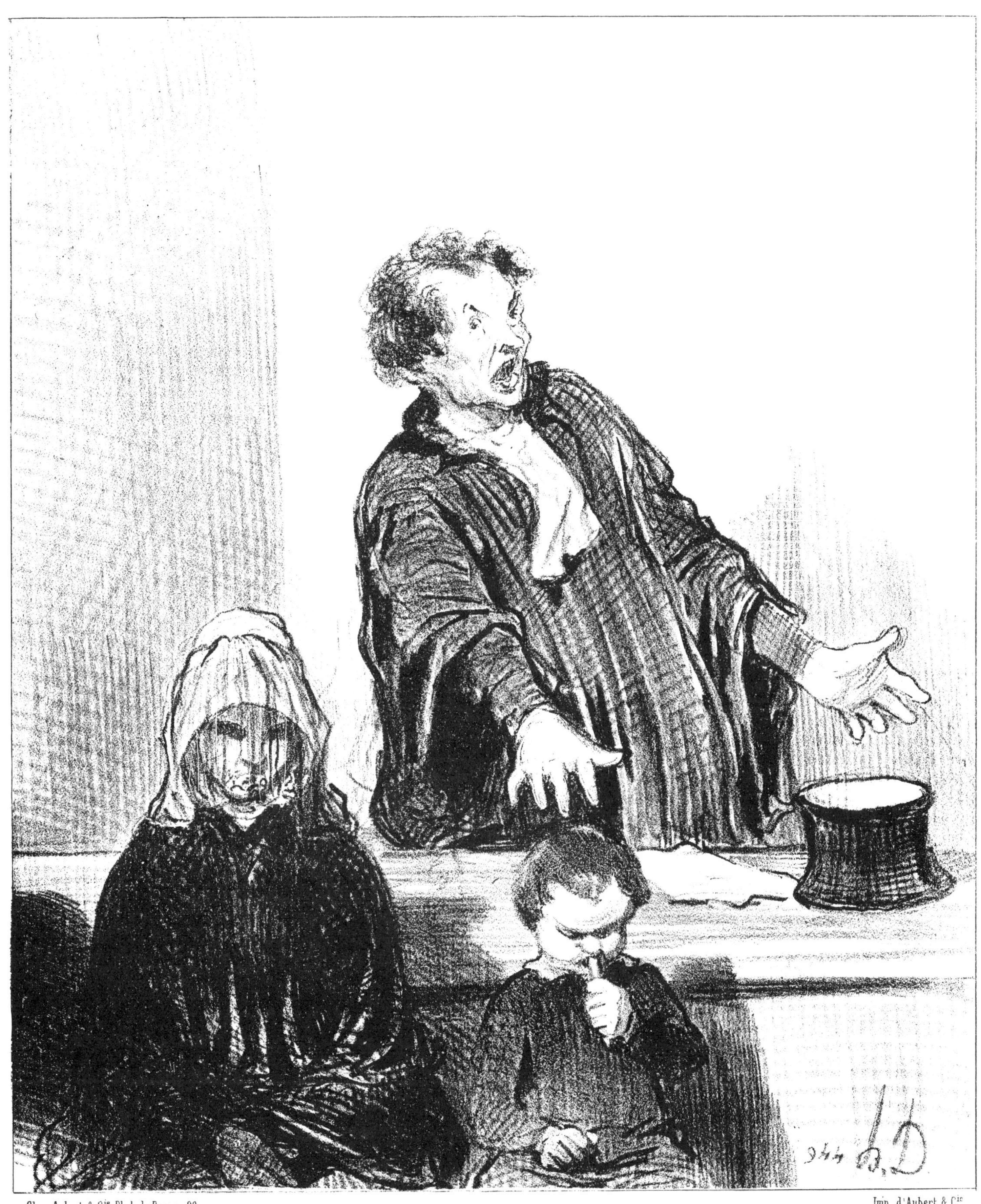

Il défend l'orphelin et la veuve, à moins pourtant qu'il n'attaque la veuve et l'orphelin.

51 The lawyer defends widows and orphans—if they are the ones paying him.
[Sept. 1, 1846]

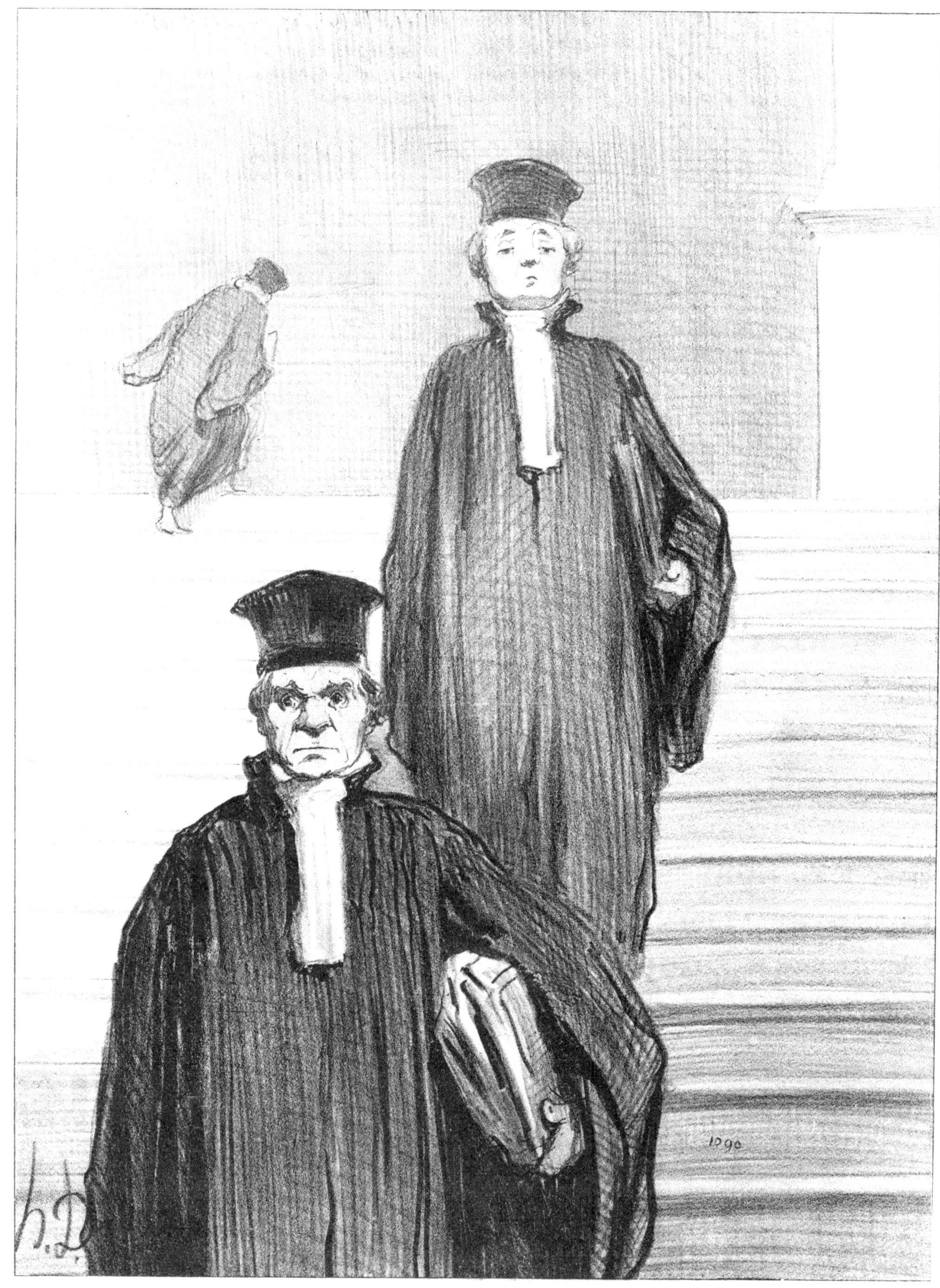

Chez Aubert, Pl. de la Bourse. Imp. Aubert & Cie

Grand escalier du Palais de justice.
Vue de faces.

52 Lawyers on the main staircase of the Palais de Justice. [Feb. 8, 1848]

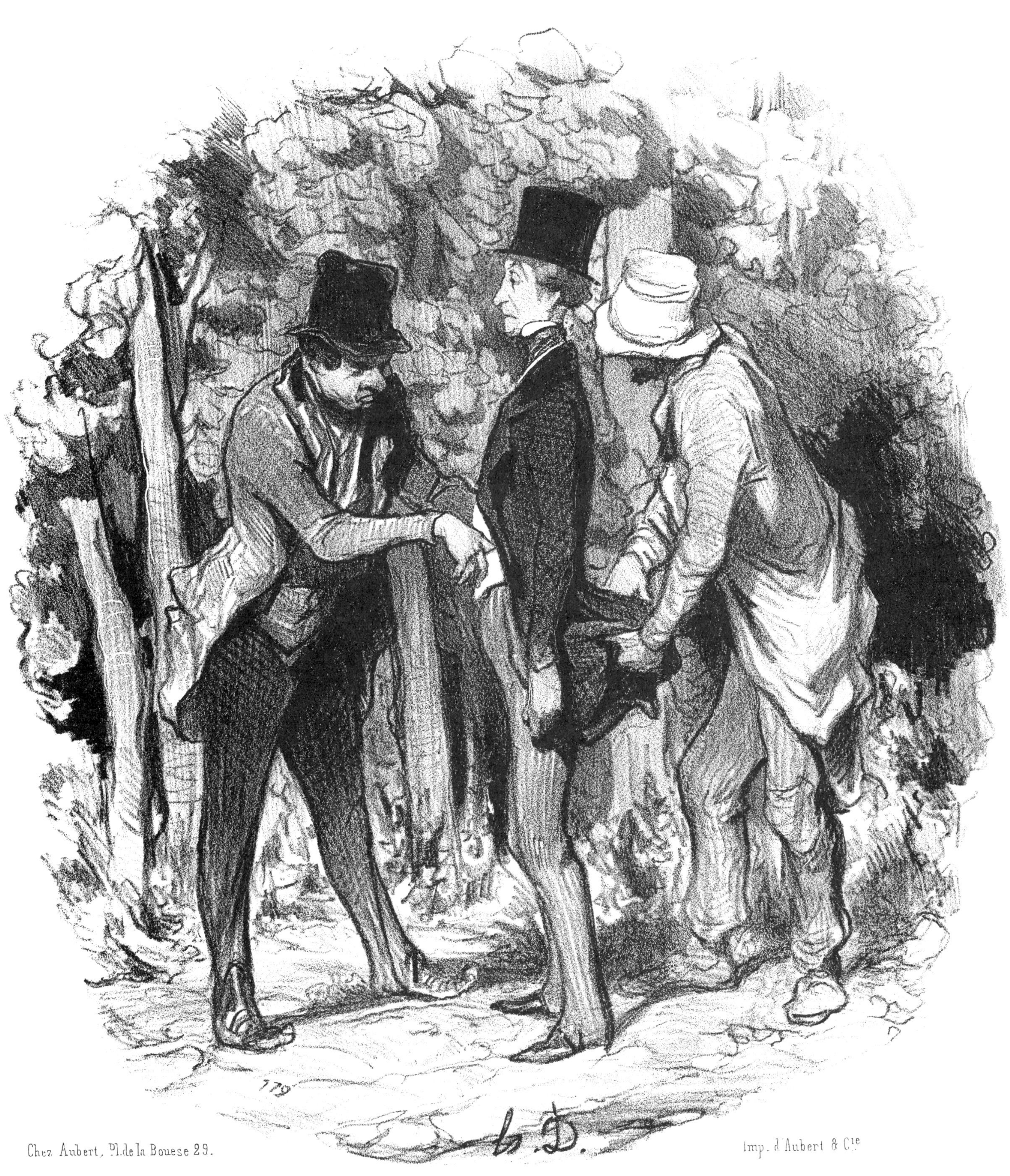

53 The dangers of a walk in rural solitude. [June 27, 1845]

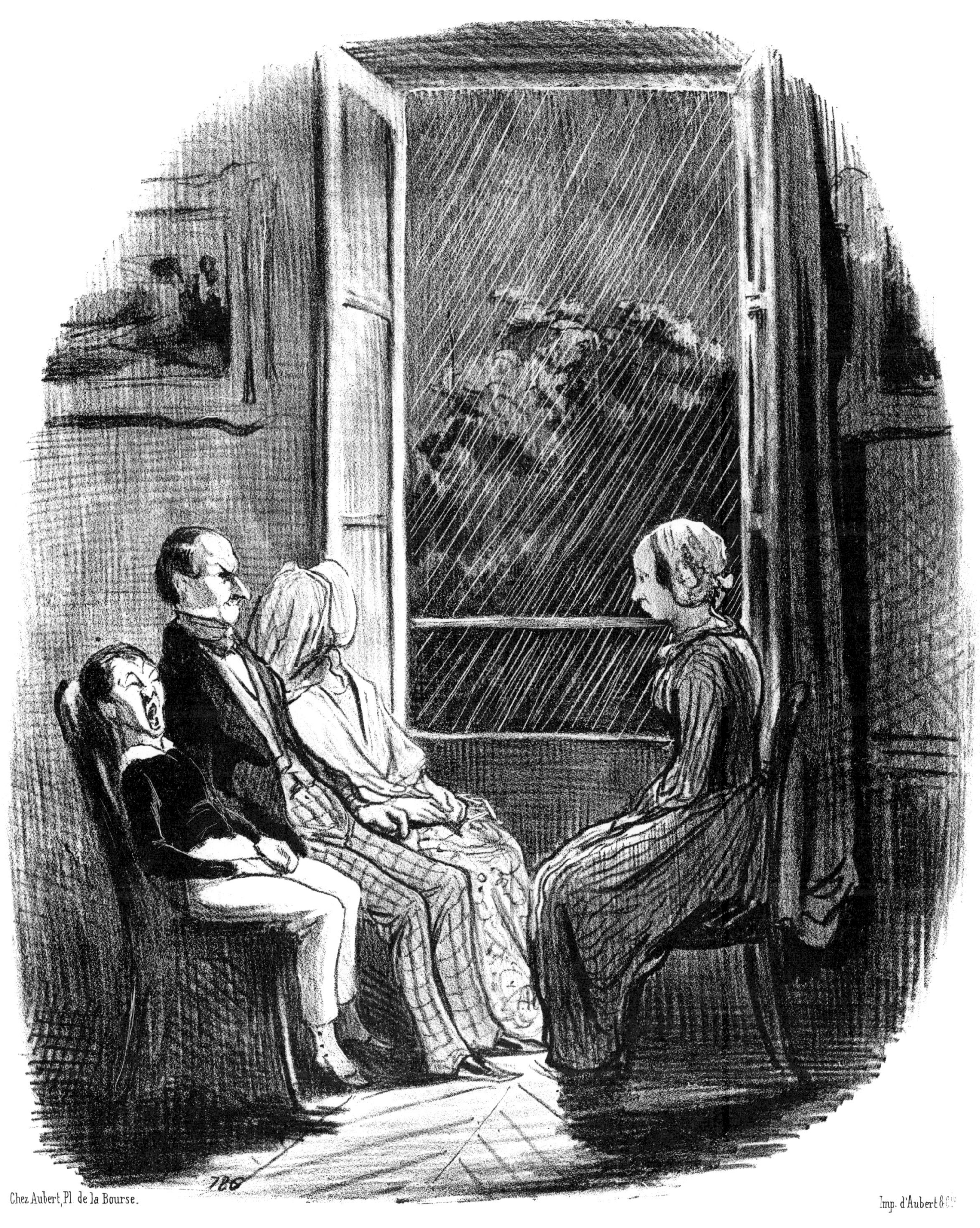

— Et dire que c'est aujourd'hui la St Médard!....

54 When it rains on a country vacation—and the rain is likely to continue! [July 10, 1845]

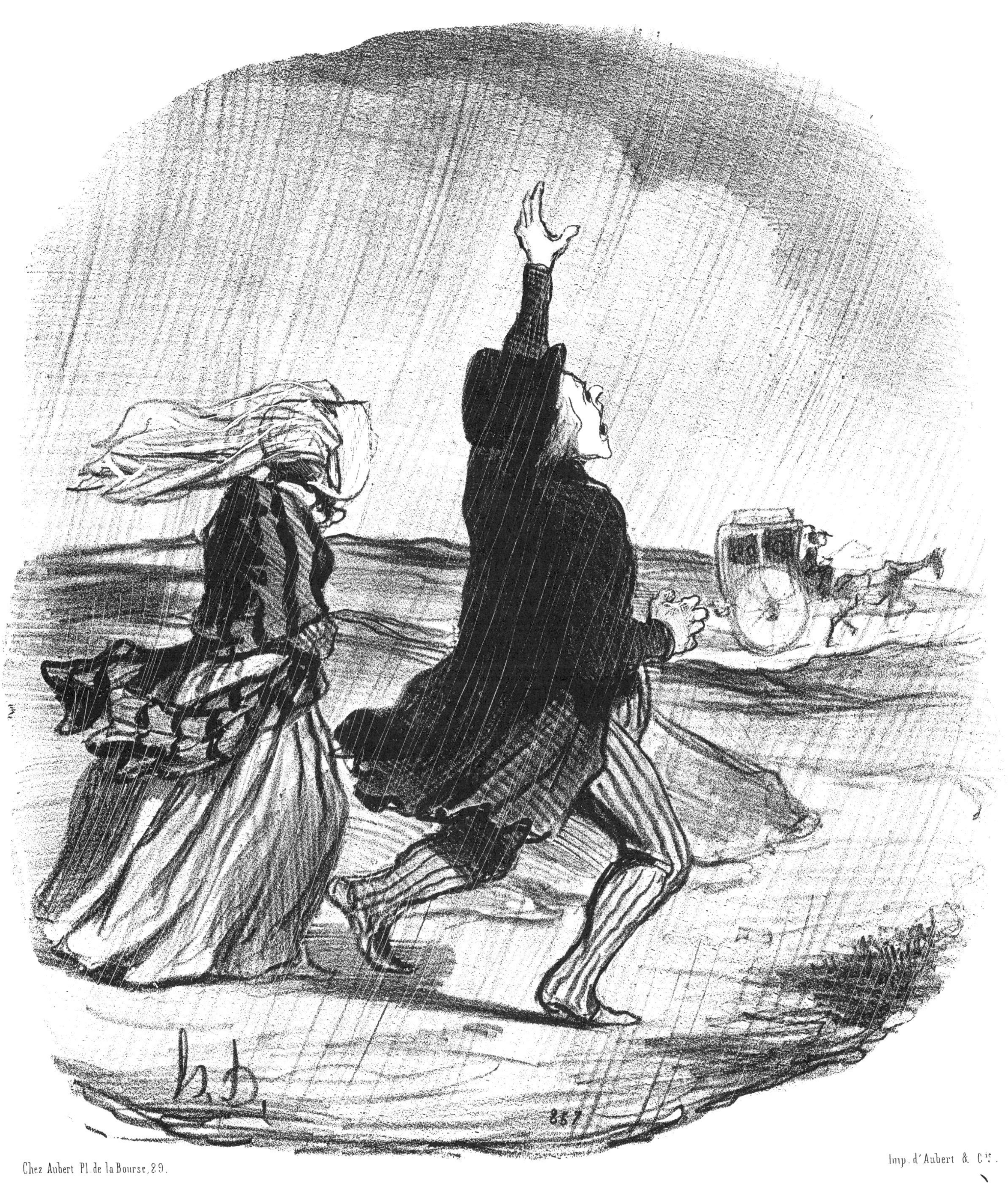

UNE COURSE AU COUCOU.

55 Trying to catch the rural coach. [Jan. 6, 1846]

Chez Aubert, Pl. de la Bourse, 29.

Imp. d'Aubert & Cie

Un jeune homme en train d'acquérir ce que l'on est convenu d'appeler un art d'agrément.

56 Sour notes and tempers at a music lesson. [June 4, 1846]

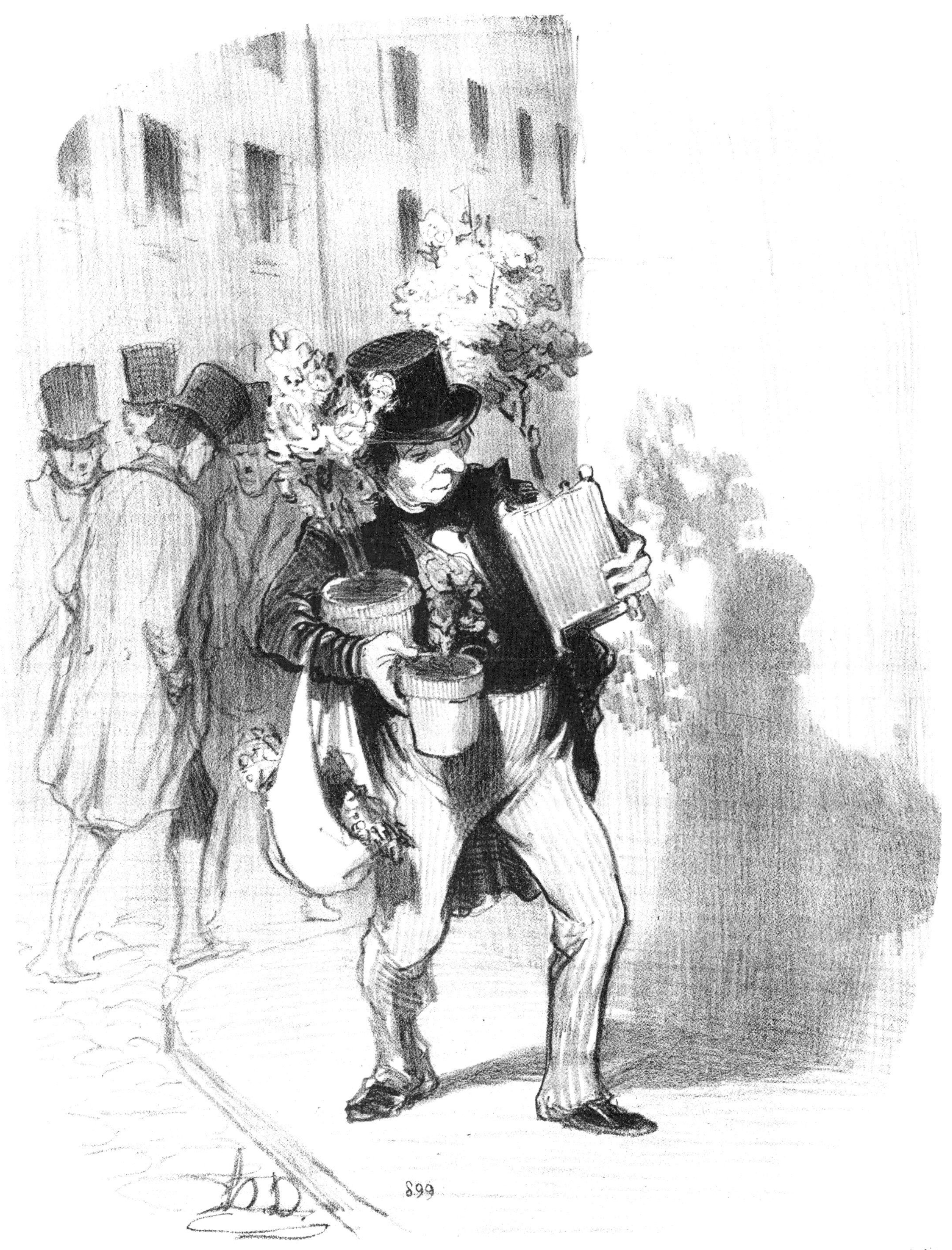

Chez Aubert Pl. de la Bourse, 29. Imp. d'Aubert & Cie

C'est demain la fête de sa femme.

57 For his wife's birthday. [June 18, 1846]

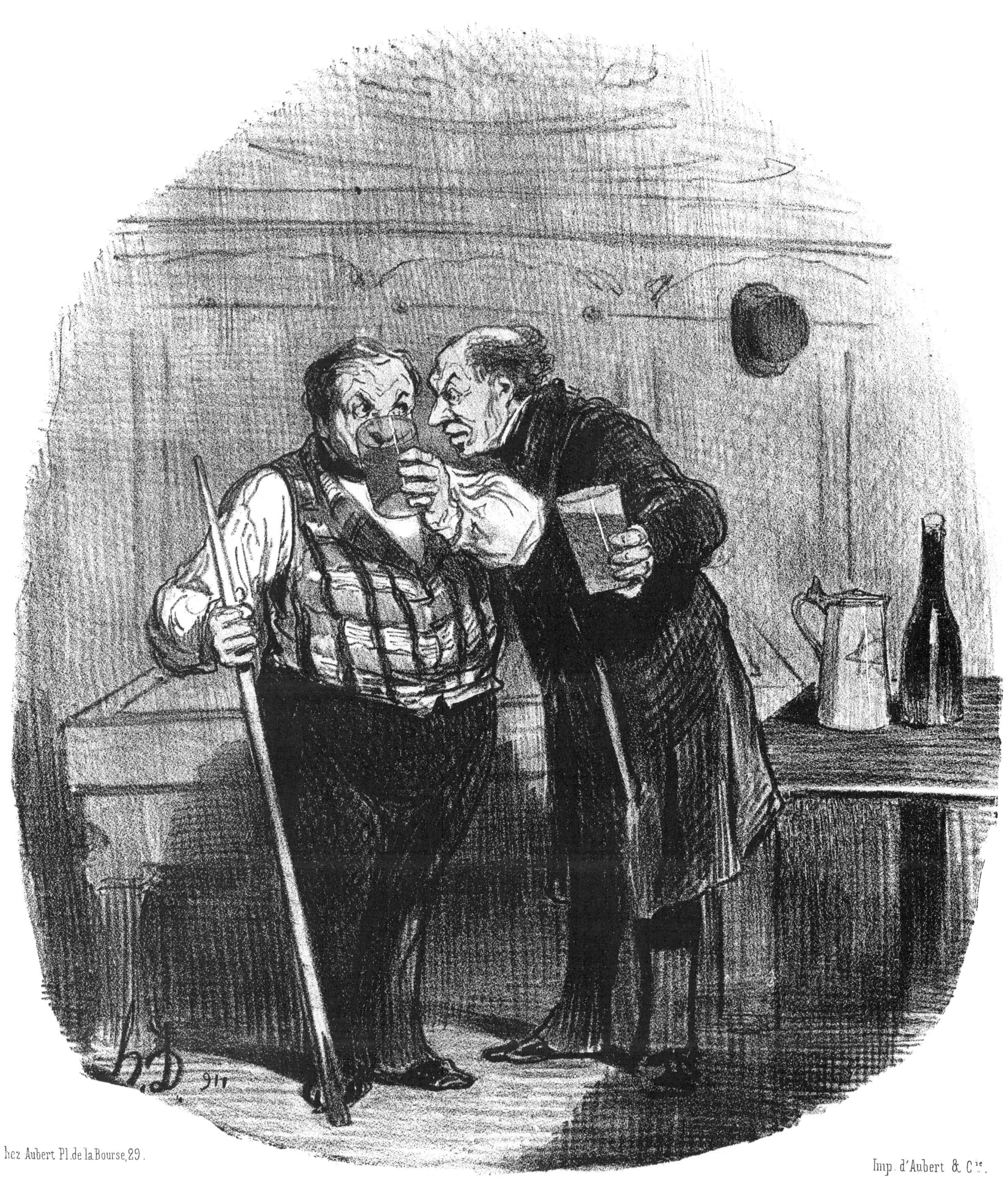

_Dites donc, Ravignard, si nos femmes nous voyaient!.. faut avouer que nous sommes de fameux mauvais sujets!..

58 Proud of their perfectly wild pleasures away from home! [Sept. 28, 1846]

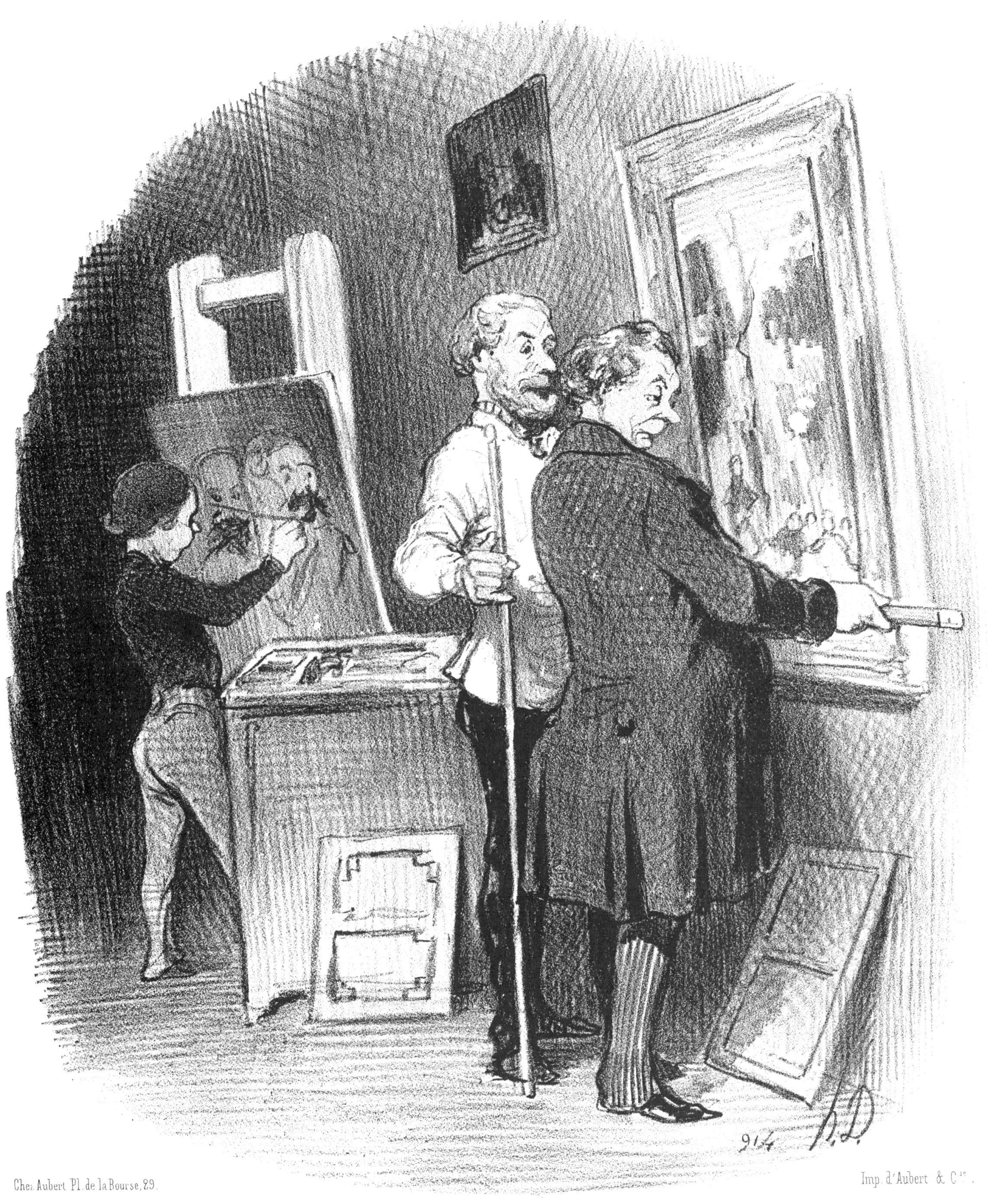

Votre tableau me plairait assez . . . . mais décidément il a une demi canne de moins que ce qu'il me faut ! . . . .

59 The painting would do if it were a little wider. [Oct. 12, 1846]

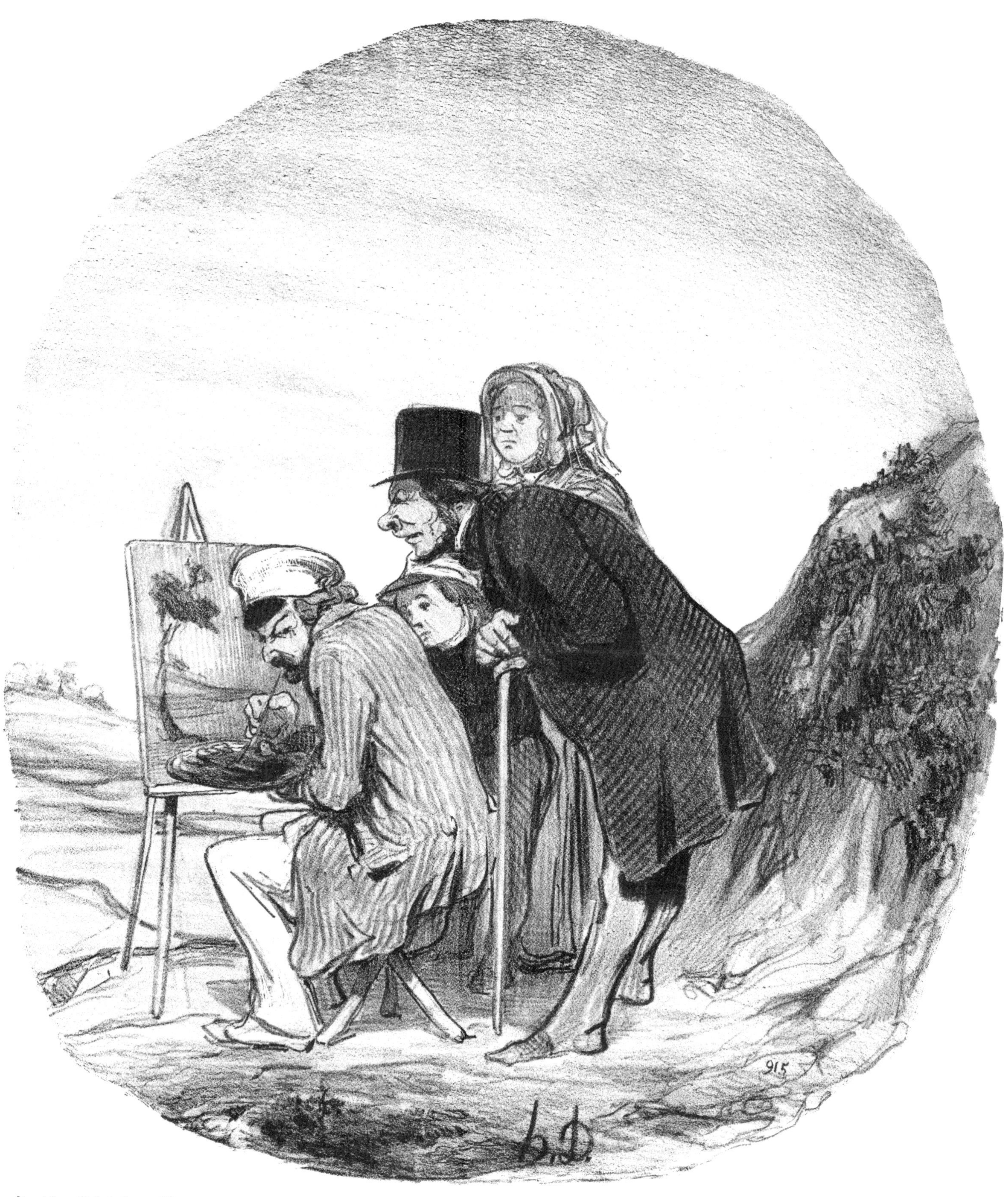

Chez Aubert Pl. de la Bourse, 29. Imp. d'Aubert & Cie.

_Mais si, ma femme, je t'assure que monsieur dessine un paysage… n'est-ce pas, monsieur, que vous dessinez un paysage?….

60 "Oh, yes, my dear, I assure you the gentleman is drawing a landscape."
[Nov. 13, 1846]

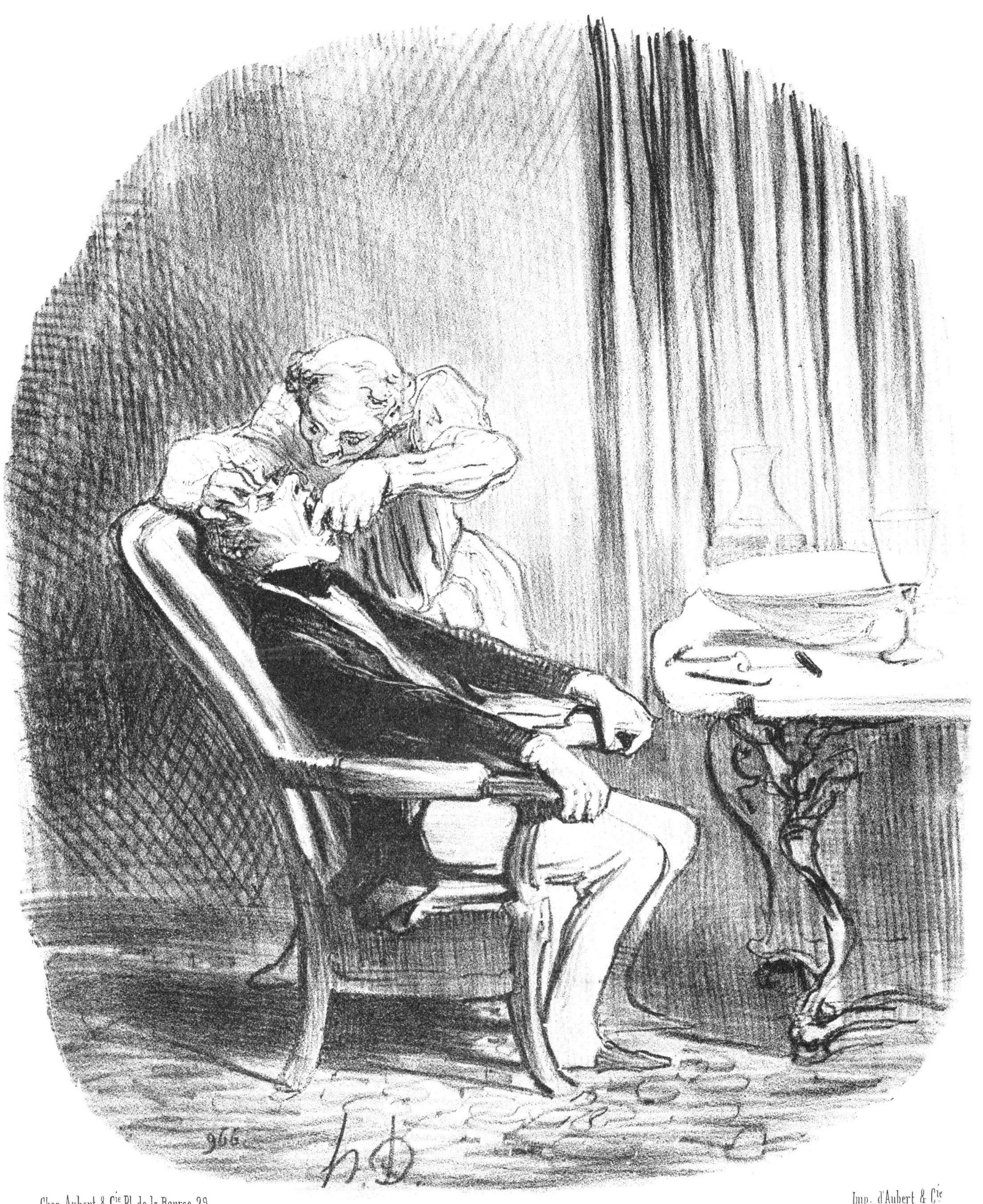

— Oh! la . . . . la . . . . ***la*** *. . . . . .* ***la !***
— Tant mieux . . . . . tant mieux . . . . ça prouve qu'elle vient ! . . . .

61 The pain proves that the tooth is coming out. [May 8, 1847]

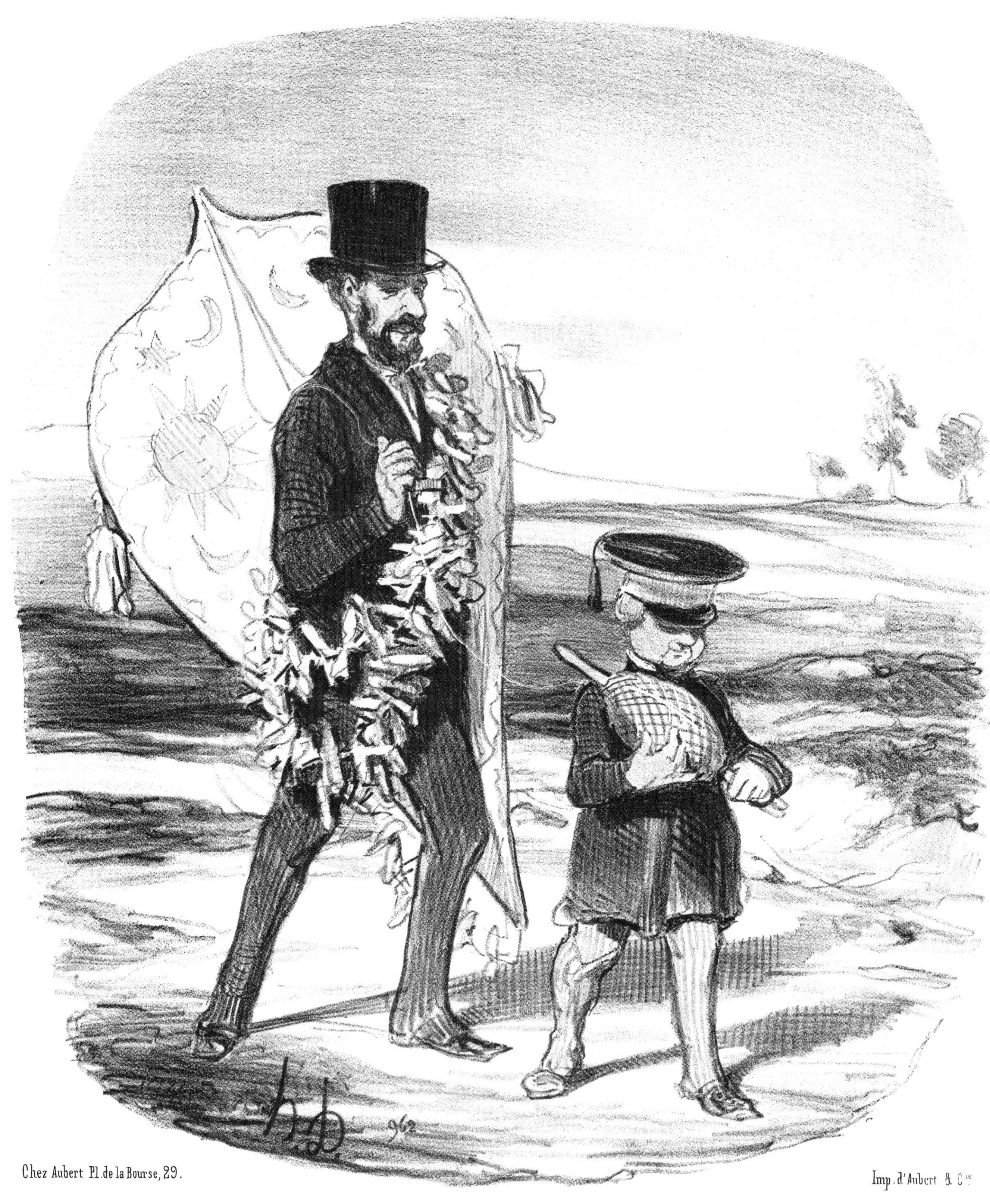

Un jour de congé.

62 A day off. [Dec. 27, 1846]

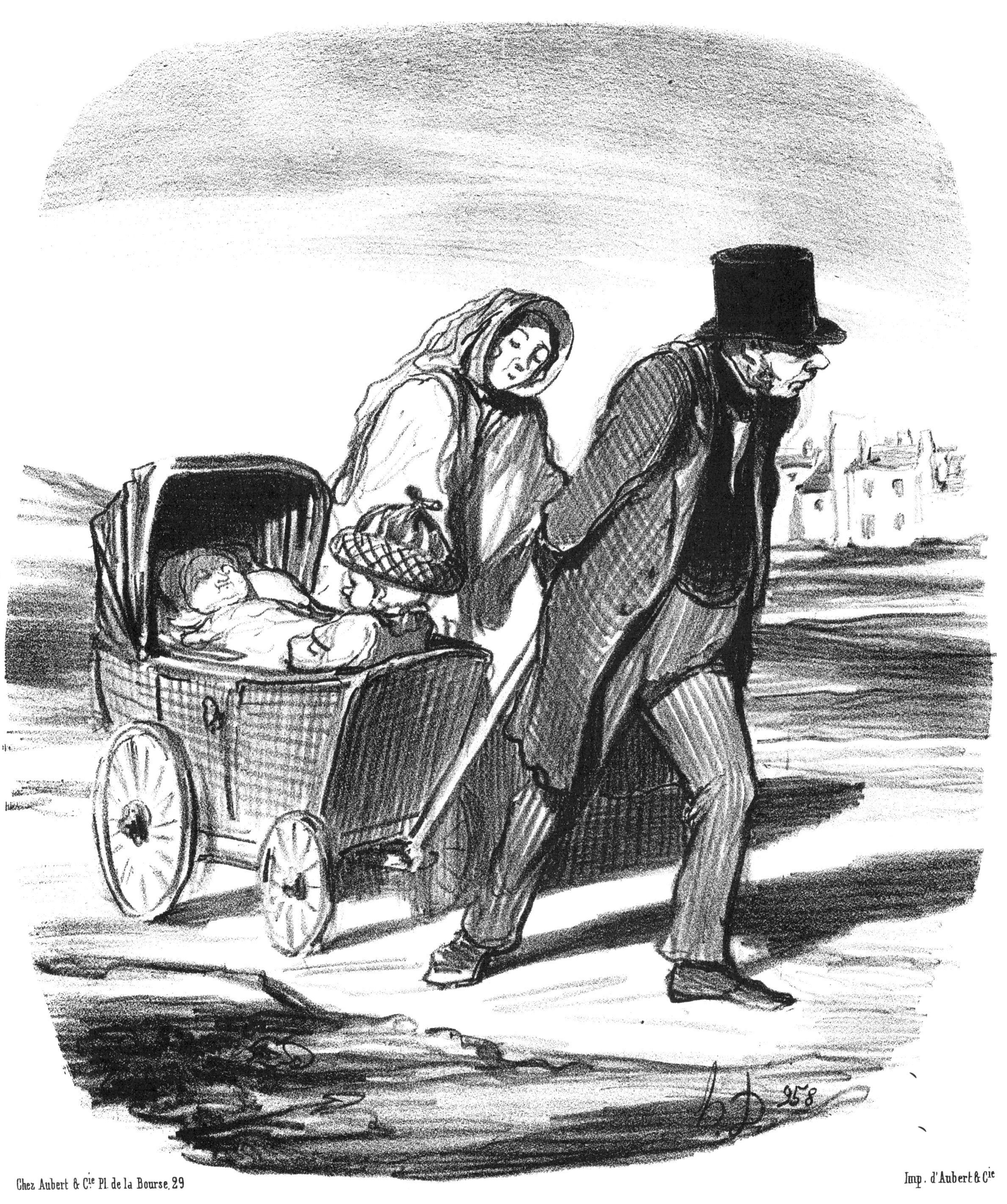

« Un père est un cheval donné par la nature! »

63 A father is a horse provided by nature! [Jan. 4, 1847]

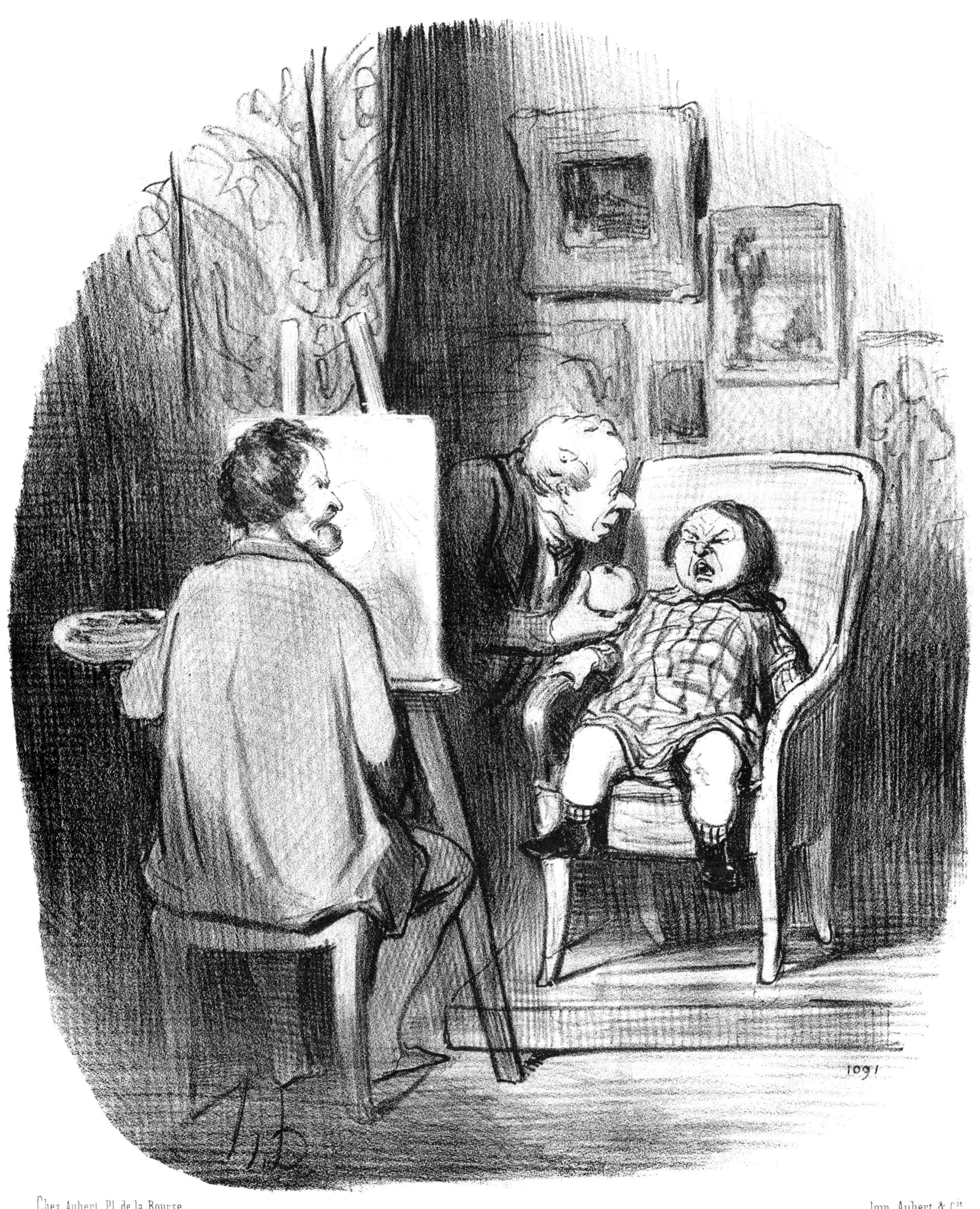

Chez Aubert Pl. de la Bourse. Imp. Aubert & Cie

Seule manière de faire poser un enfant avec fruit.

64 Trying to get a child to pose with fruit. [Aug. 24, 1847]

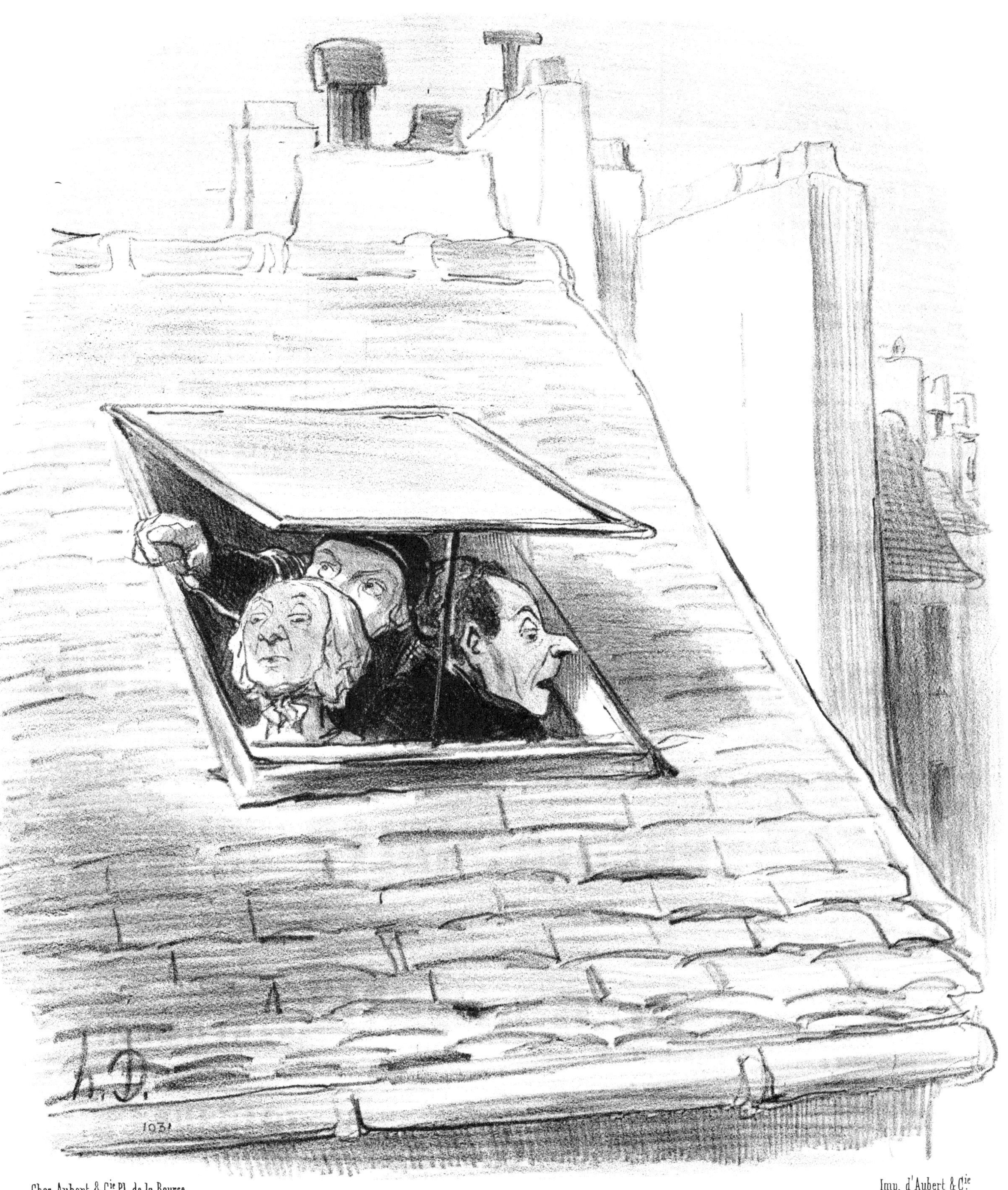

De ce côté-là, vous voyez la tour St Jacques la Boucherie!......

65 Pointing out the wonderful view to prospective tenants. [Apr. 19, 1847]

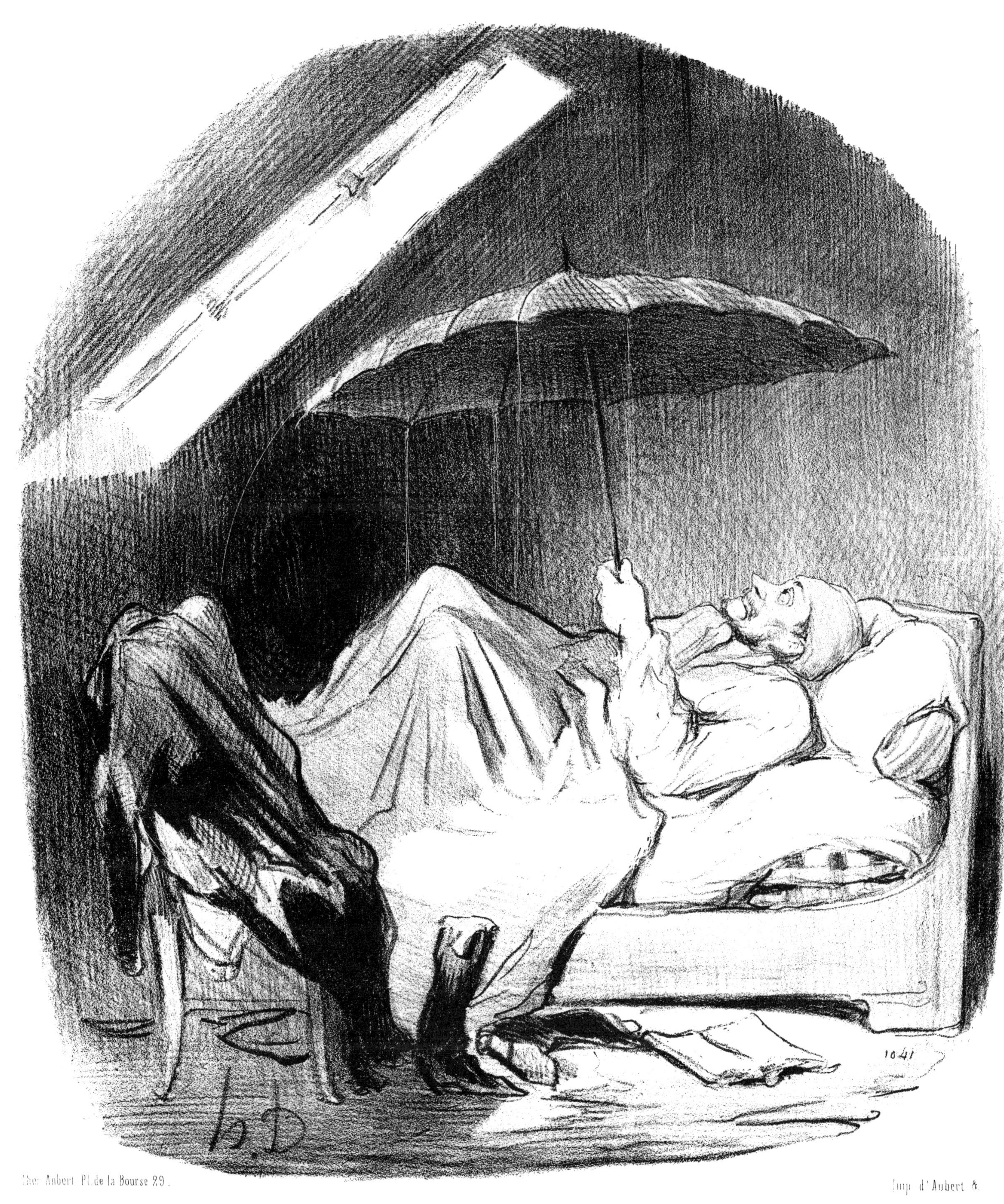

Brigand de propriétaire.... qui ne veut me faire faire des réparations qu'au beau temps !...

66 Cursing the landlord who refuses to repair the leak. [May 26, 1847]

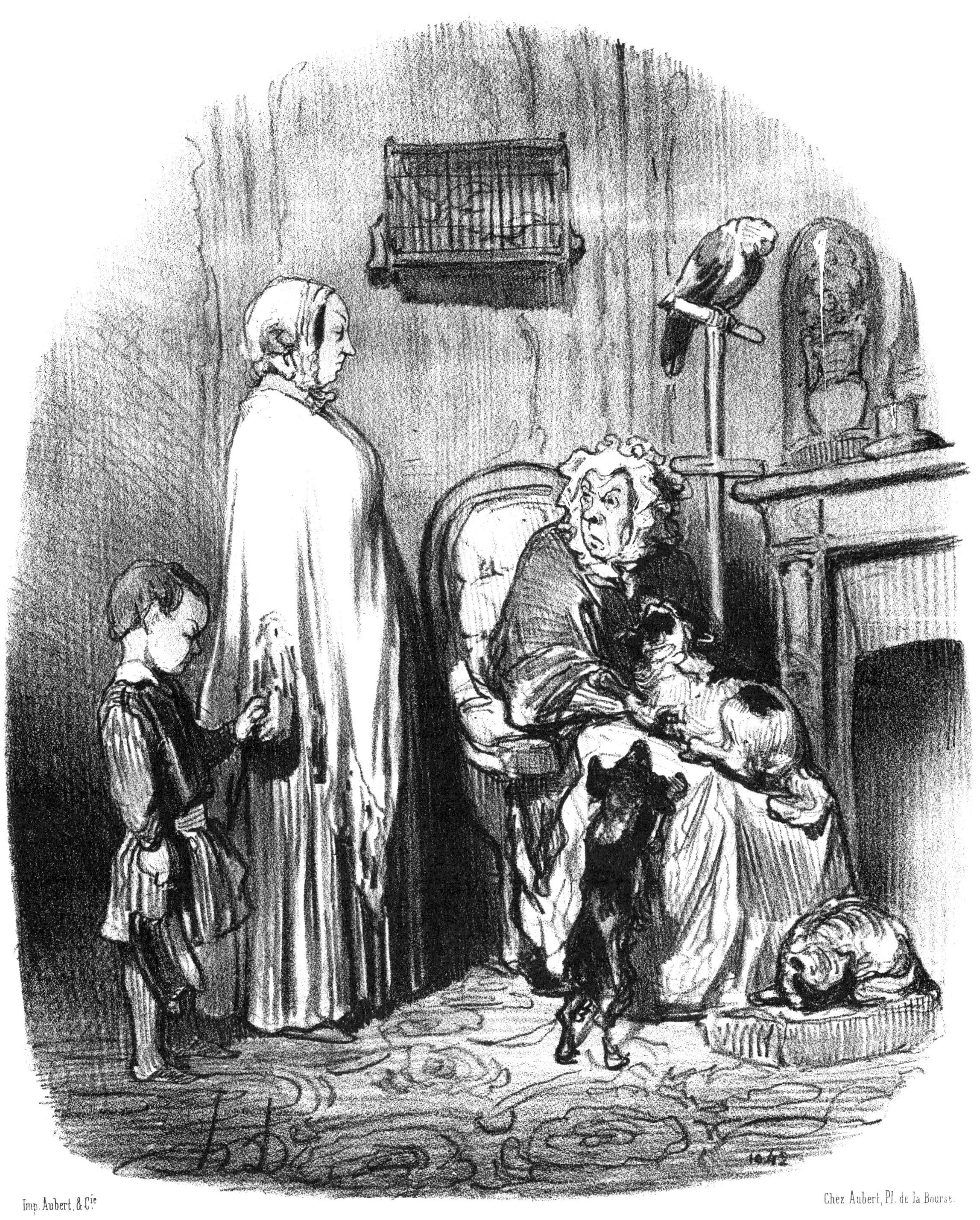

– Je ne loue pas aux gens qui ont des enfants ! . . . .

67 "I never rent to people who have children!" [June 24, 1847]

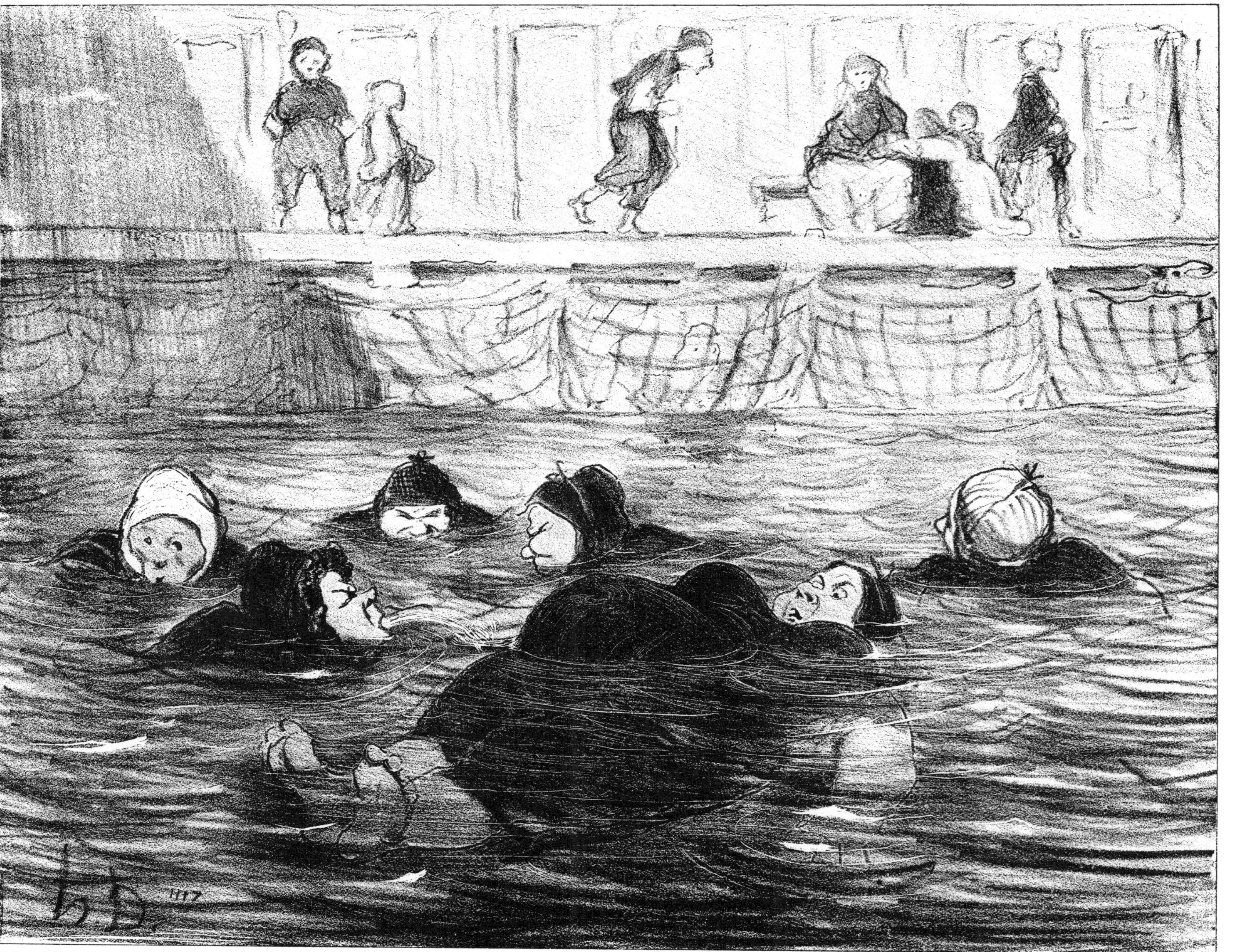

Chez Aubert, Pl. de la Bourse. Imp. Aubert & Cie

Nayades de la Seine.

68 Women bathers in the Seine. [July 14, 1847]

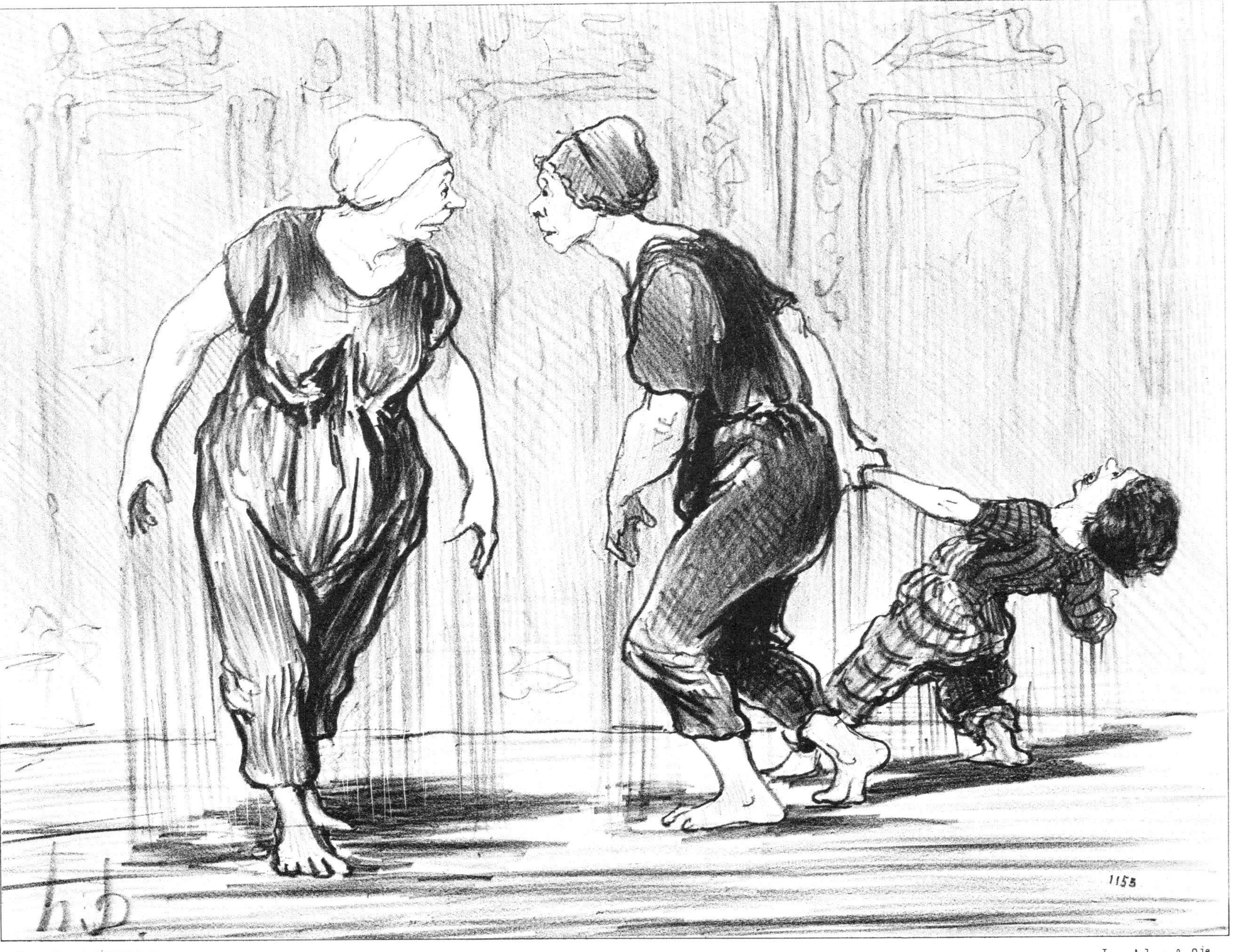

Chez Aubert & Cie Pl. de la Bourse. Imp. Aubert & Cie

— Ma p'tite me donne bien du mal, mame Radiguet ... elle ne mord pas à l'eau.

69 Her little girl doesn't take to swimming. [Aug. 1847]

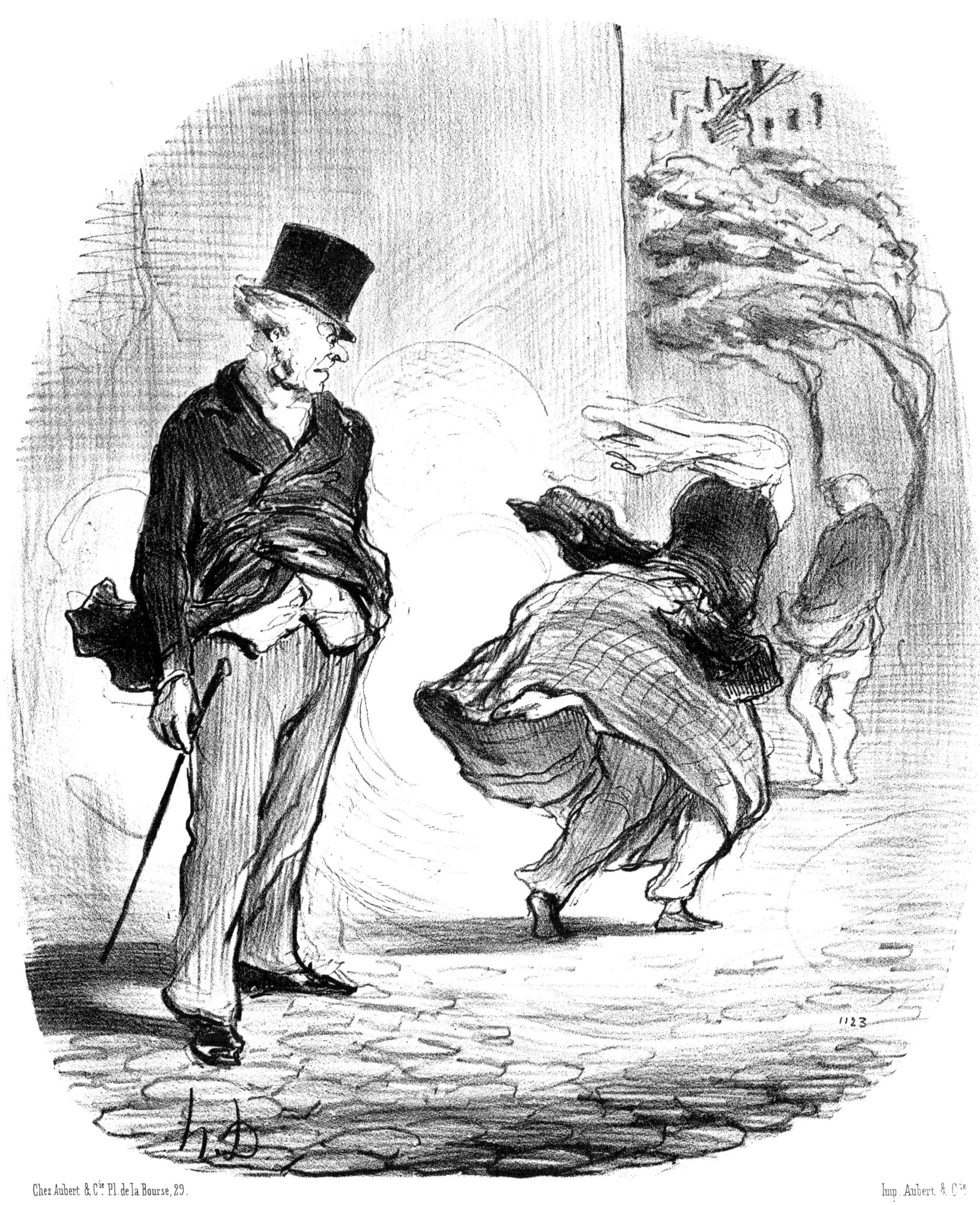

– Tiens . . . vla un homme qui s'est déguisé en femme ! . .

70 The pantalets cause confusion about the wearer's sex. [1848]

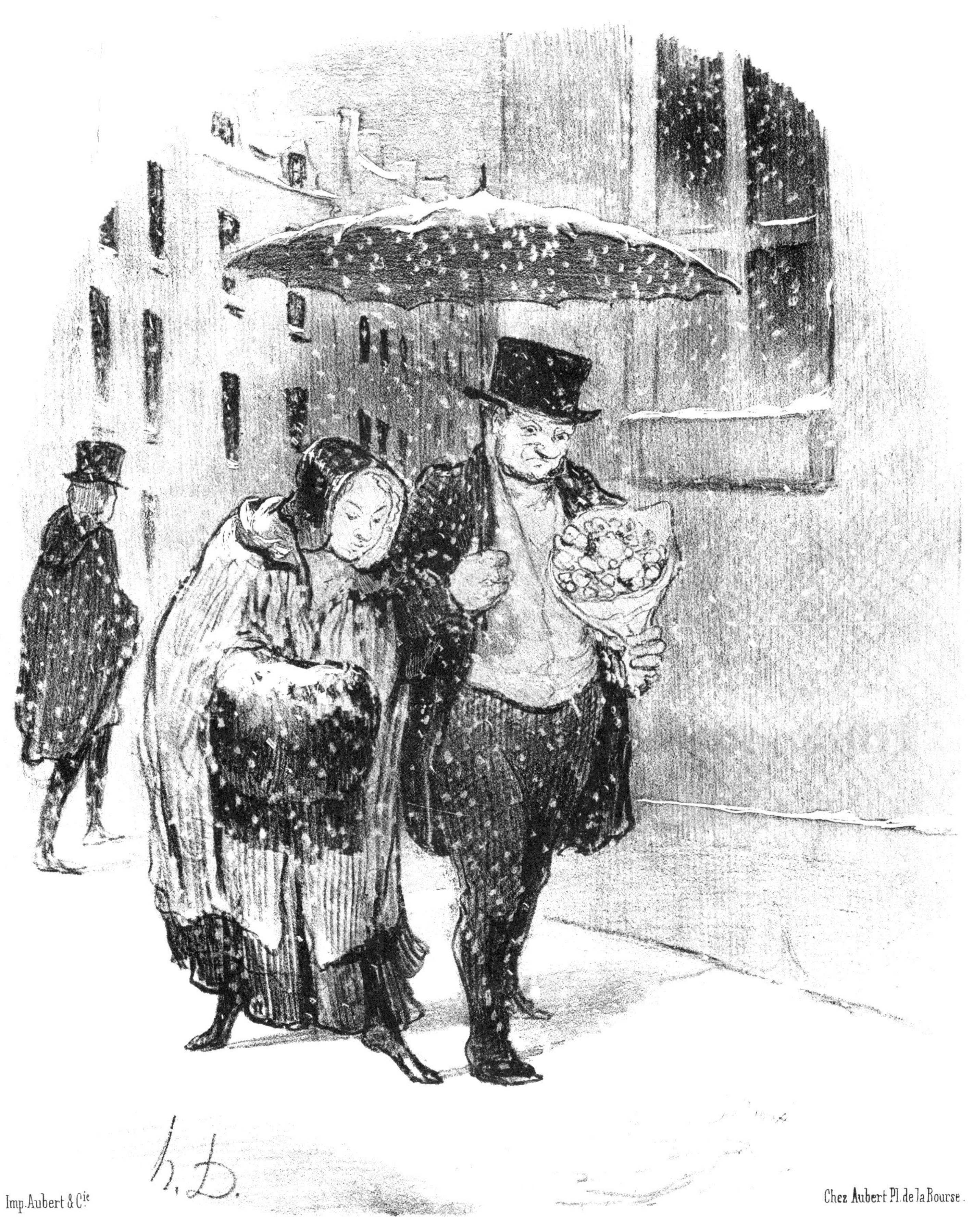

Inconvénient d'avoir un parent qui se nomme **Babylas**, ce qui oblige à aller lui porter un bouquet le **24** Janvier.

71 Bringing a name-day bouquet to a relative in January snows. [Jan. 29, 1850]

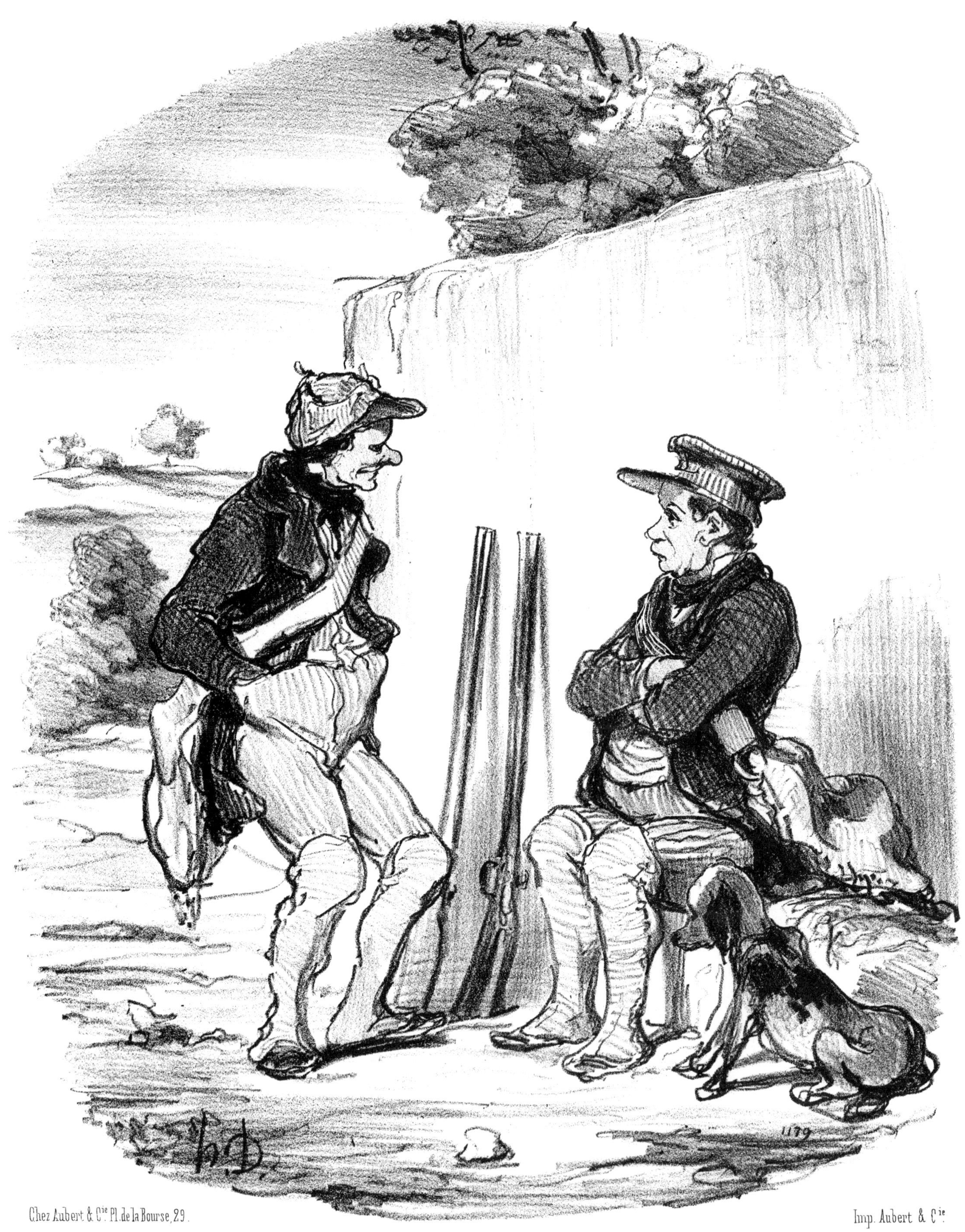

_ Dire que je n'ai pas pu tirer seulement un coup de fusil depuis c'matin ! . . .
_ Oh ! moi c'est différent . . . . j'ai tué mon chien ! . . .

72 One hunter shot nothing all day, the other shot his own dog. [Feb. 18, 1848]

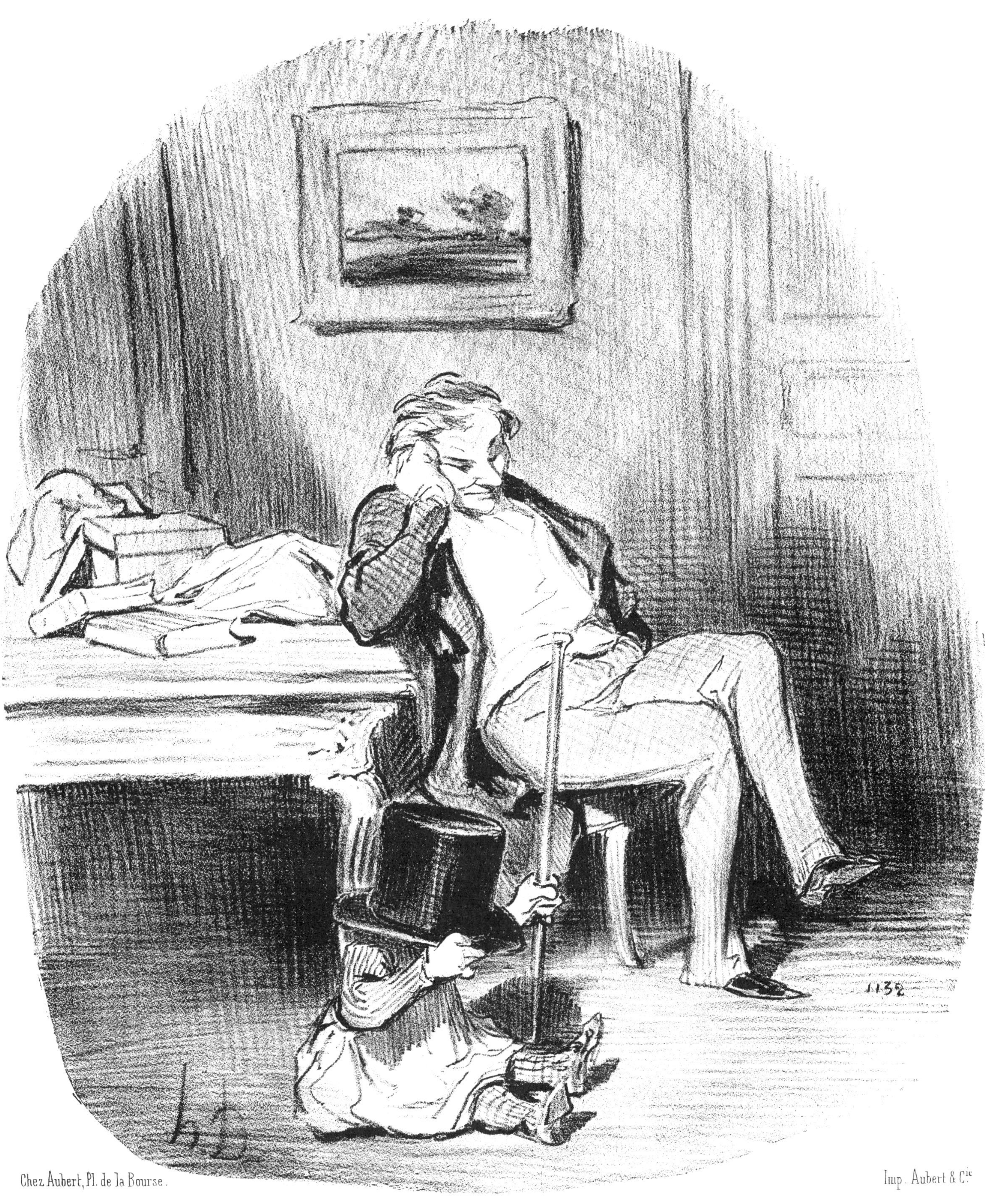

– Ma femme reste bien long-temps à ce banquet . . . . . . voilà bientôt quarante huit heures qu'elle est partie !

73 The husband of a socialist woman is worried about her 48-hour absence. [June 9, 1849]

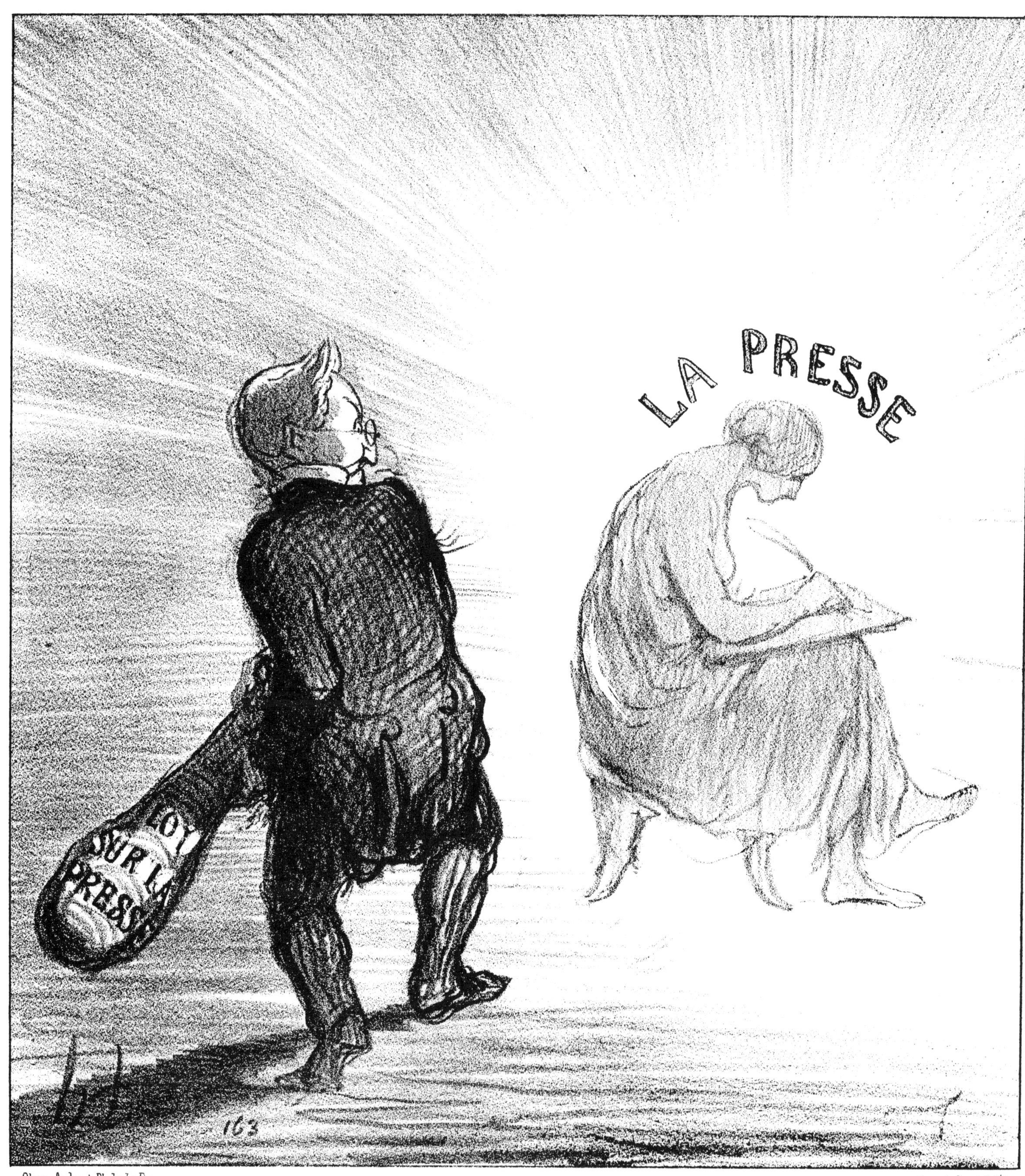

Un parricide.

74 Thiers, once a liberal journalist, now appears as a censor of the press. [Apr. 16, 1850]

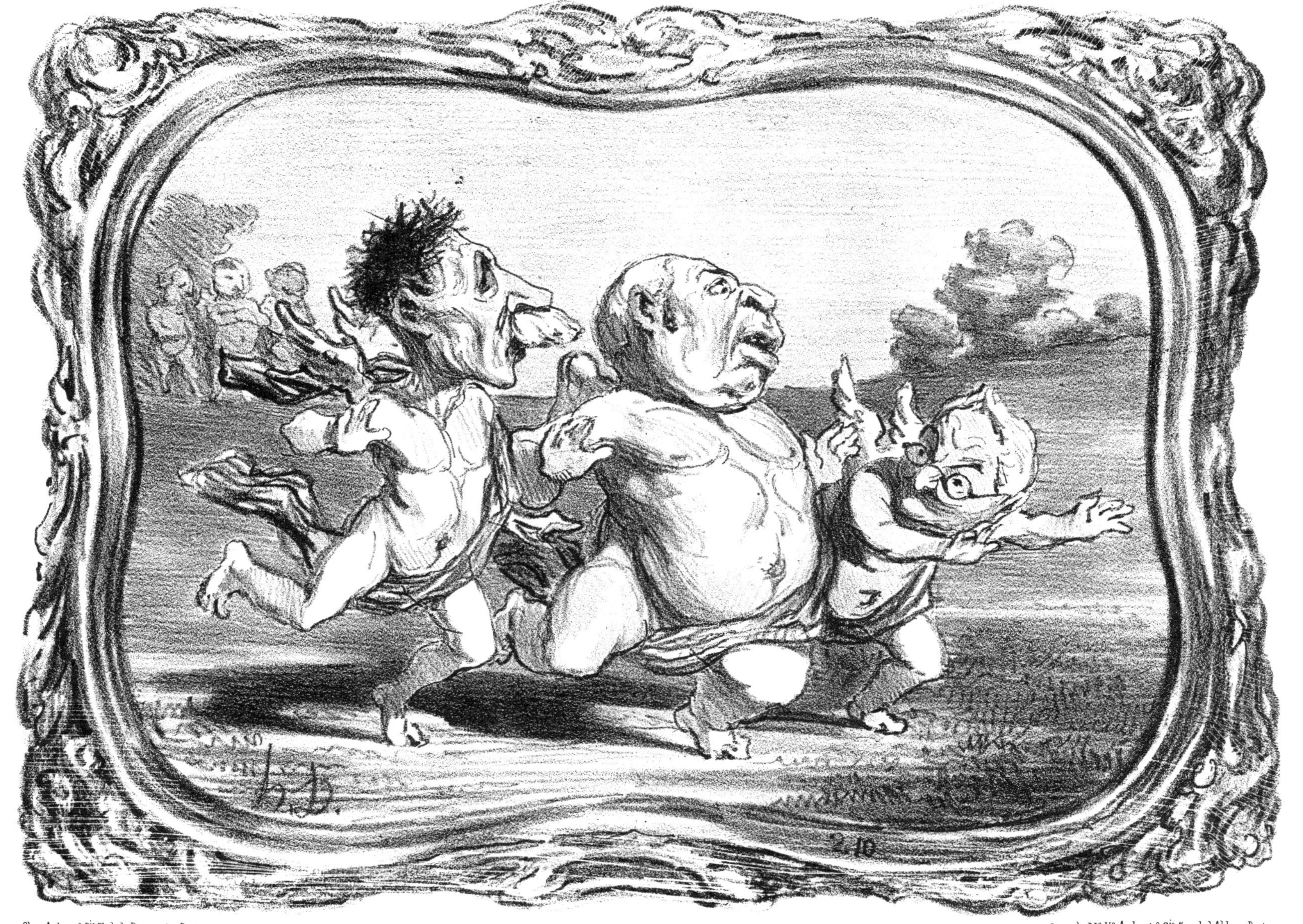

Empire, Orléanisme et Légitimité
Se disputent le prix en une ardente lutte,
Oubliant le dicton, si fréquemment cité,
Au bout du fossé la culbute.

(Quatrain trouvé dans la boîte de l'Elysée.)

75 In the chaotic period after the Revolution of 1848, partisans of Empire, Orleanism and Legitimacy race for power. [Nov. 4, 1850]

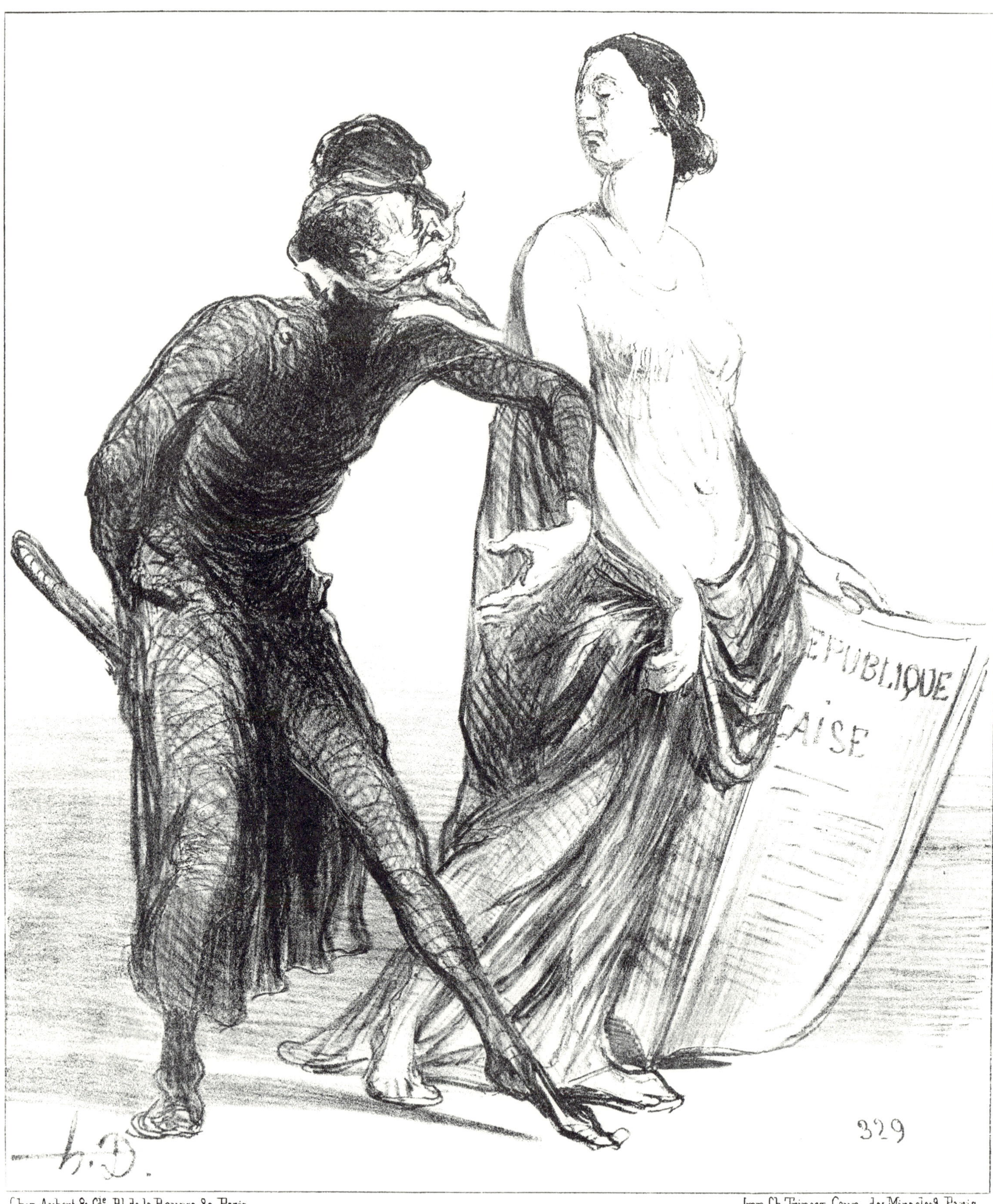

— Belle dame, voulez-vous bien accepter mon bras ?
— Votre passion est trop subite pour que je puisse y croire !

76 The Second French Republic is suspicious of the attentions of Ratapoil, agent of Louis-Napoléon. [Sept. 25, 1851]

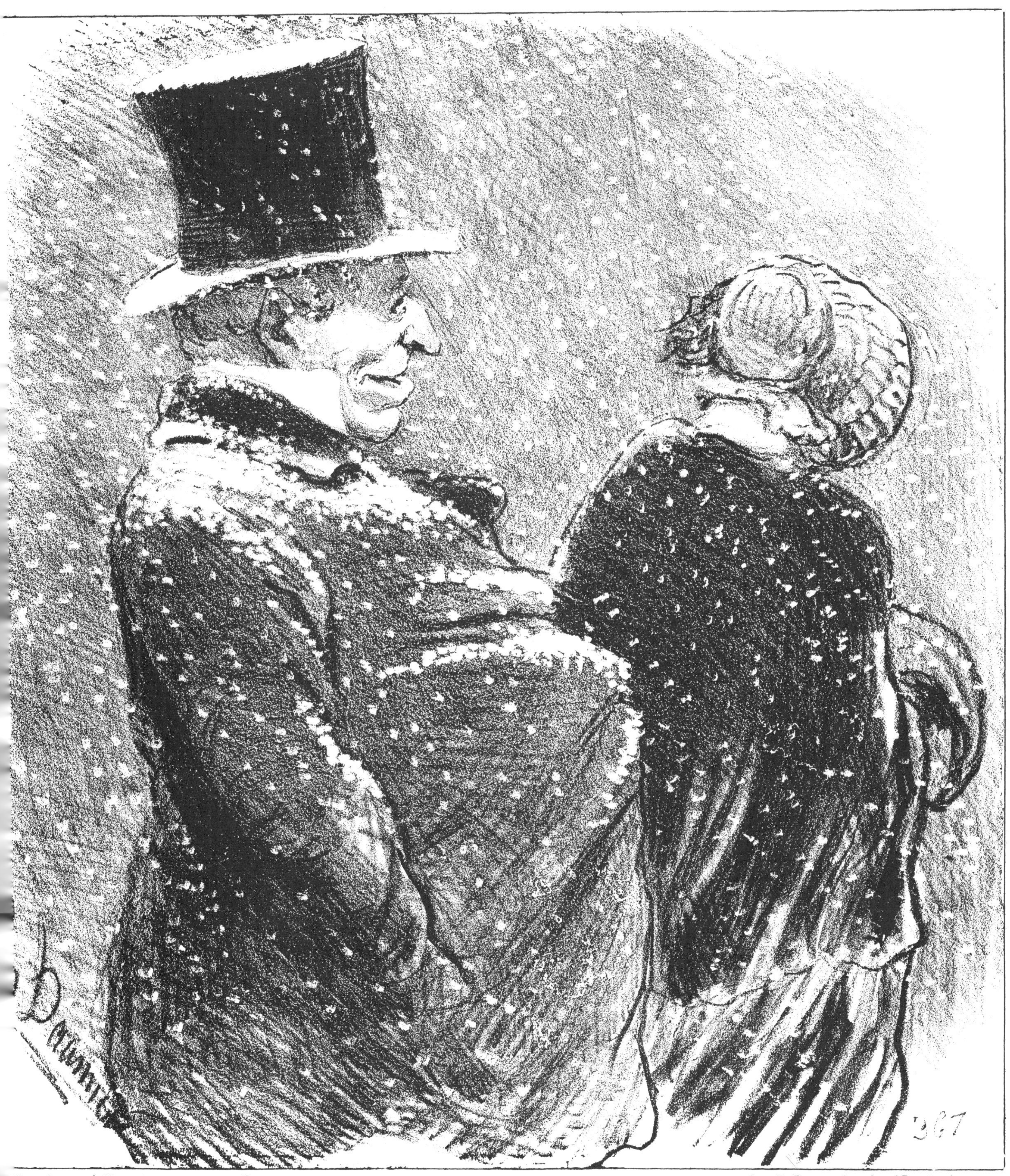

Un monsieur qui s'enflamme en toute saison.

77 A gentleman who gets hot in any season. [Jan. 14, 1852]

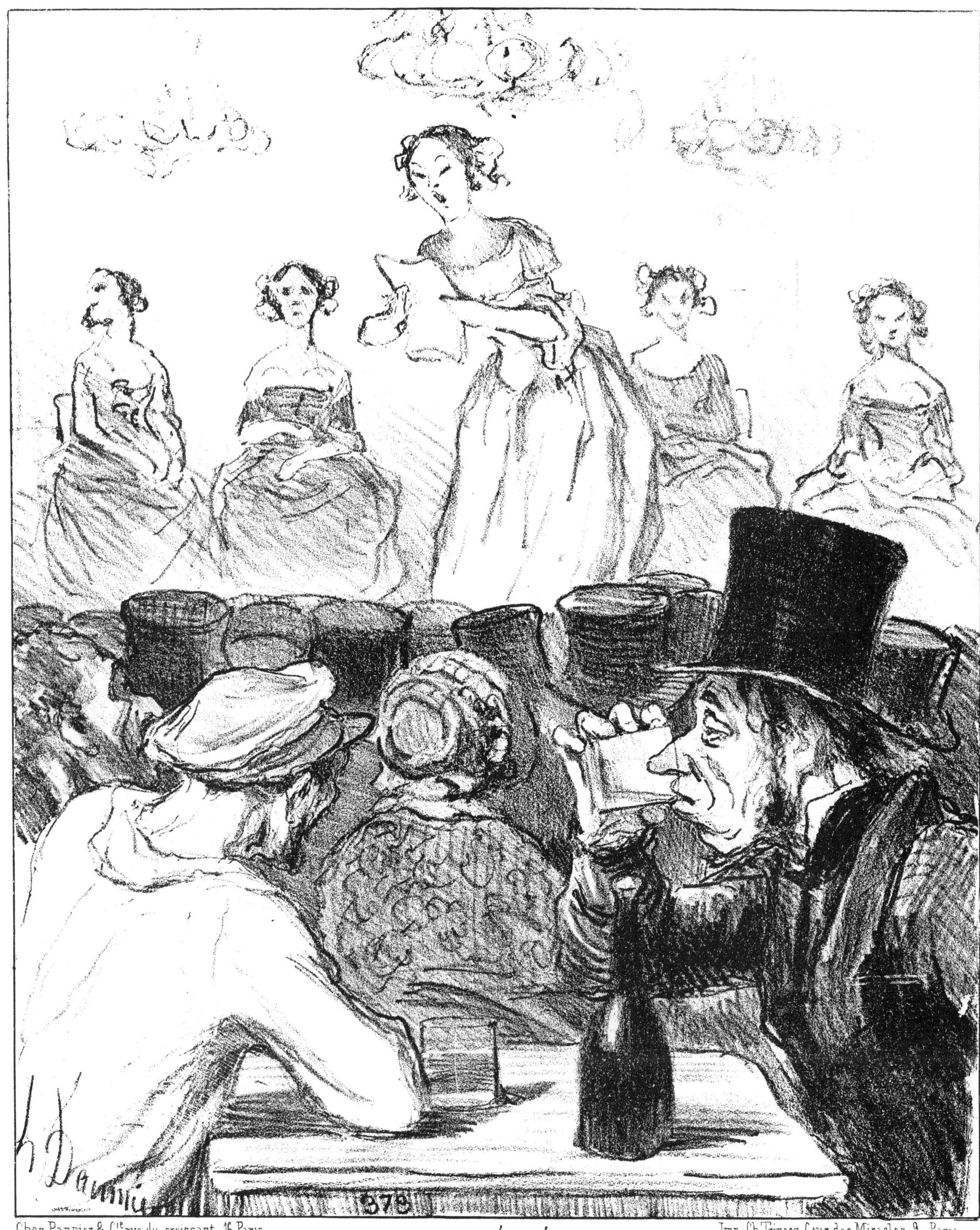

78 Does the entertainment sell the mediocre beer, or vice versa? [Feb. 13, 1852]

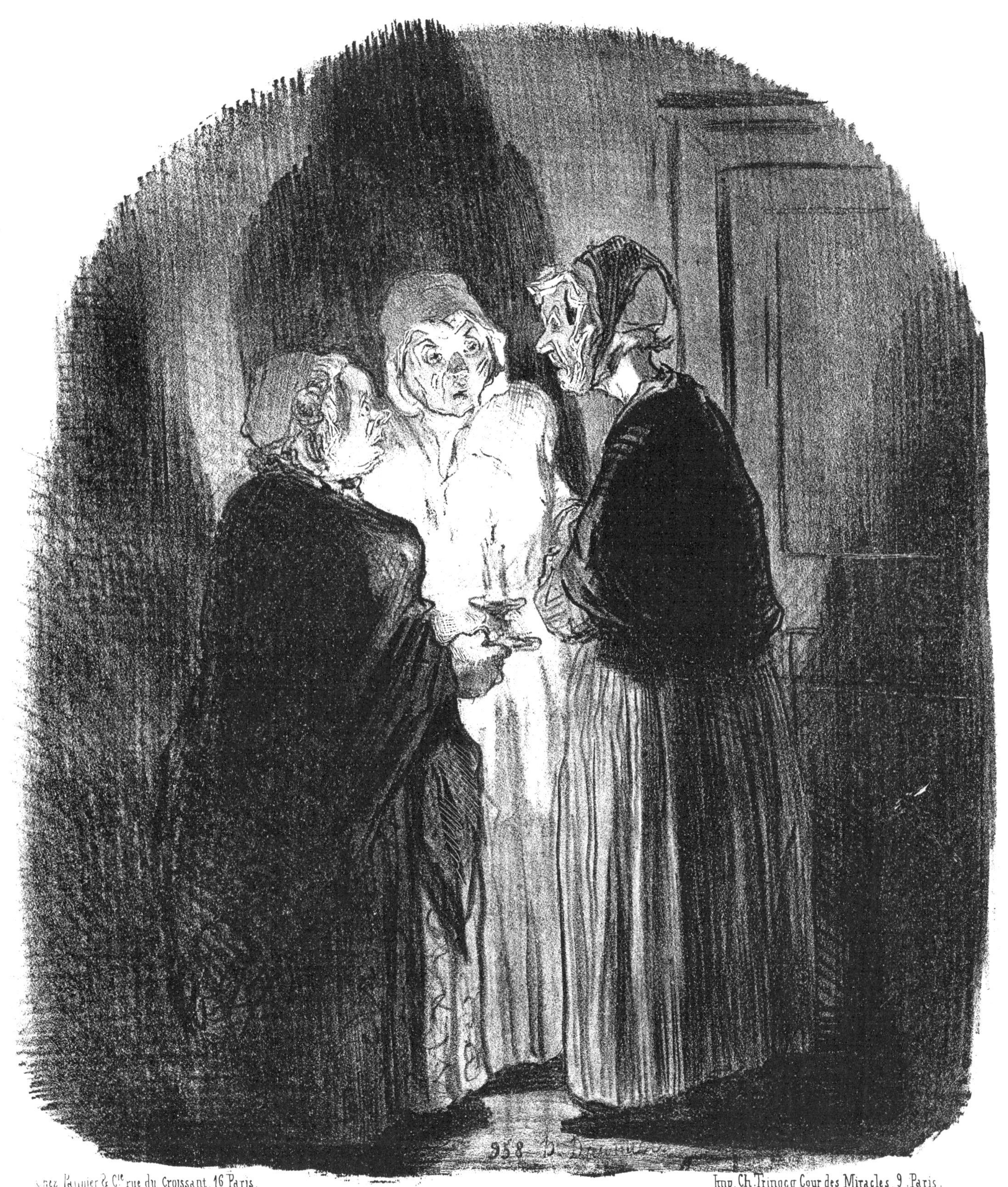

— Oui, madame Fribochon, il y a évu, il y a trois semaines, un tremblement d'terre très conséquent à Bordeaux, et pas pus tard qu'avant z'hier, entre minuit et trois heures du matin, j'ai ressenti des secousses qui ne sont pas naturelles dans mon lit... l'herboriste, m'sieu Potard, m'a expliqué ce Phénomène... y prétend que ça tient à ce que le gouvernement laisse trop creuser la terre en Californie et que ça finira par nous jouer à tous un mauvais tour aux Batignolles!...

79 A misinformed discussion of an earthquake threat to Paris. [Mar. 17, 1852]

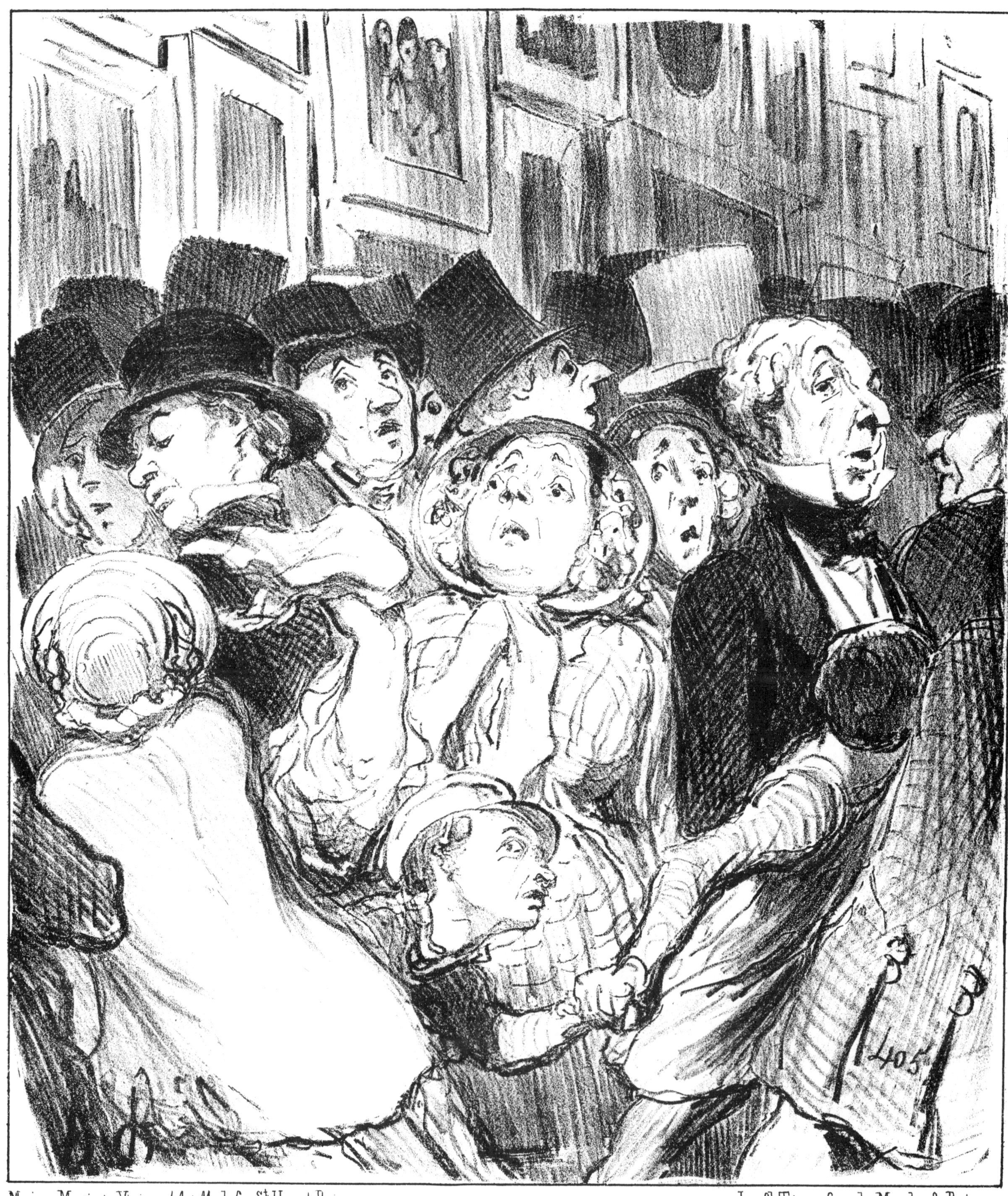

Maison Martinet, r. Vivienne 41 et 11 r. du Coq St Honoré. Paris. Imp. Ch. Trinocq Cour des Miracles, 9. Paris.

Un jour où l'on ne paye pas. — Vingt-cinq degrés de chaleur.

80 A very hot free-admission day at the art Salon. [May 17, 1852]

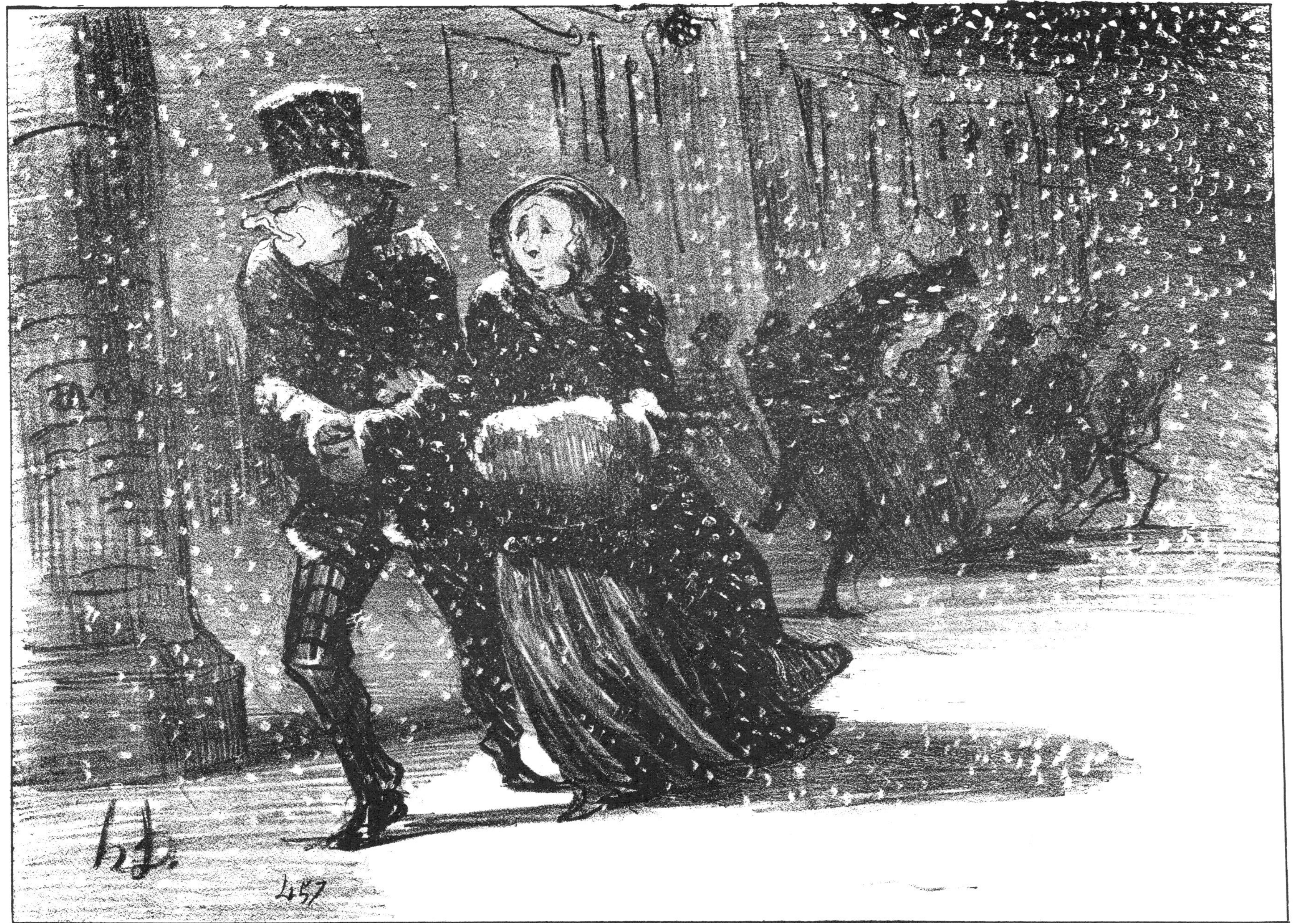

Maison Martinet, r. Vivienne, 41, et r. du Coq, 11.

Imp. Ch. Trinocq, Cour des Miracles, 9, Paris.

— Qui diable se serait jamais douté qu'il neigerait encore à Paris !...

81 Snowfall in Paris later in the season than usual. [Feb. 21, 1853]

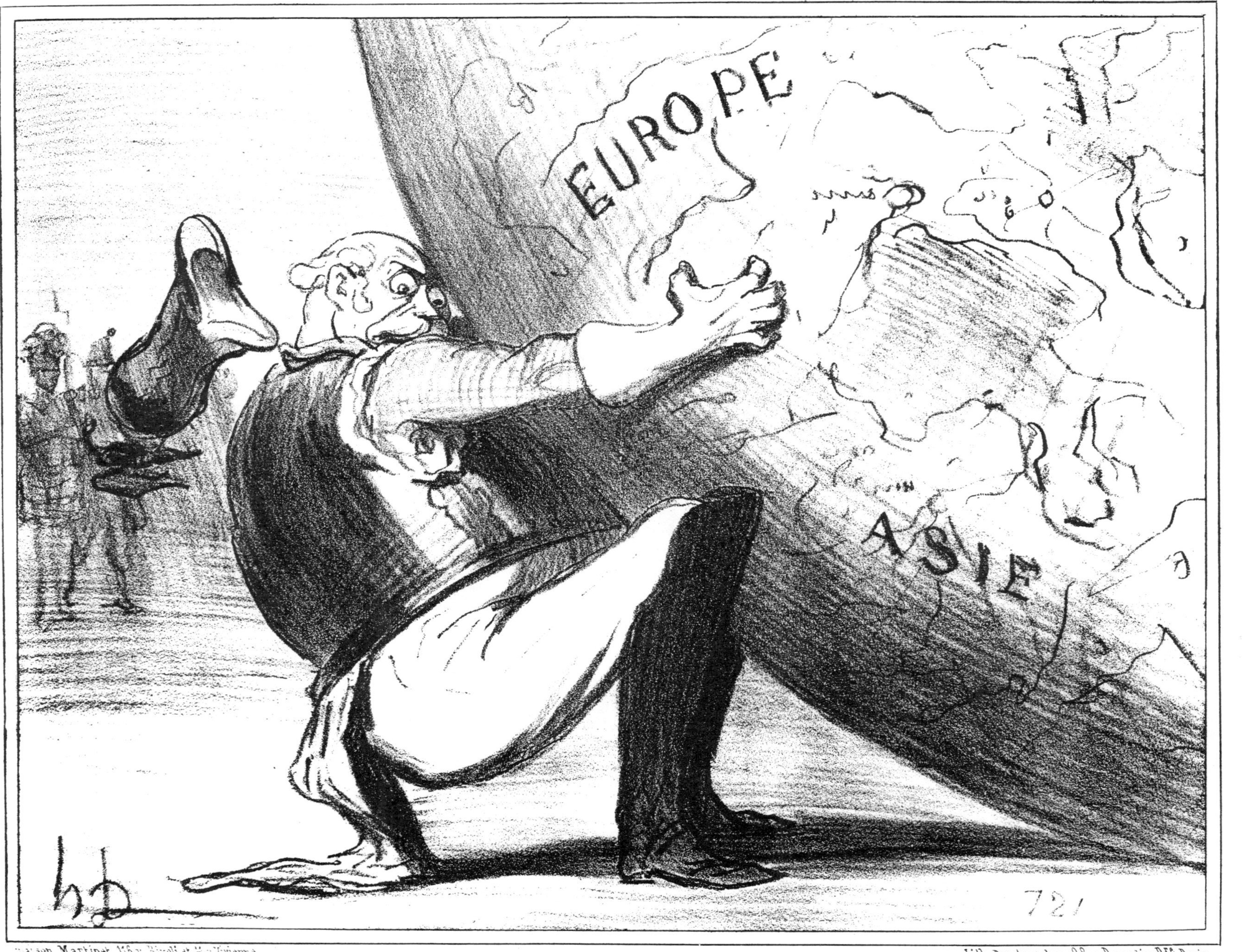

— Bigre!.....j'ai eu tort de me mettre toute l'Europe sur les bras!.....

82 Czar Nicholas I afraid he has overextended himself in the Crimean War. [Jan. 2–3, 1855]

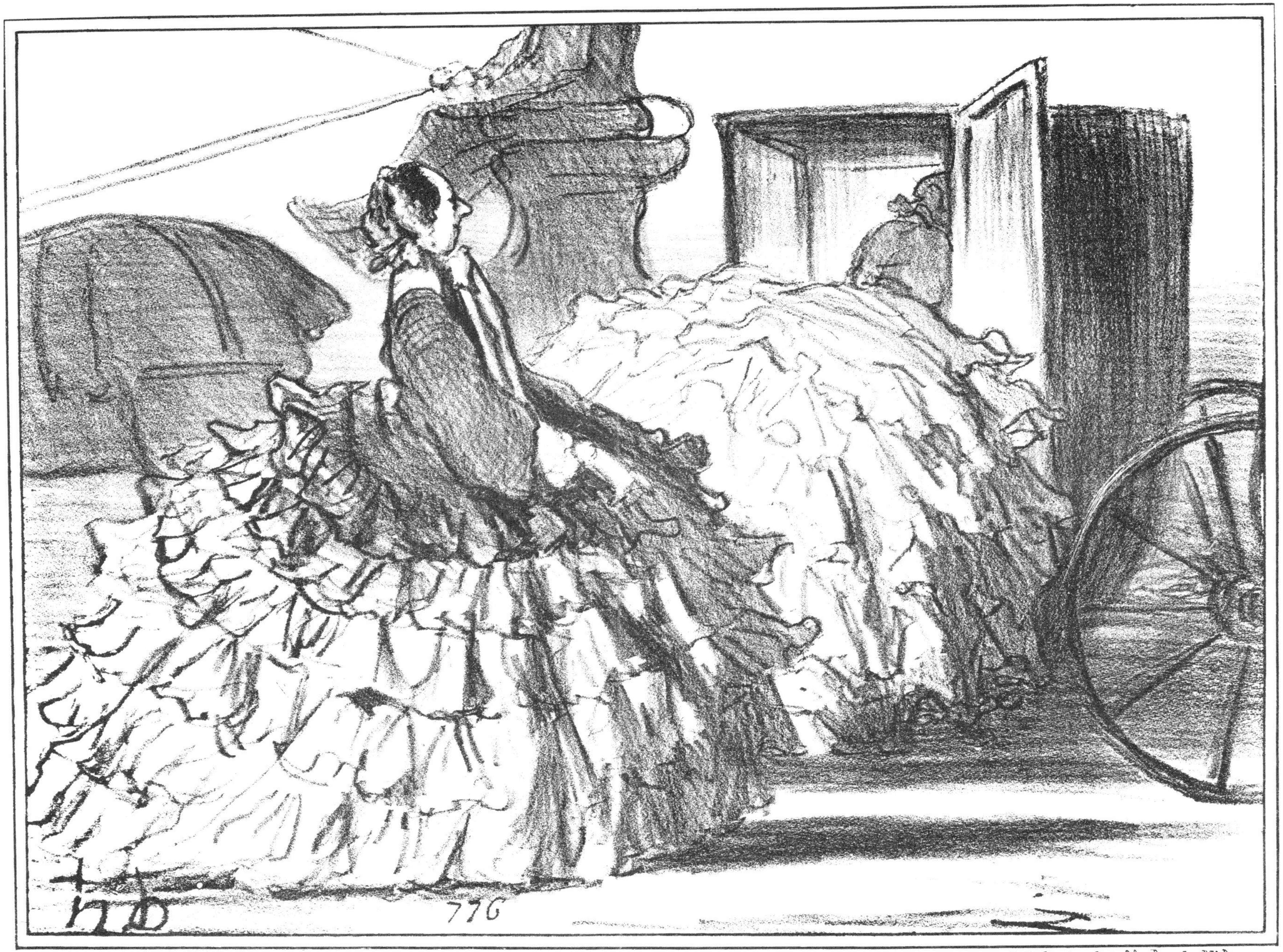

Maison Martinet, 41b r Rivoli et 41 r Vivienne — Lith. Destouches 28 r Paradis Pre Par.

Des dames d'un demi-monde, mais n'ayant pas de demi-jupes.

83 Fashionable courtesans wearing the brand-new crinolines. [May 11, 1855]

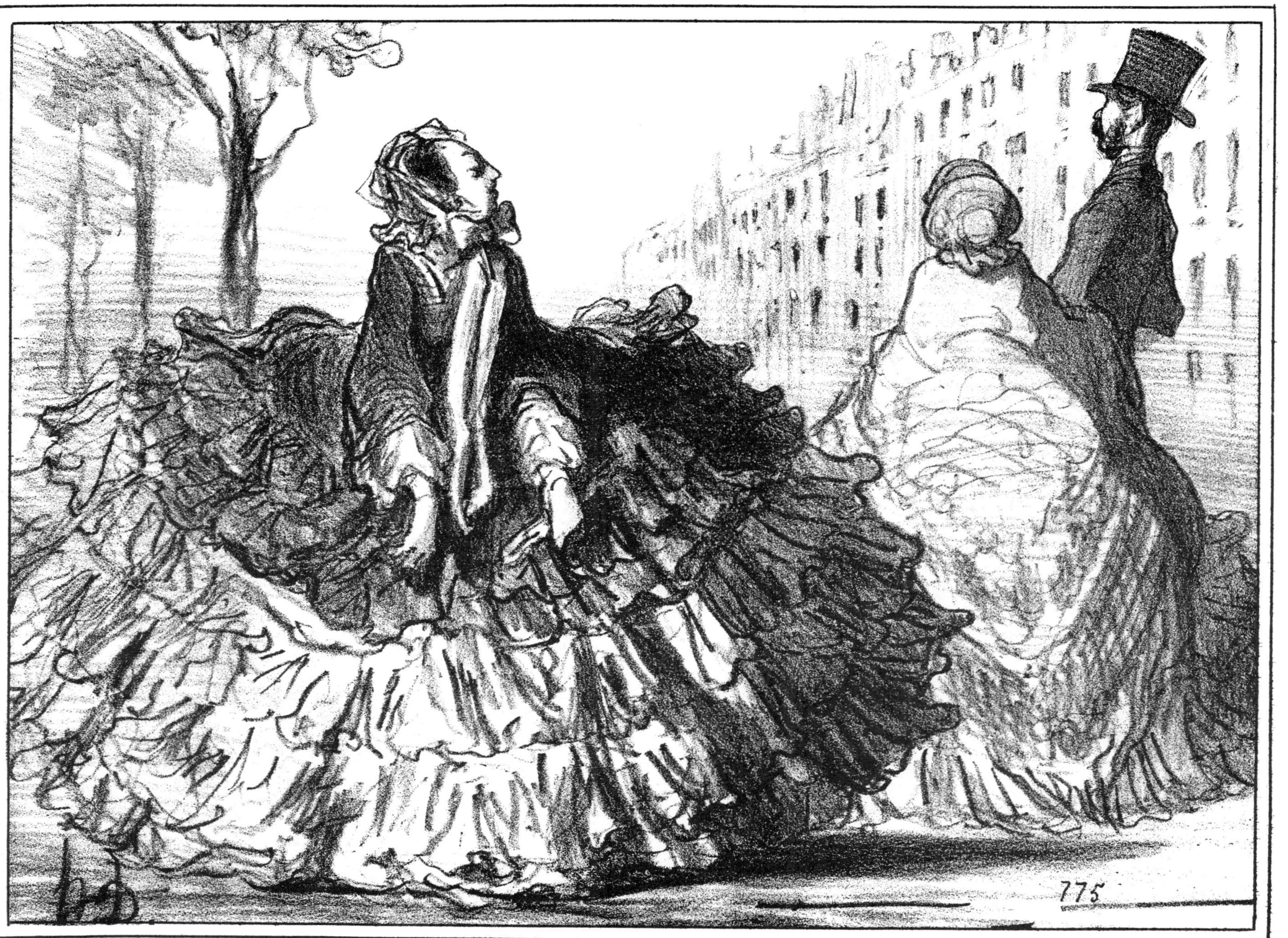

Modes du printemps de 1855 — Le dernier chic.

84 Spring fashions, 1855. [May 14, 1855]

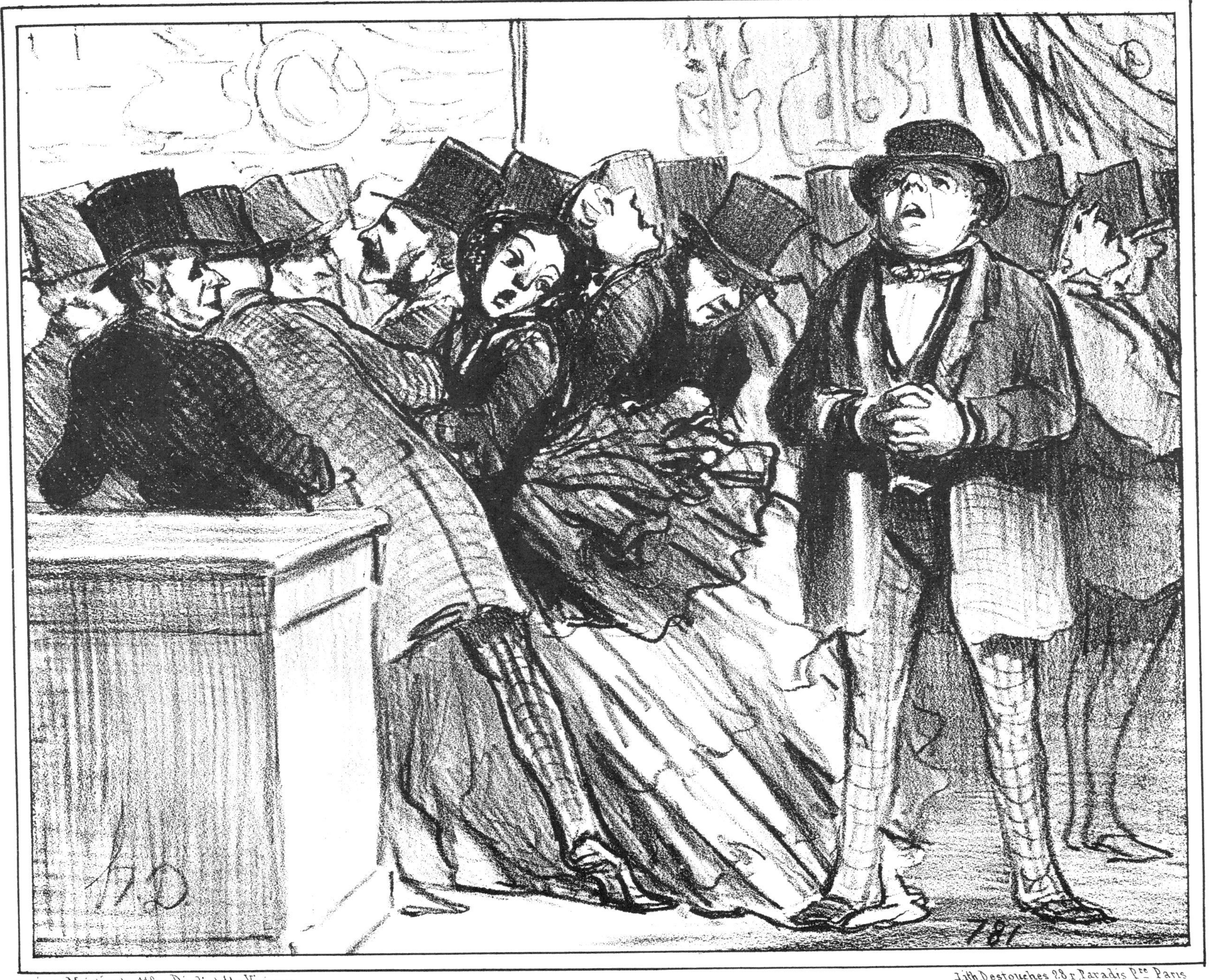

Comme quoi un jour d'entrée à quatre sous, on n'en est pas quitte à moins d'une robe de soixante francs.

85 When admission to the 1855 World's Fair is cheap, there is expensive wear and tear on clothing. [June 12, 1855]

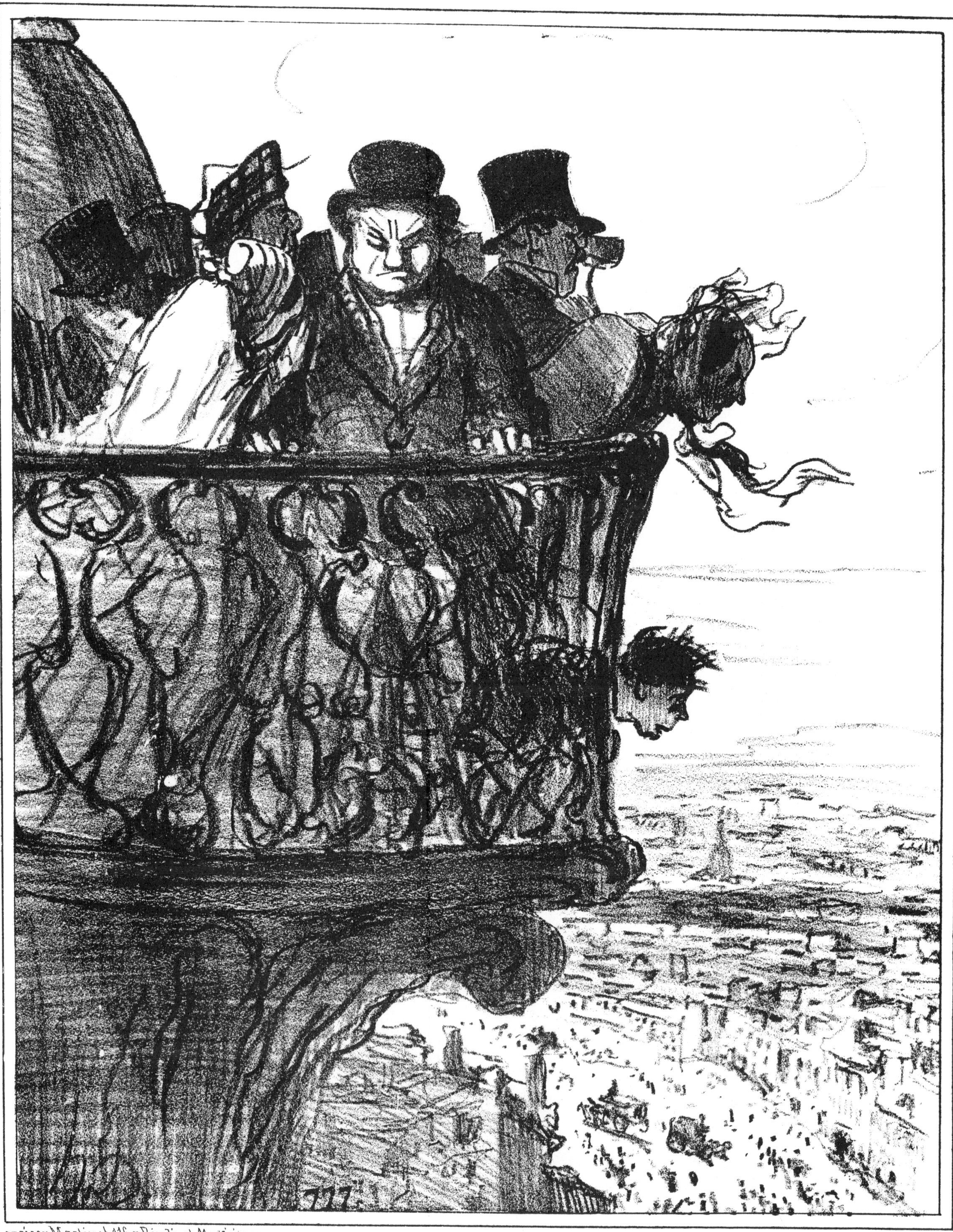

86 Killing time on the Vendôme Column before the World's Fair opens.
[May 15, 1855]

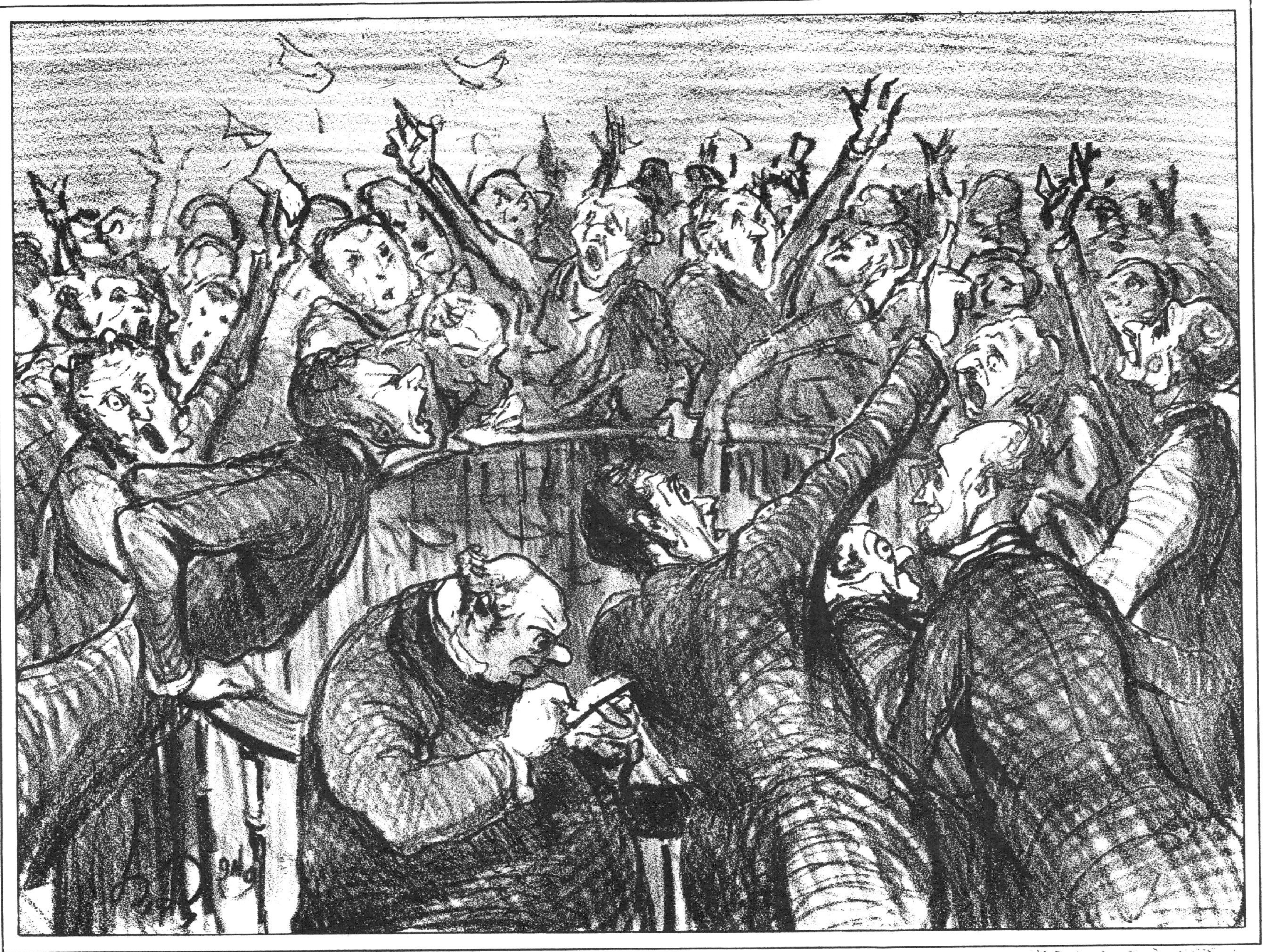

À LA BOURSE.

Ce qu'on appelle une corbeille _ pas de fleurs en tout cas.

87 The heart of the Parisian Stock Exchange. [July 25, 1856]

mon Martinet, 146 r. Rivoli et 41, r. Vivienne.

Lith. Destouches, 28 r. Paradis P.re Paris.

— Quinze centimes un bain complet ...... parole, c'est pas payé ! ....

88 A bath as well as a bus ride for fifteen centimes. [Aug. 30, 1856]

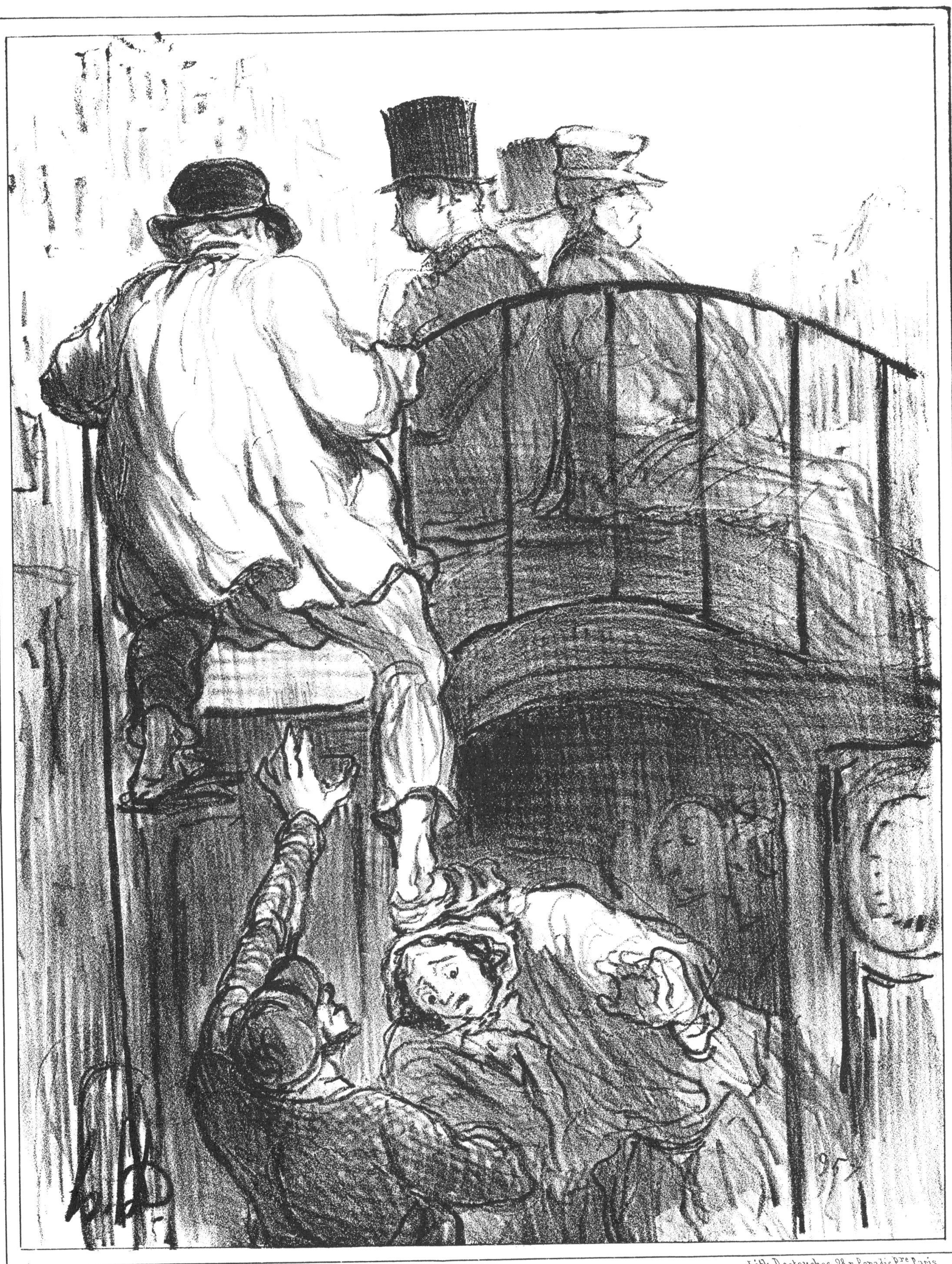

maison Martinet, 146, r. Rivoli et 41, r. Vivienne — Lith. Destouches, 28, r. Paradis Pre Paris

Le mauvais côté des nouveaux omnibus

89 An unpleasant aspect of double-decker buses. [Sept. 4, 1856]

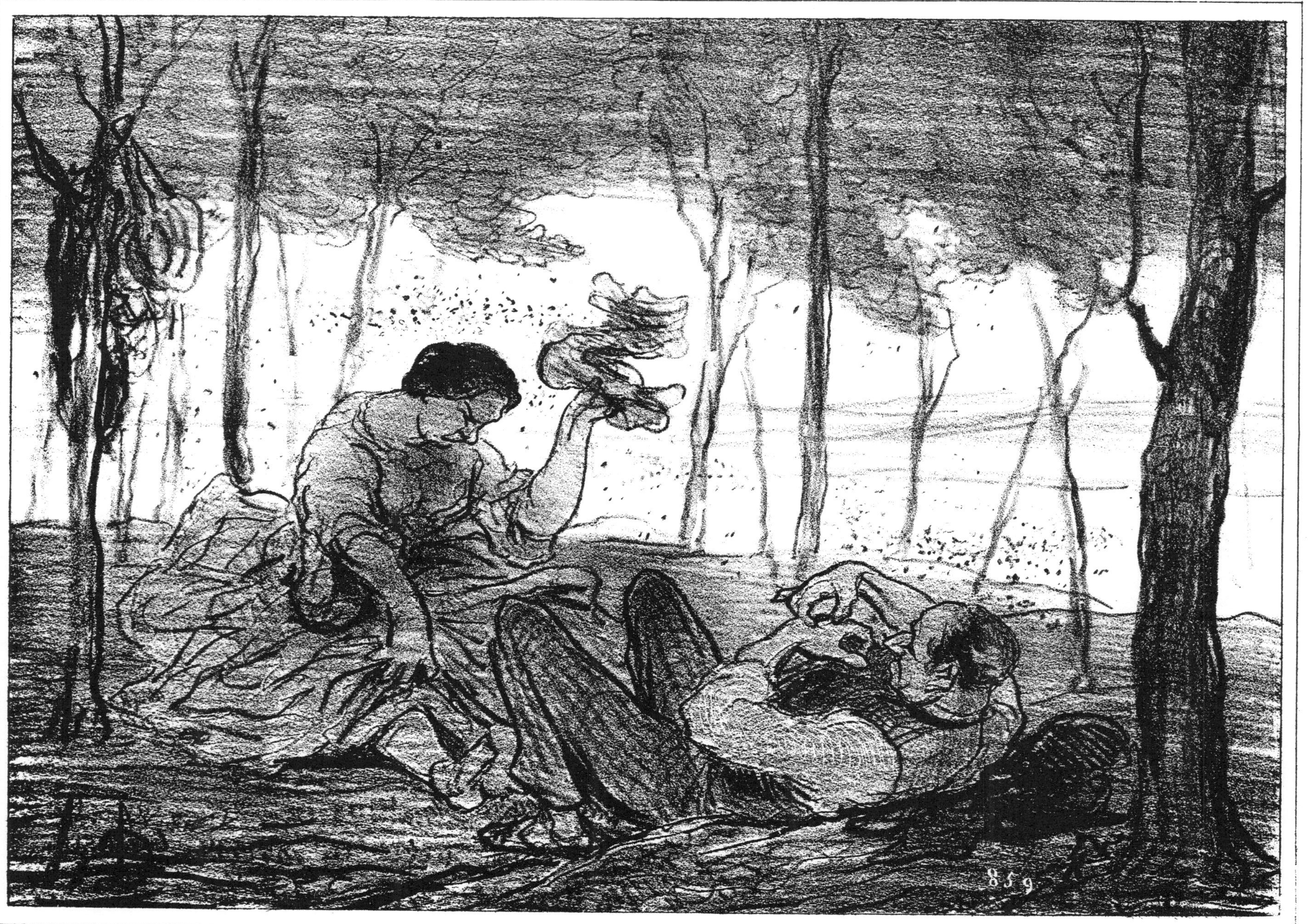

Ayant eu la fâcheuse idée d'aller faire la sieste au bord de l'eau

90 They wanted to take a nap by the river. [Aug. 25 & Sept. 3, 1856]

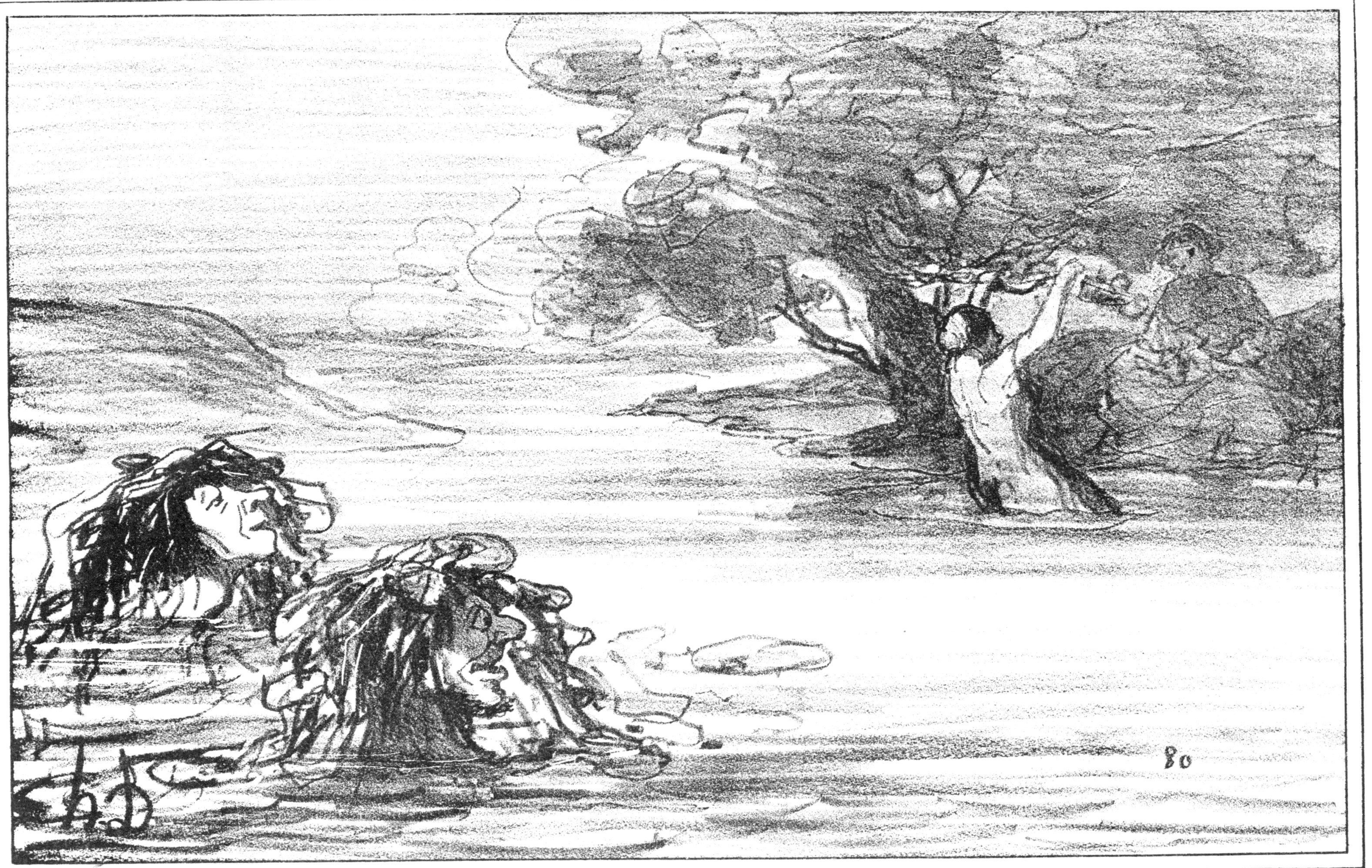

Mon Martinet, 172, Rivoli et 41, r. Vivienne
Lith Destouches, 28, r. Paradis Pre Paris

Divertissement aquatique renouvelé des Grecs.

91 Aquatic amusement borrowed from the Greeks. [Aug. 16–17, 1857]

Mon Martinet, 172, r. Rivoli et 41, r. Vivienne

Lith. Destouches, 28, r. Paradis Pre Paris.

Faisant son apprentissage au tourniquet de la bourse, pour être cantonnier d'un chemin de fer Russe ......

92 Guarding the Stock Exchange turnstile is a cold job. [Feb. 6, 1857]

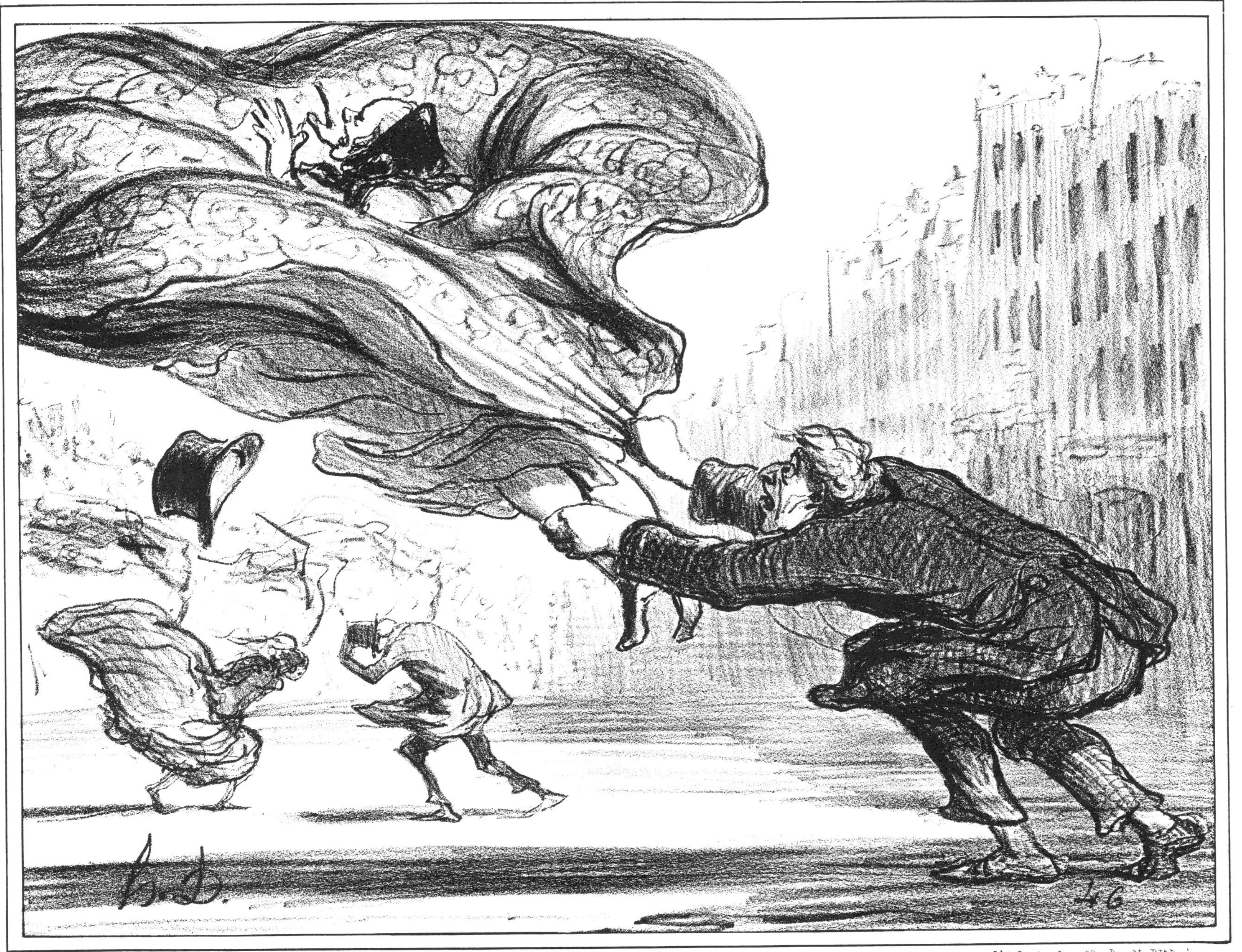

Maison Martinet, 172, r. Rivoli et 41, r. Vivienne — Lith. Destouches, 28, r. Paradis Pre Paris.

Danger de porter des jupons-ballons à l'époque des coups de vent de l'équinoxe.

93 The danger of balloon petticoats in windy weather. [Apr. 3, 1857]

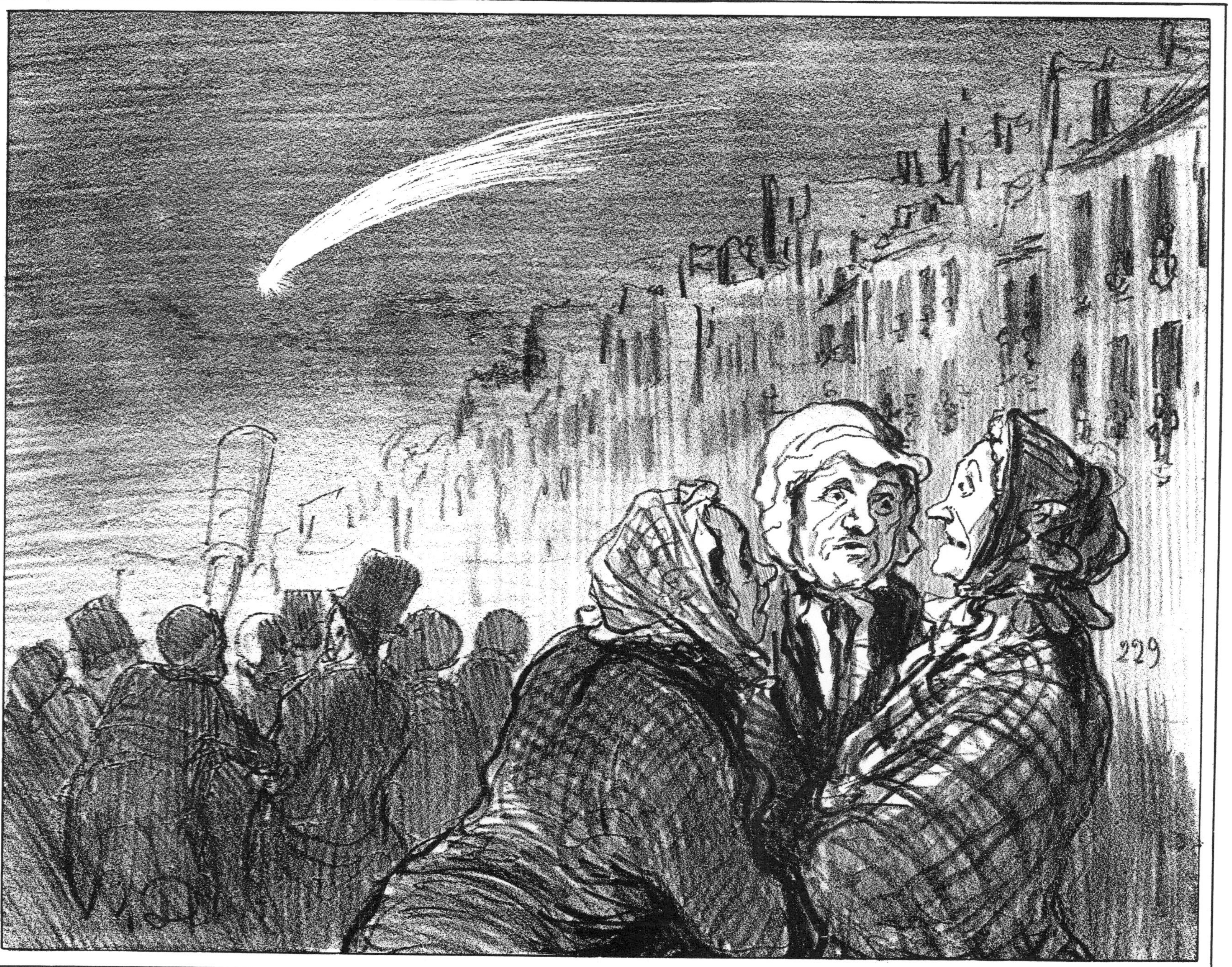

maison Martinet, 172, r. Rivoli et 41, r. Vivienne.

Lith. Destouches, 28, r. Paradis P^re Paris

– Ah !... les comètes ......, ça annonce toujours quelques grands malheurs !..... je n'm'étonne plus que c'te pauv' madame Galuchet est morte subitement hier soir !....

94 Discussing the disasters caused by the appearance of comets. [Oct. 30, 1858]

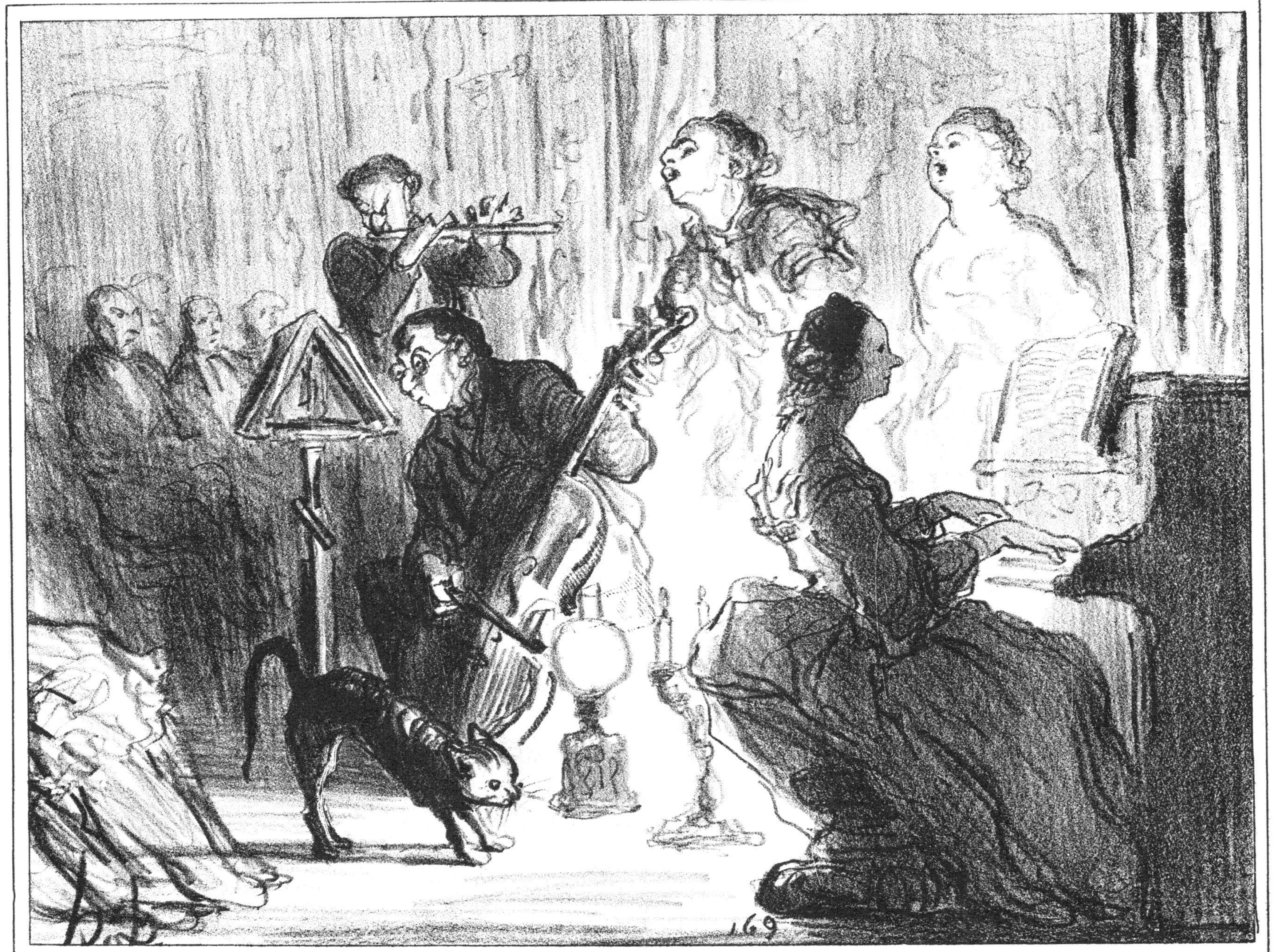

Mon Martinet, 172, r. Rivoli et 41, r. Vivienne — Lith. Destouches, 28, r. Paradis Pre Paris.

Un orchestre dans une maison très comme il faut, où l'on se passe la fantaisie de jouer l'opérette.

95 An operetta performed by amateurs in a wealthy home. [Apr. 20, 1858]

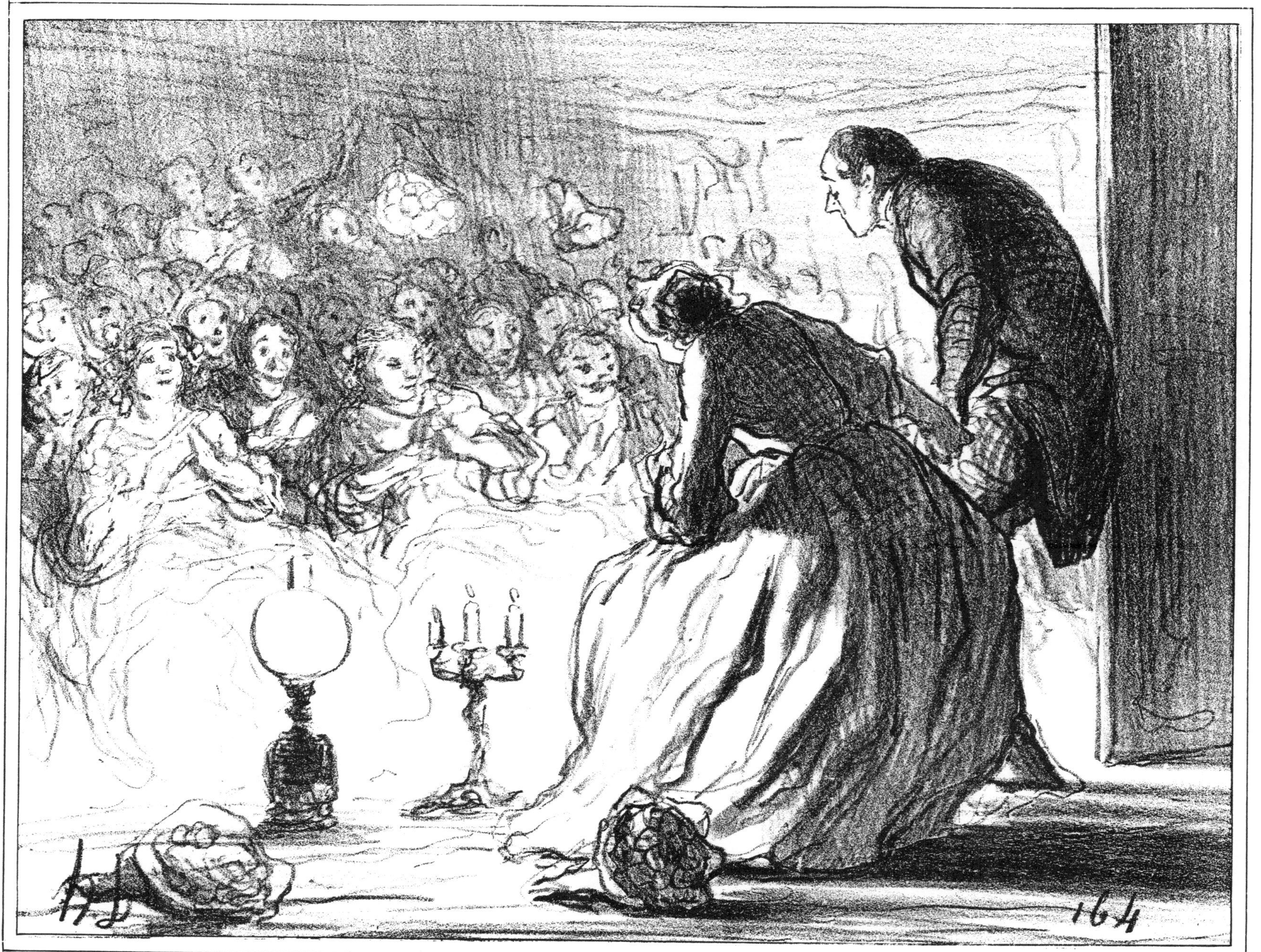

Rappelés avec enthousiasme !....... et pas un claqueur ..... voilà ce qui s'appelle un vrai succès...... et on dit que l'art dramatique dépérit ..... allons donc !....

96 A curtain call after an amateur performance. [Apr. 30 & May 1, 1858]

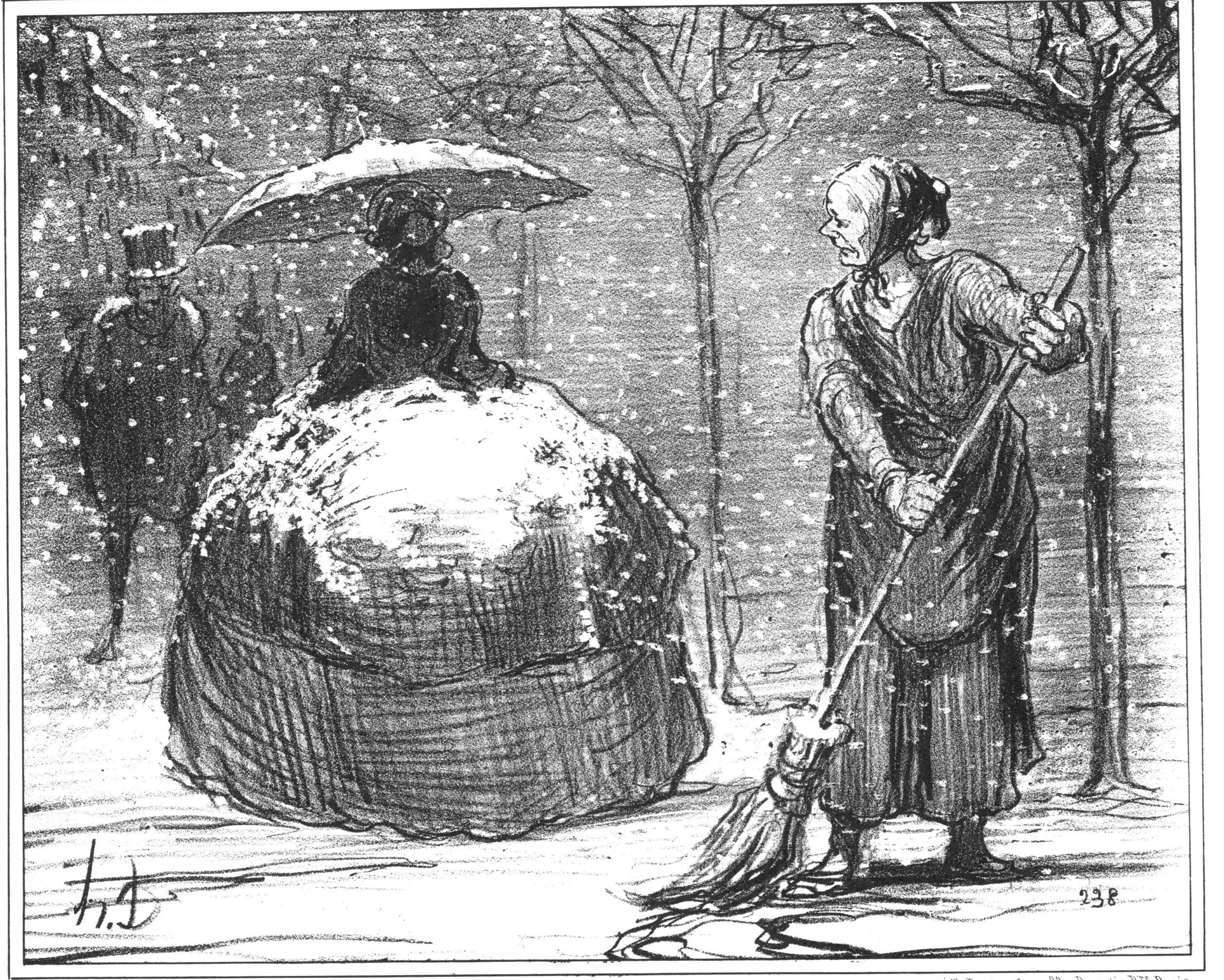

Mon Martinet, 172, r. Rivoli et 41, r. Vivienne.

Lith. Destouches, 28, r. Paradis Pre Paris.

LA CRINOLINE EN TEMPS DE NEIGE

– Ma belle dame..... faut-y vous donner un coup d' balai ?.....

97 The crinoline in snowy weather. [Nov. 13, 1858]

maison Martinet, 172, r Rivoli et 41, r Vivienne. Lith. Destouches, 28 r Paradis Pre Paris.

UN AMATEUR — Mais quel est donc ce tableau...., on n'y voit rien que du noir ?...

LE CRIEUR. — C'est l'empereur Soulouque tiré au daguerréotype.

98 Picture connoisseurs at an auction room. [Mar. 16, 1859]

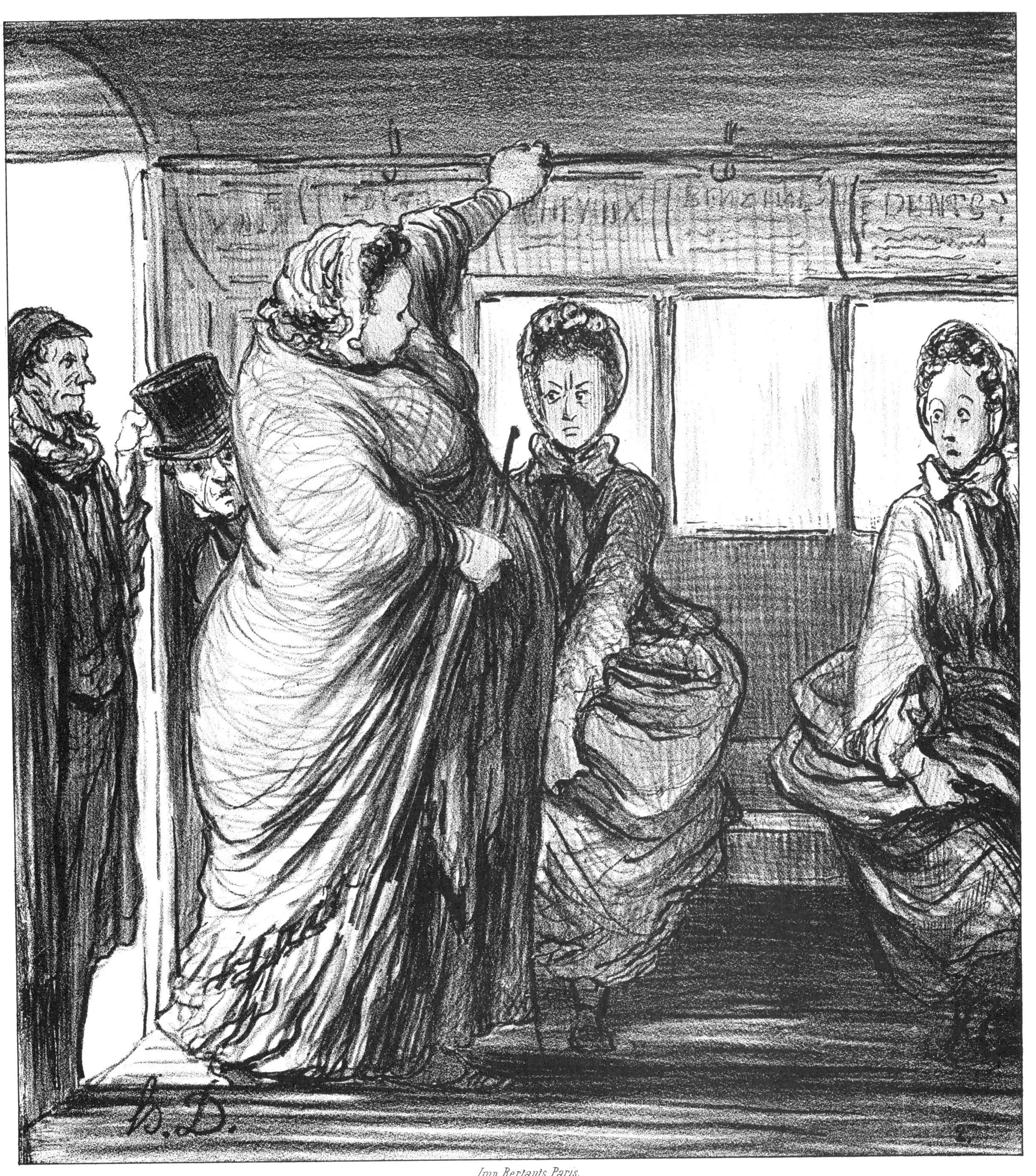

Imp. Bertauts, Paris.

Un zeste, un rien.... et l'omnibus se trouve complet.

99 A trifle, a mere nothing . . . and the omnibus is already filled! [Mar. 16, 1862]

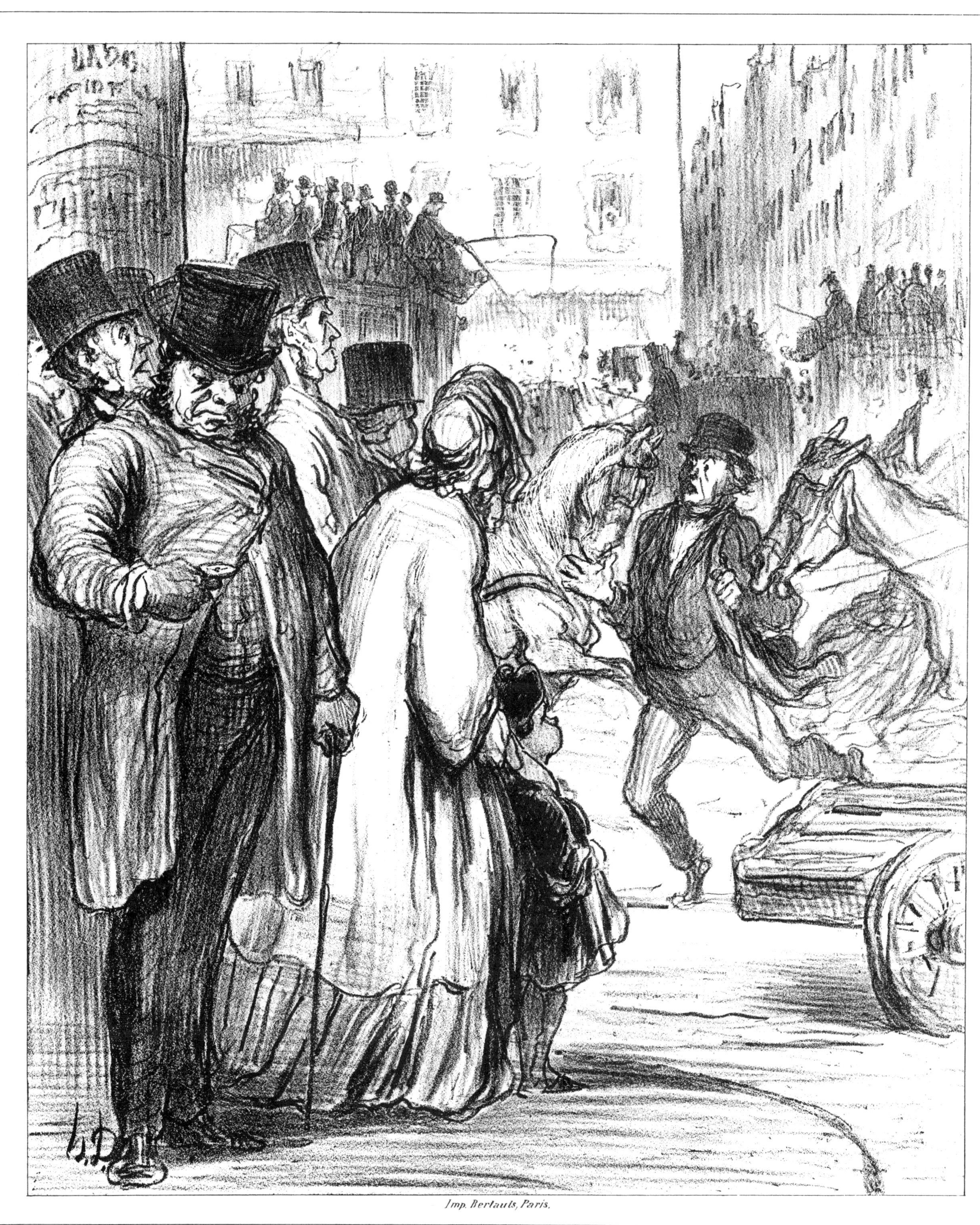

Comme c'est heureux pour les gens pressés, qu'on ait élargi les voies de communication!!!.

100 How fortunate that the thoroughfares have been widened! [Apr. 6, 1862]

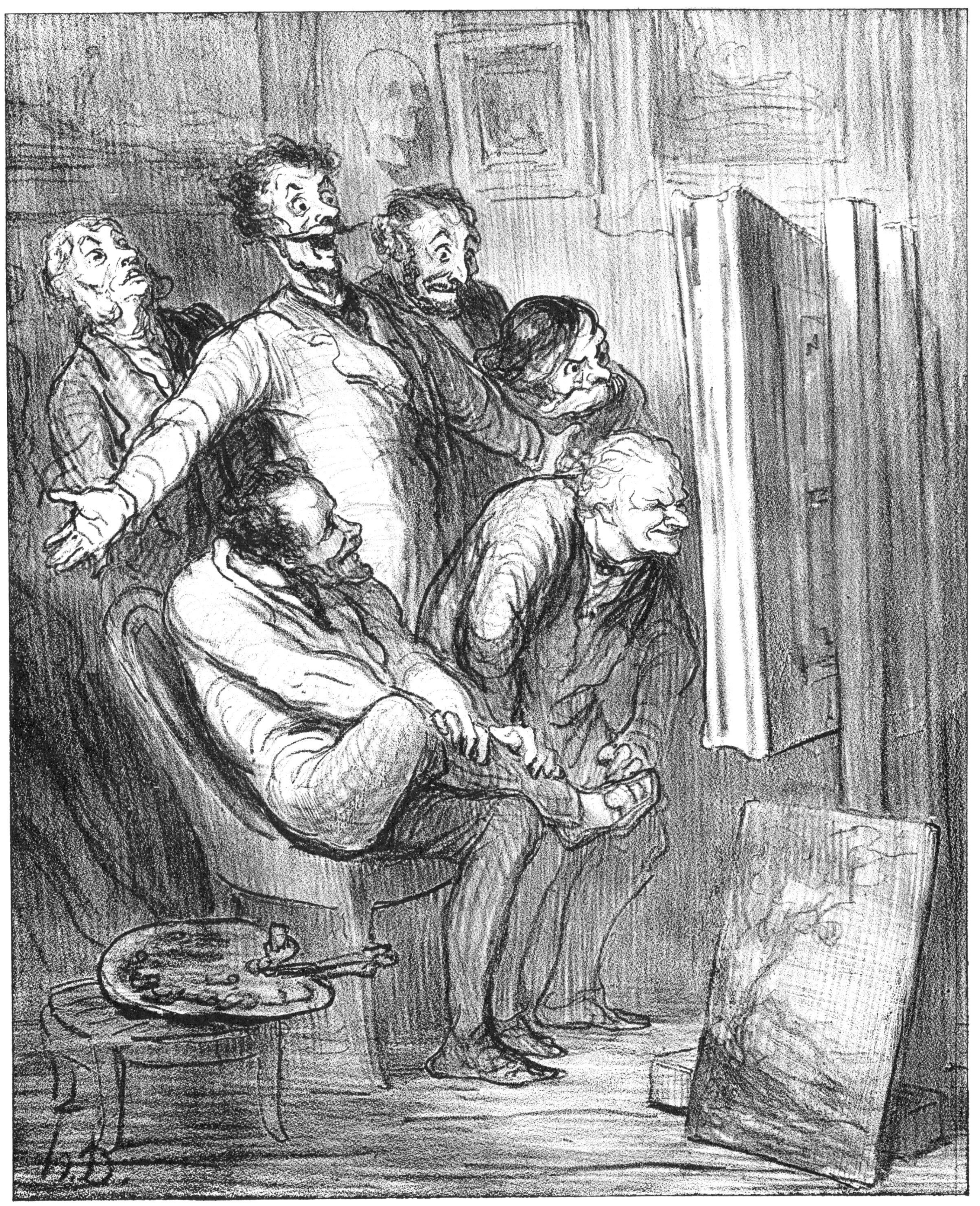

Imp. Bertauts, Paris.

Fichtre !... Epatant !... Sapristi !... Superbe !... ça parle !...

101 Unqualified admiration of a new painting in the artist's studio. [Apr. 20, 1862]

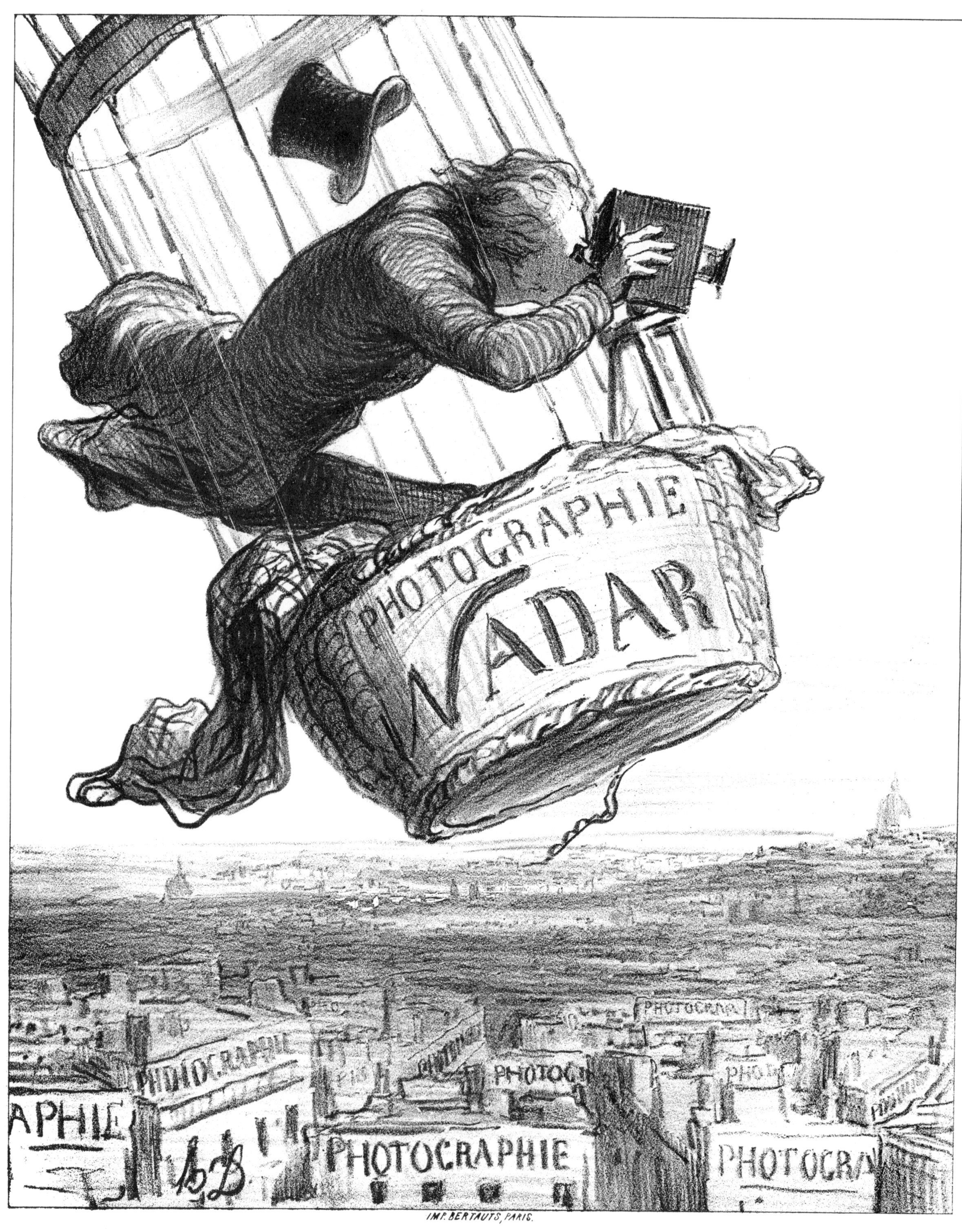

NADAR élevant la Photographie à la hauteur de l'Art

102 Nadar raising photography to the level of art. [May 25, 1862]

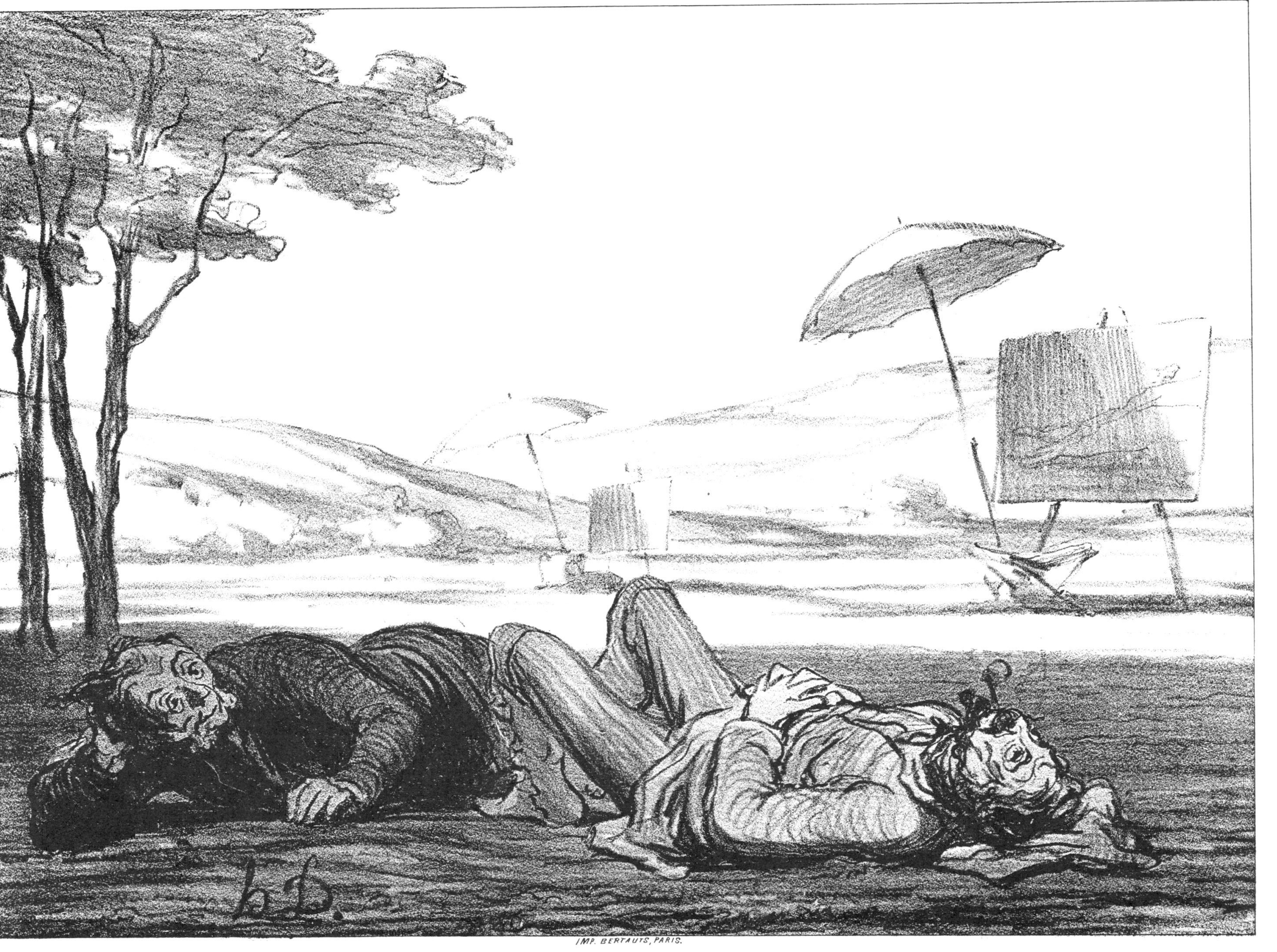

Paysagistes au travail...

103 Landscapists at work. [Aug. 17, 1862]

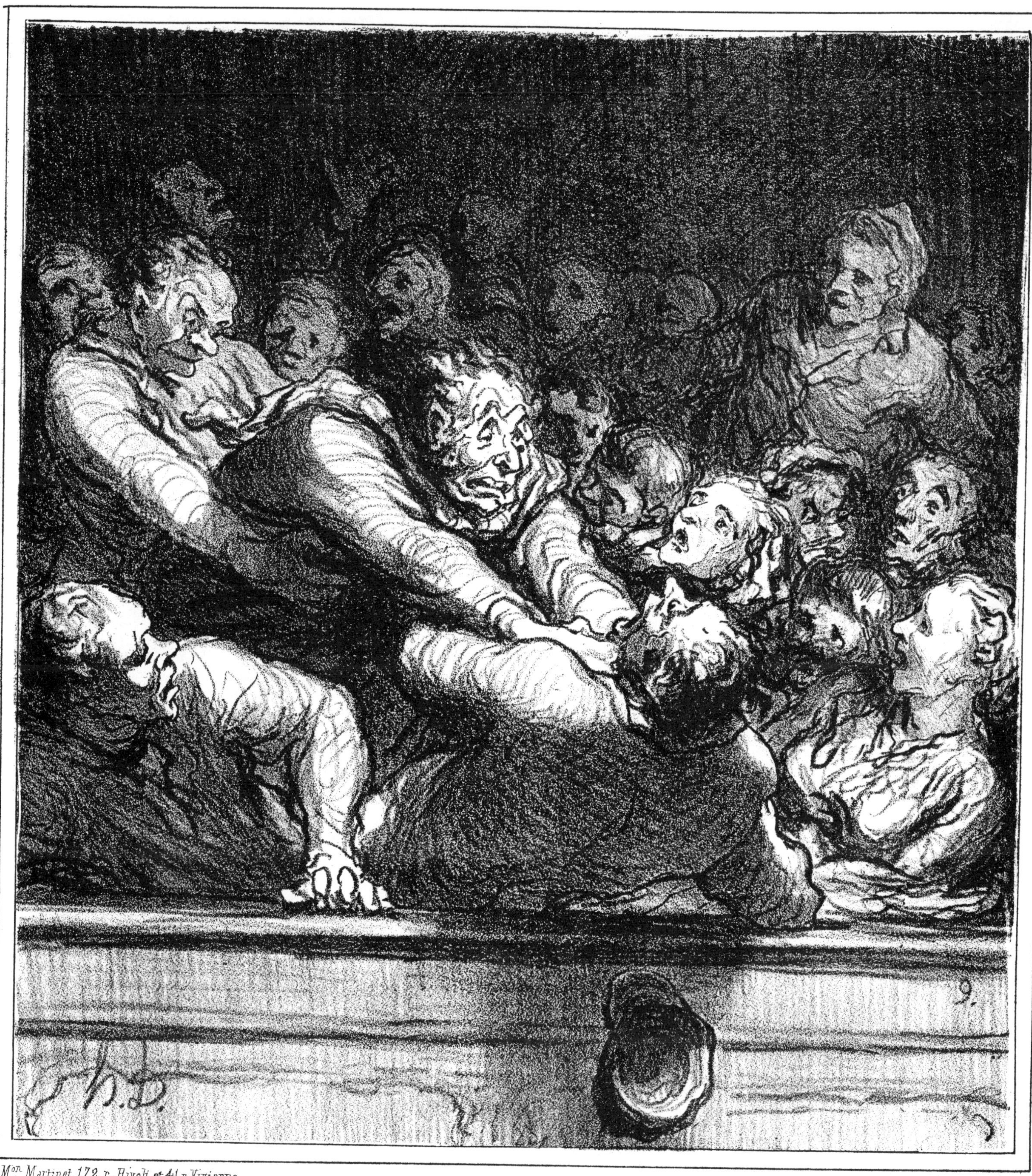

Mon. Martinet, 172, r. Rivoli et 41 r Vivienne

Lith. Destouches 28 r Paradis P.re

Une discussion littéraire à la deuxième Galerie.

104 A literary discussion in the second balcony. [Feb. 27, 1864]

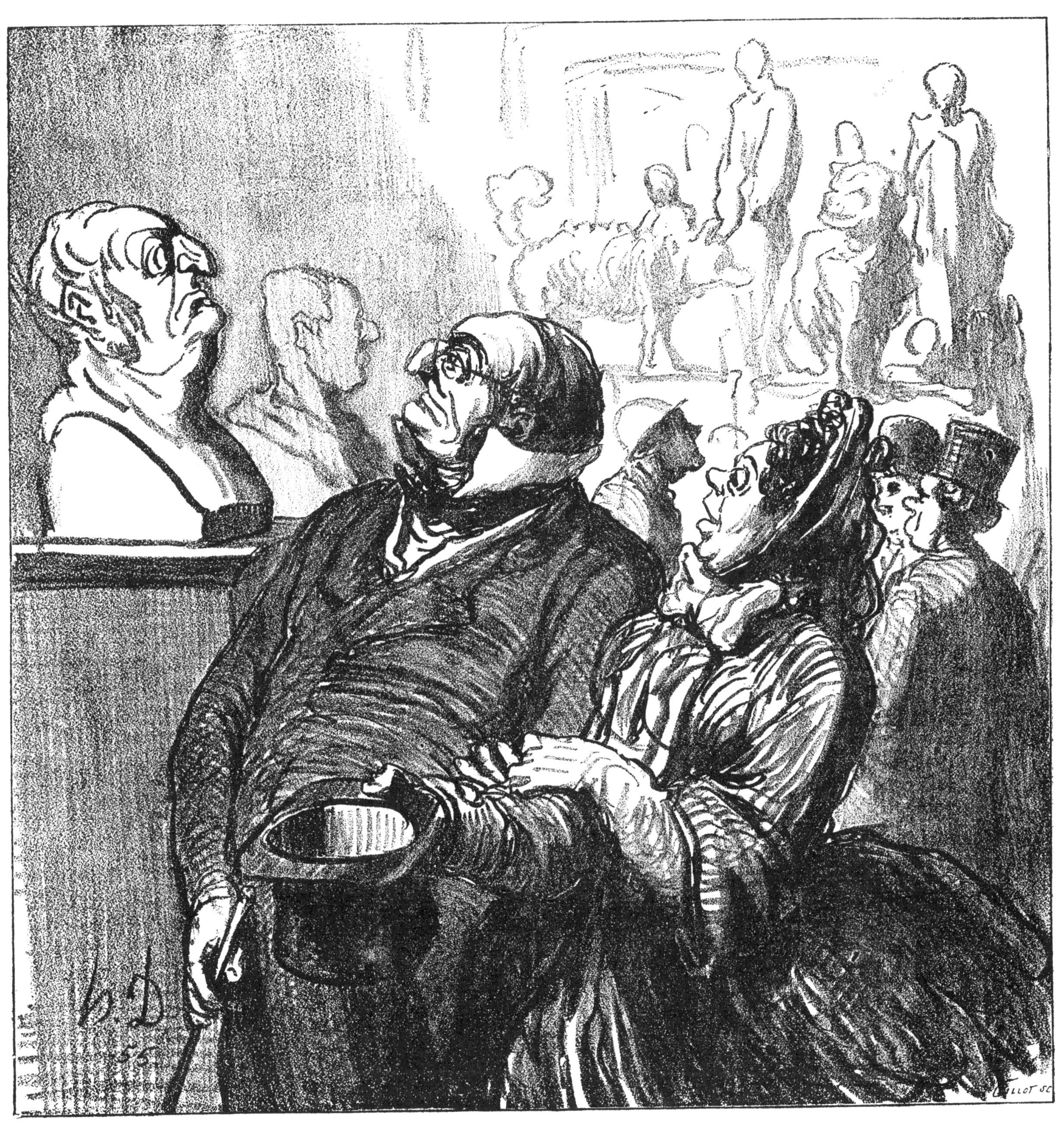

— Il n'y a pas à dire, c'est bien moi, c'est bien mon galbe; mais je regretterai toujours que l'artiste ait eu l'entêtement de ne vouloir pas reproduire mes lunettes, non plus que mon faux col!...

105 Joseph Prudhomme, the typical bourgeois, admires his bust at the Salon.
[June 18, 1864]

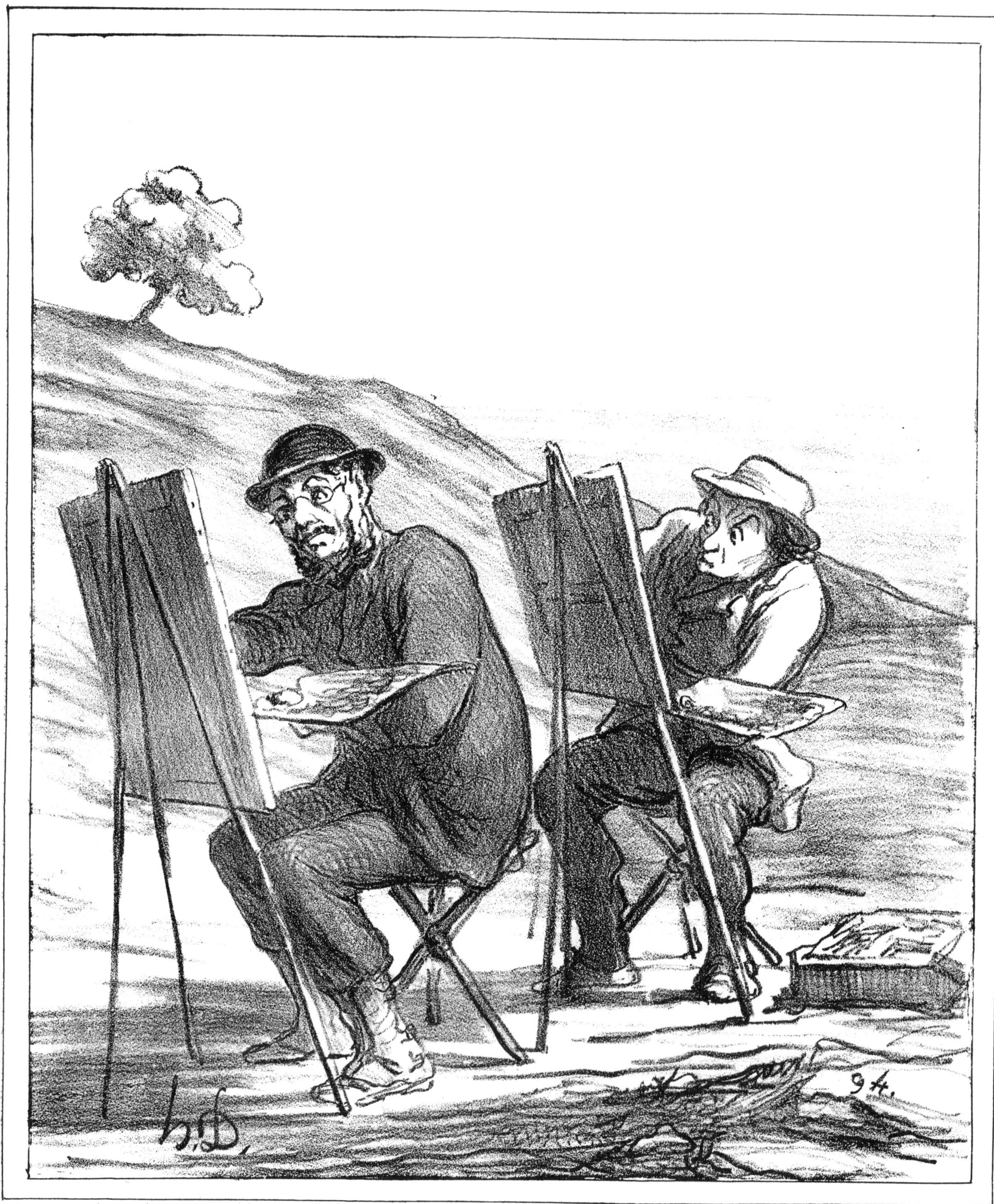

Mon Martinet, 172, r. Rivoli et 41, r. Vivienne — Lith. Destouches, 28, r. Paradis Pre

LES PAYSAGISTES

Le premier copie la nature, le second copie le premier.

106 One landscape artist copies nature, the second copies the first. [May 12, 1865]

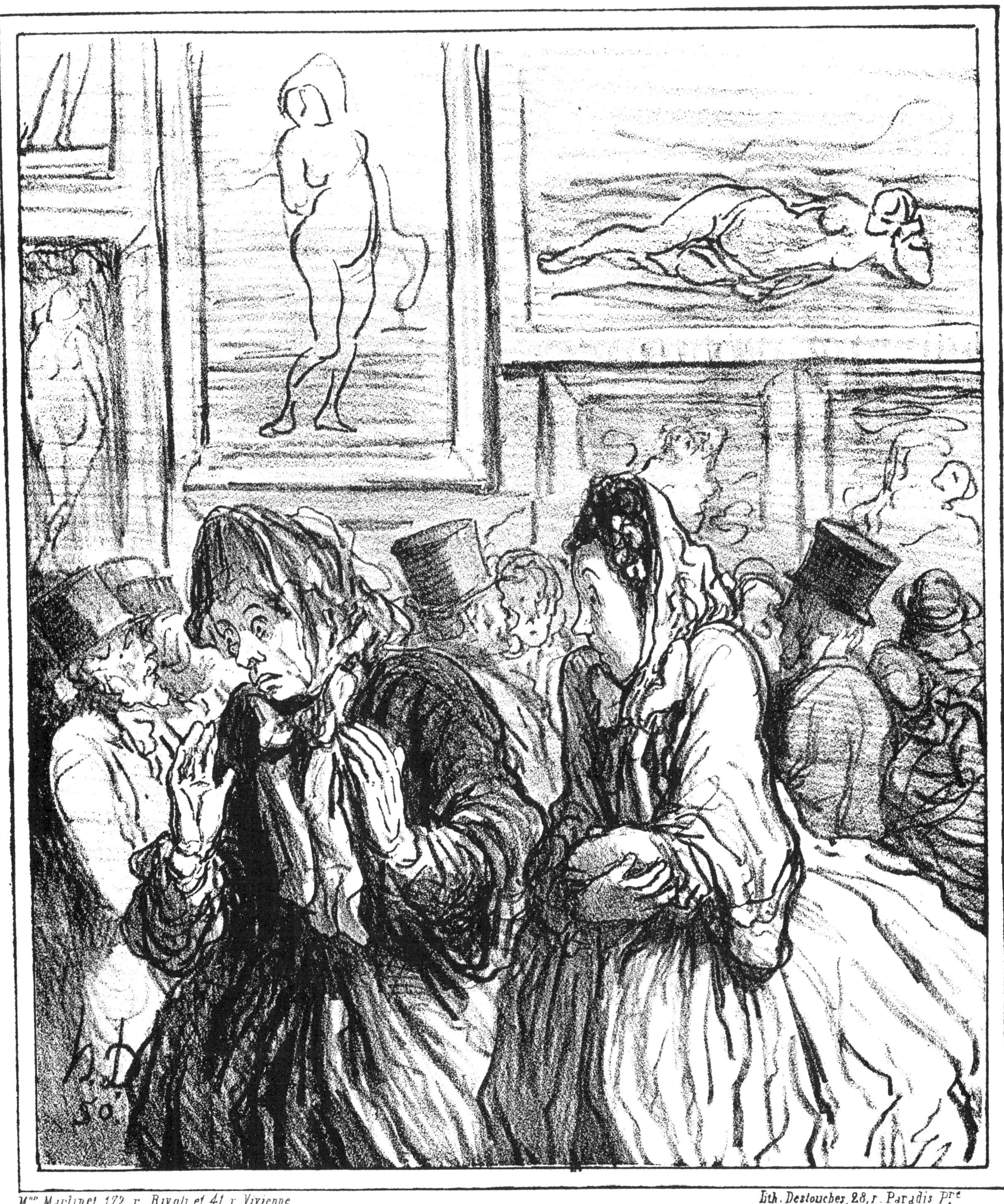

Mon Martinet 172, r. Rivoli et 41, r. Vivienne — Lith. Destouches, 28, r. Paradis Pre

— Cette année encore des Vénus.... toujours des Vénus!... comme s'il y avait des femmes faites comme ça!....

107 Too many pictures of Venus at the Salon! [May 10, 1864]

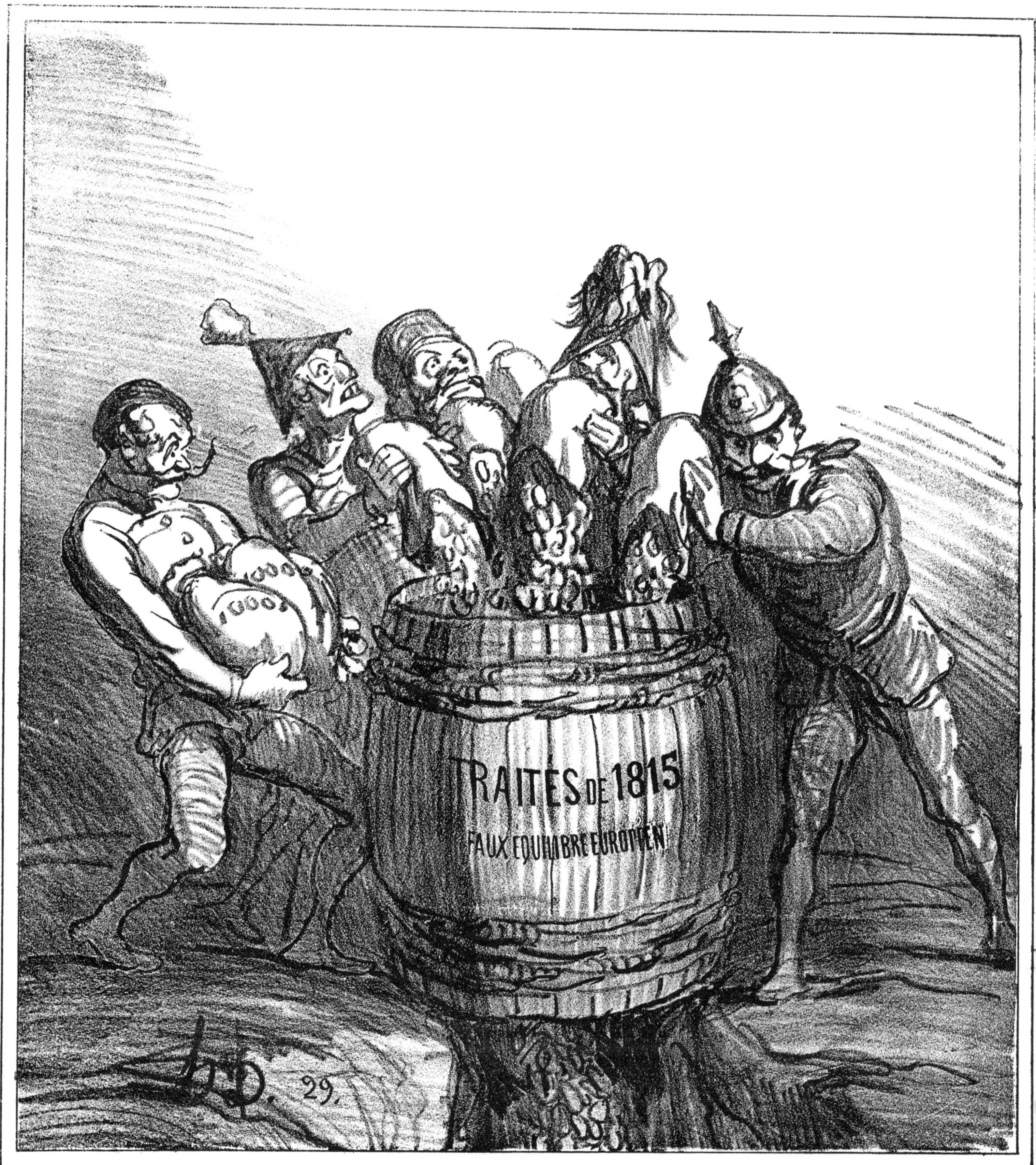

A de Vresse R. Rivoli 55.

Lith Destouches r. Paradis Pon

Renouvelé des petites Danaïdes.

108 The European heads of state pour gold into the bottomless cask that symbolizes the obsolete balance of power. [June 26, 1866]

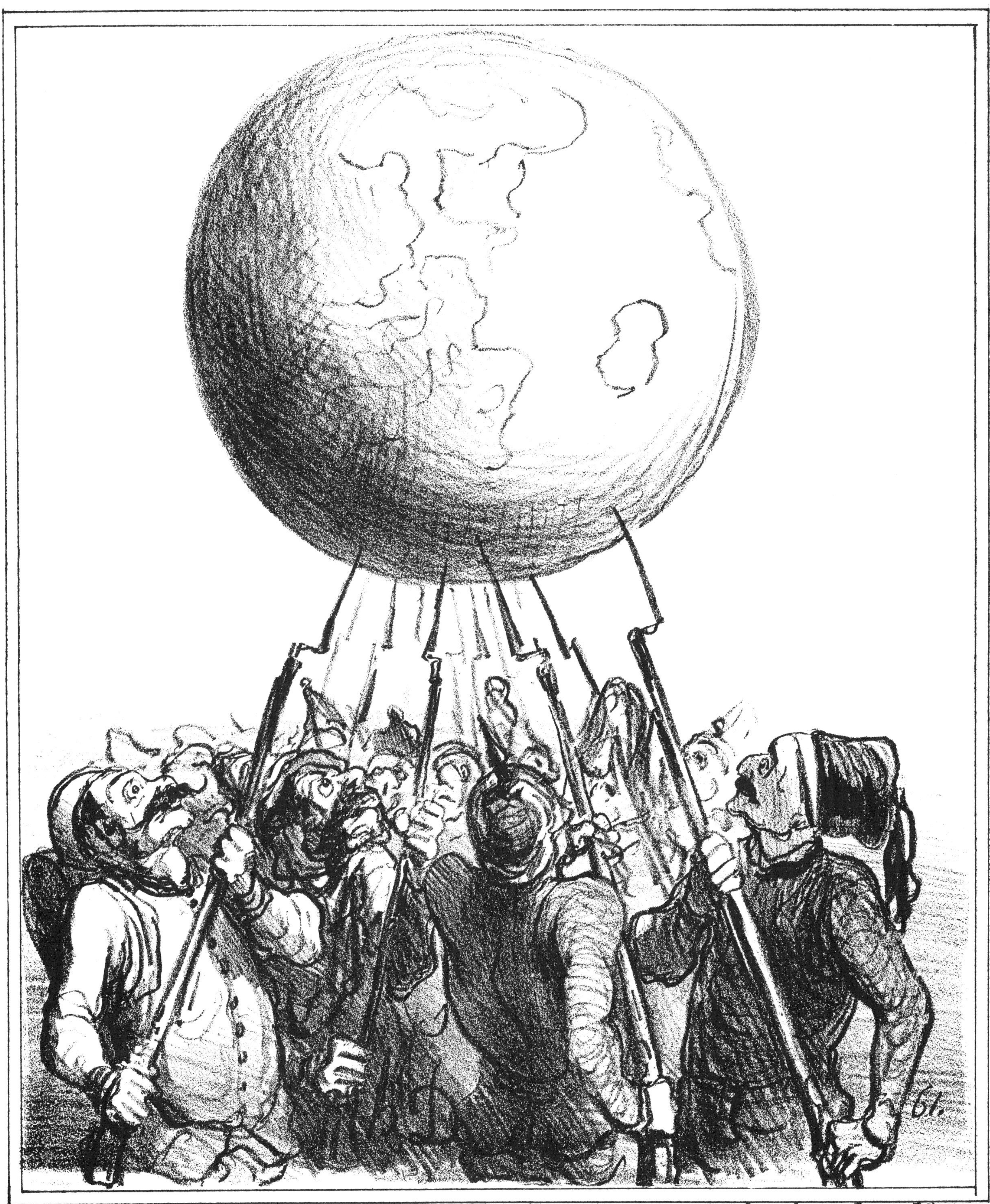

L'Equilibre Européen.

109 The European balance of power. [Dec. 1, 1866]

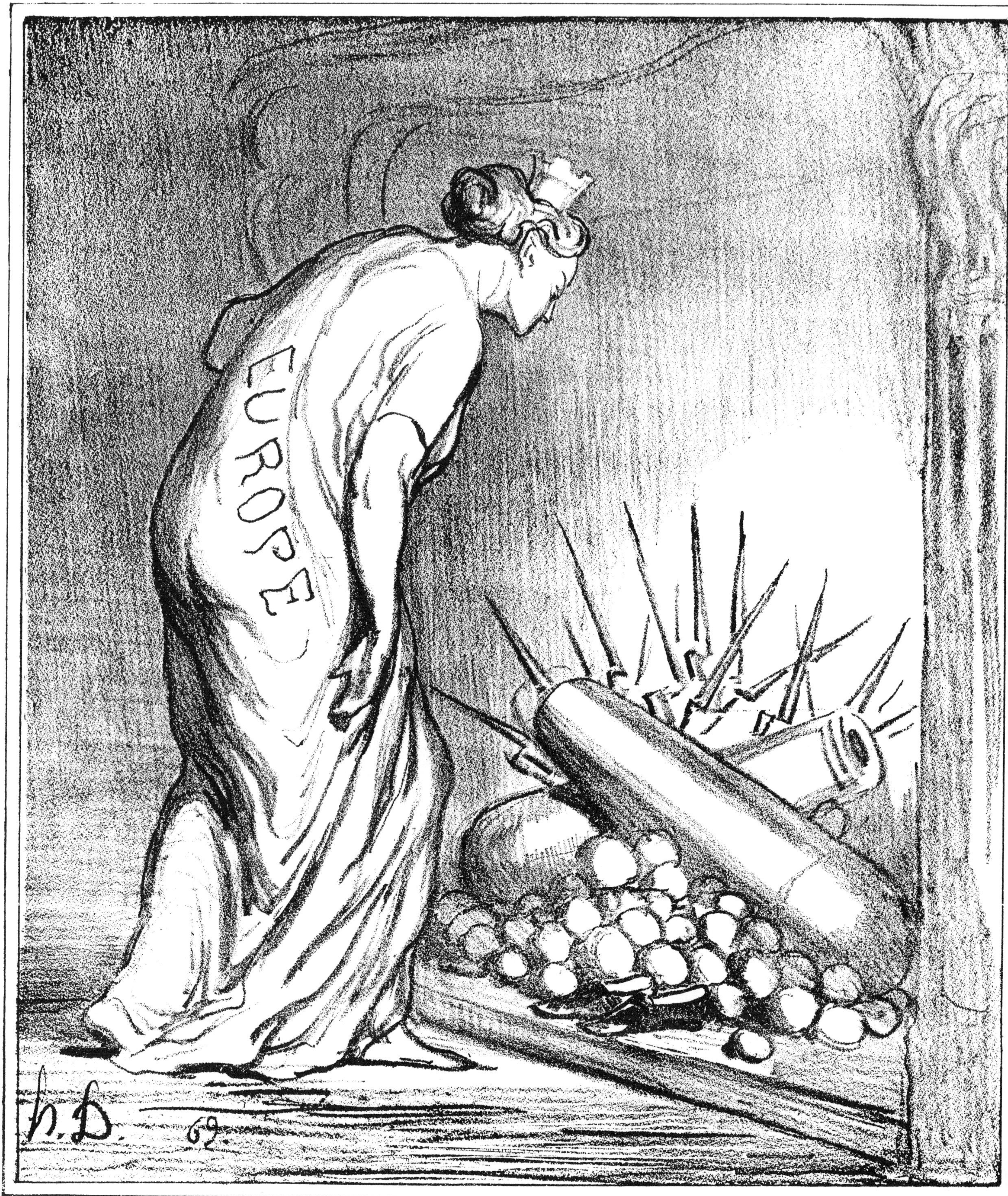

110 The gifts for Christmas 1868. [Dec. 25, 1868]

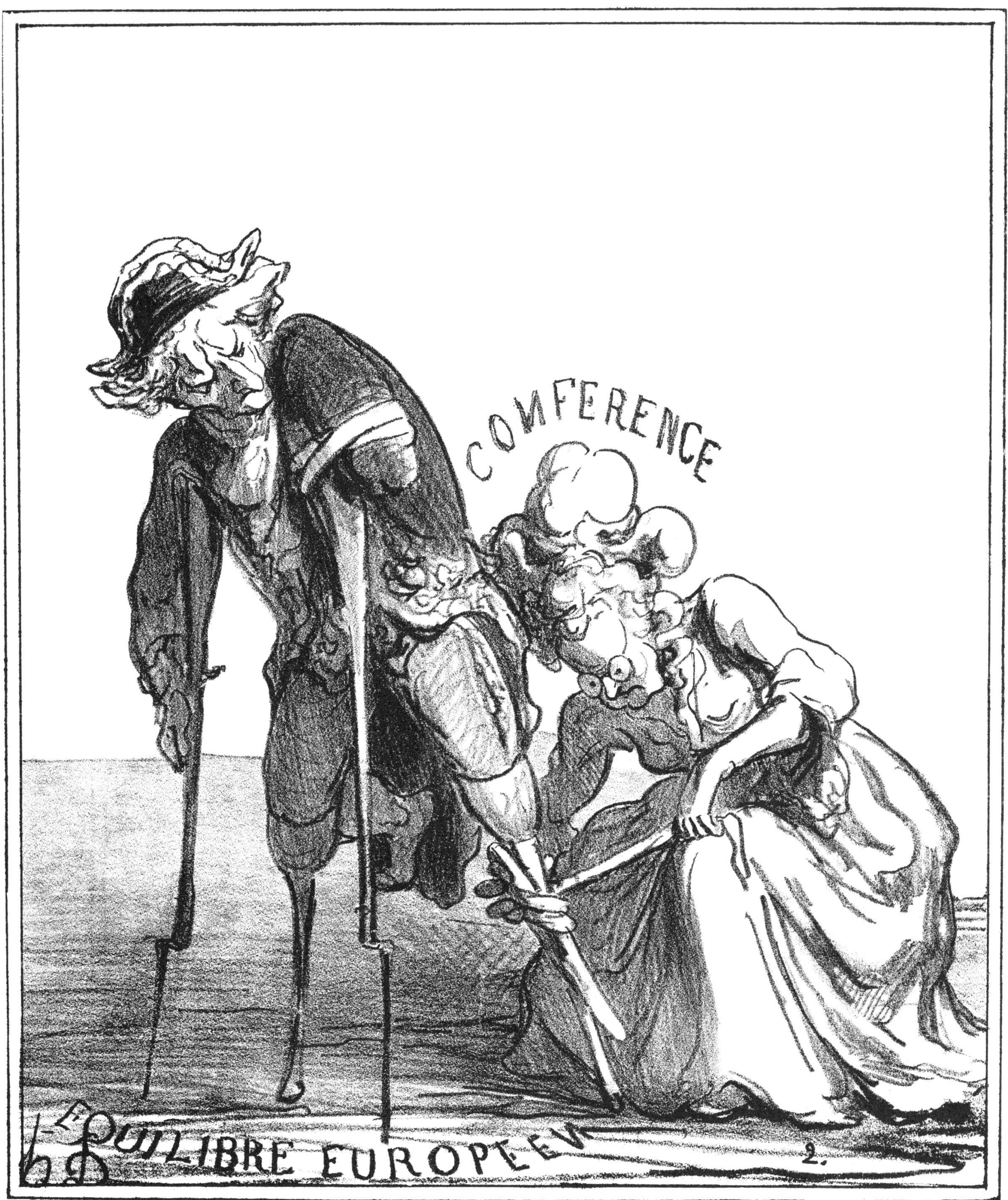

– Pauvre vieux!

111 An old, dazed "Conference" attempts to patch up the battered veteran "European Balance of Power." [Jan. 26, 1869]

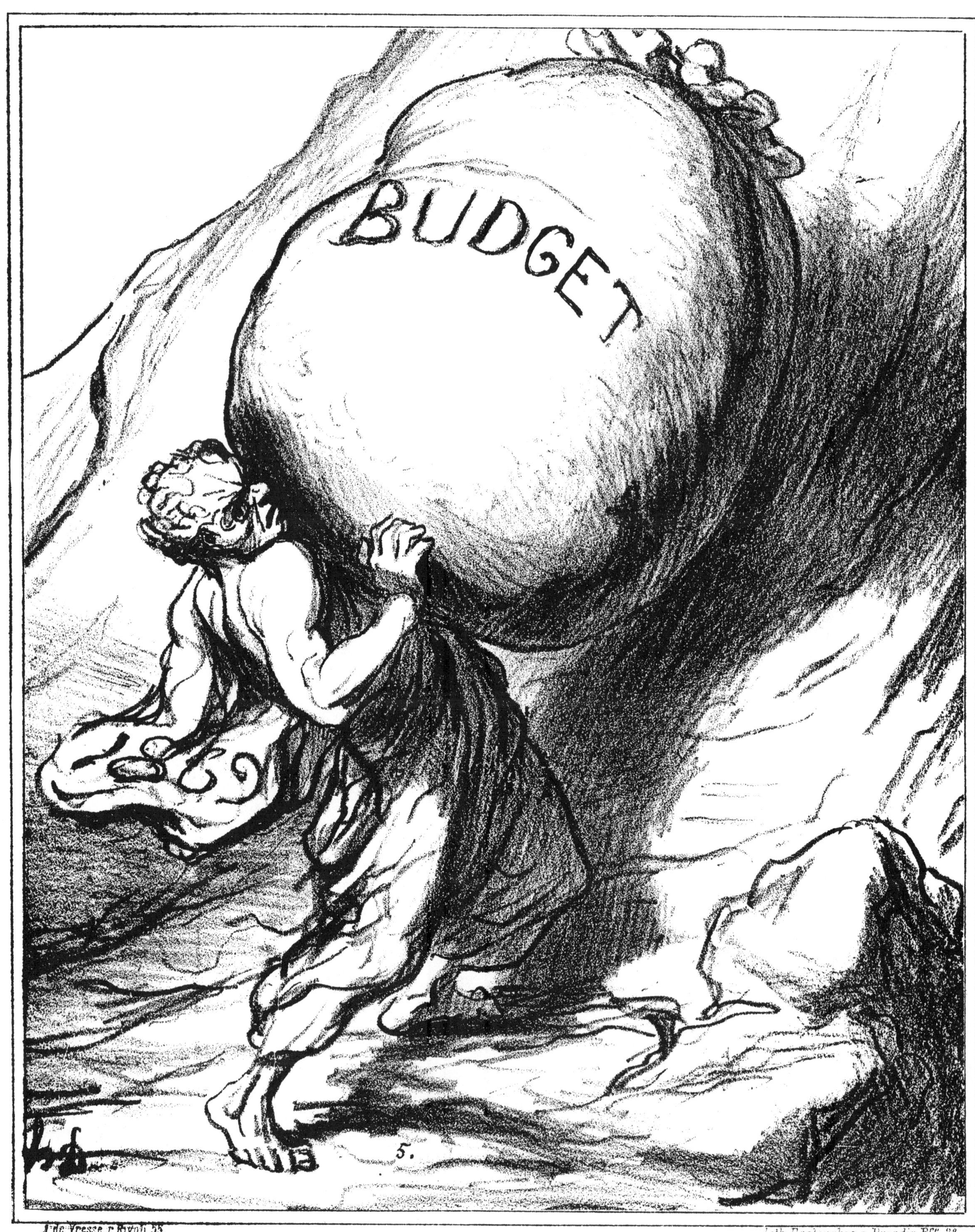

Comme Sisyphe.

112 Like Sisyphus. [Feb. 25, 1869]

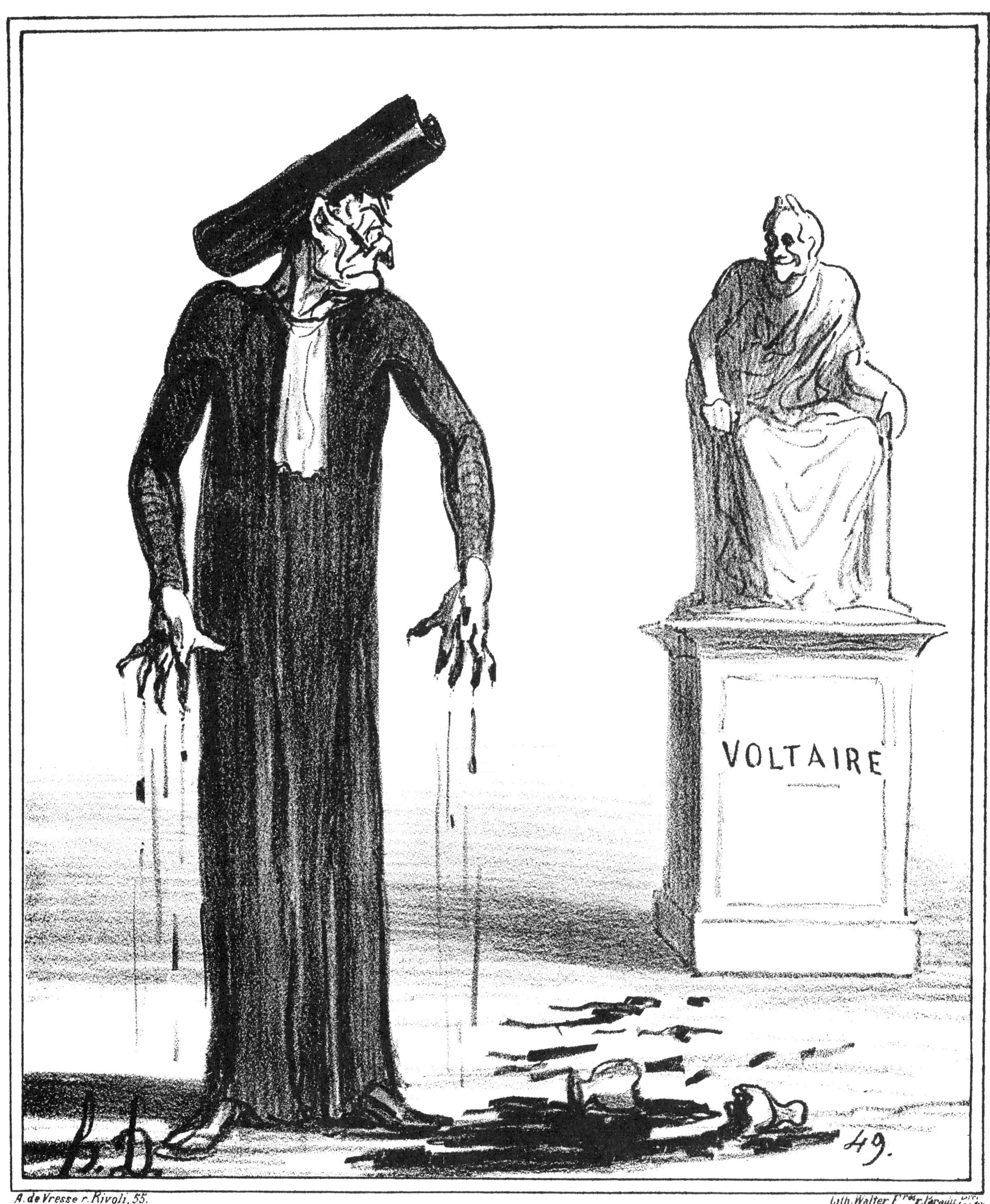

Je voulais la lui jeter et c'est moi qui me suis sali.

113 The Jesuit who wanted to bespatter the statue of Voltaire has only succeeded in soiling himself. [Sept. 22, 1869]

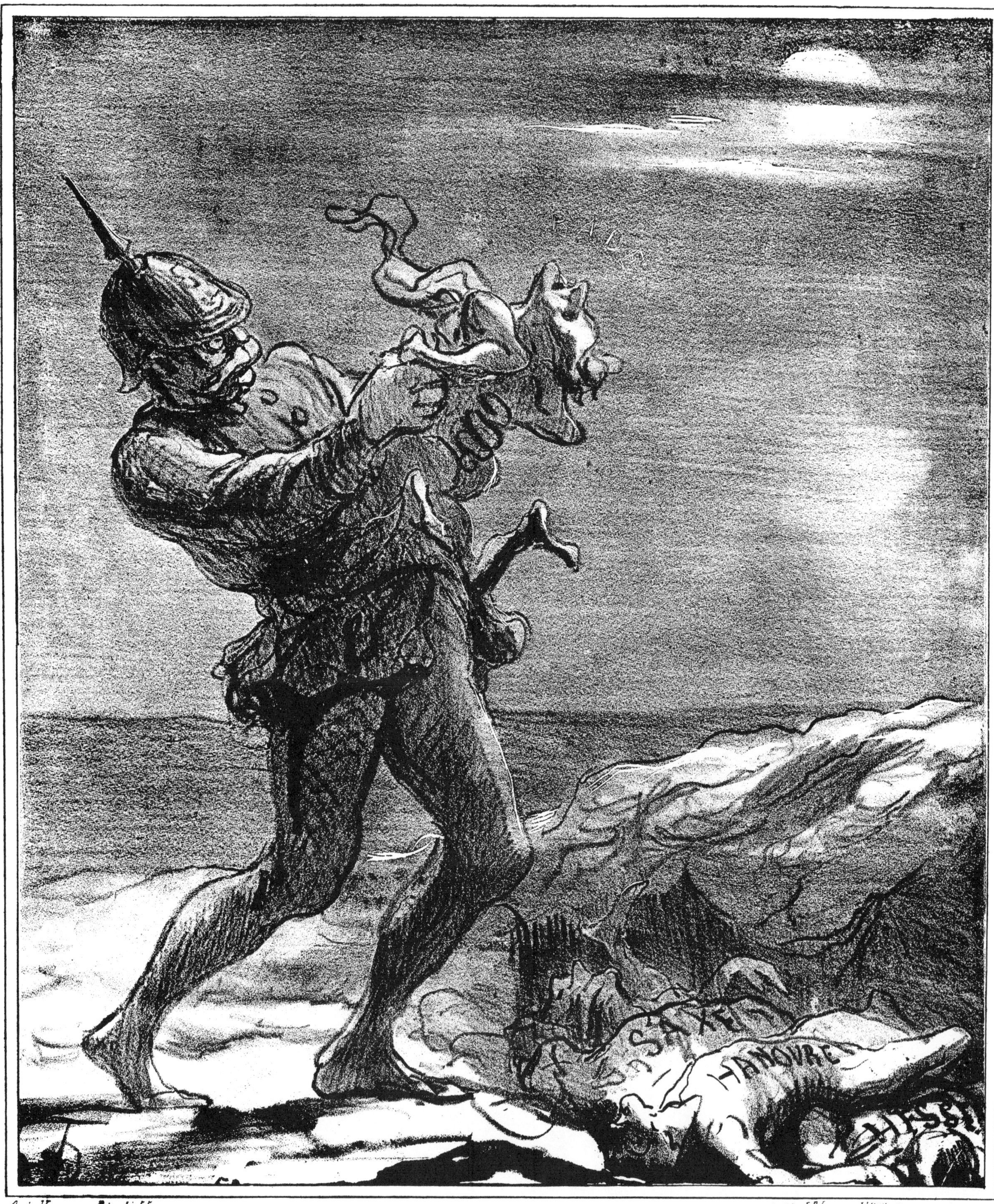

A l'instar de Pantin.

114 The Prussian Bismarck crushing the independent German states. [Oct. 12, 1869]

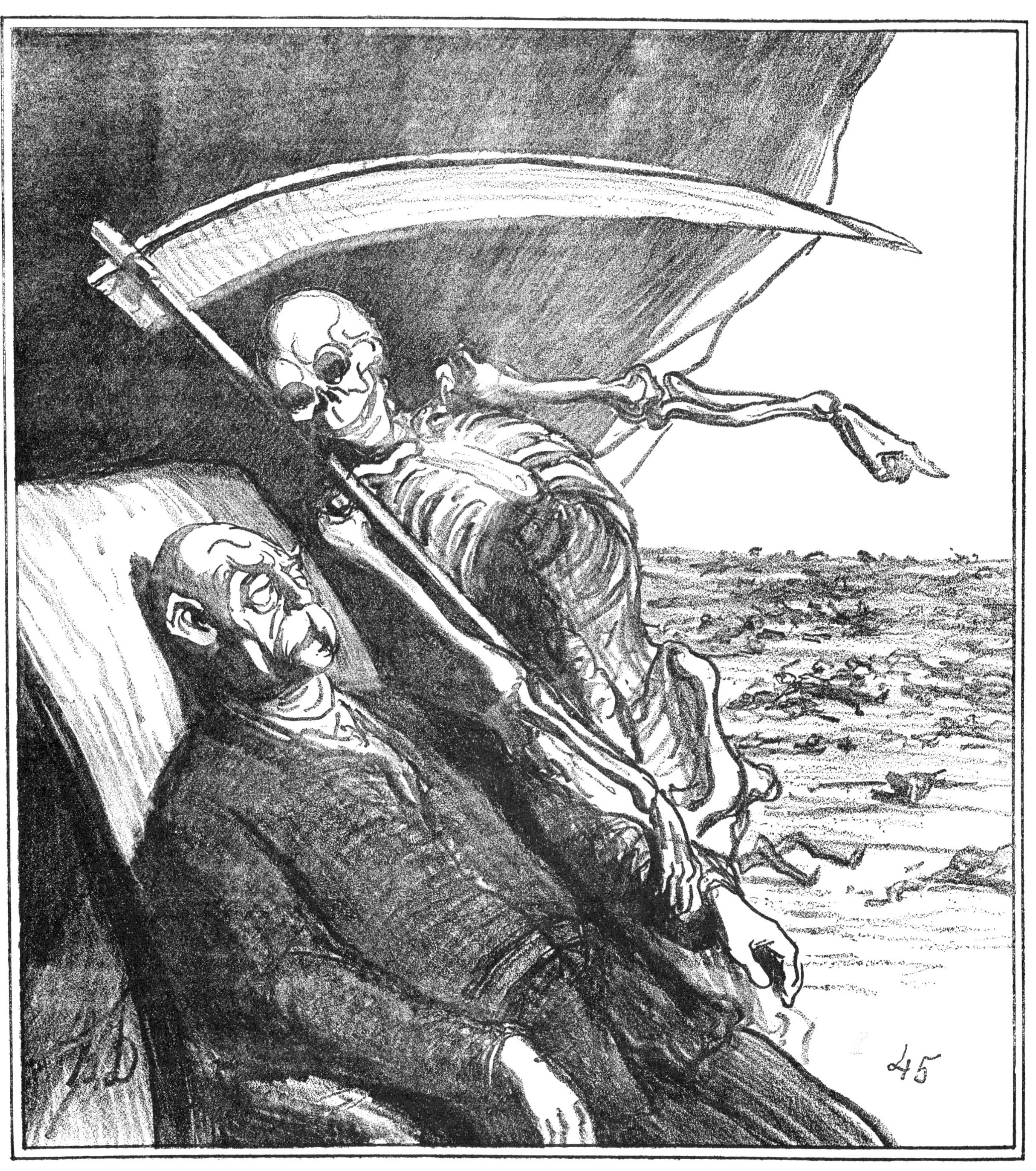

UN CAUCHEMAR DE M. DE BISMARK.

— Merci !...

115 In a dream, Death thanks Bismarck for the wars he has fomented. [Aug. 22, 1870]

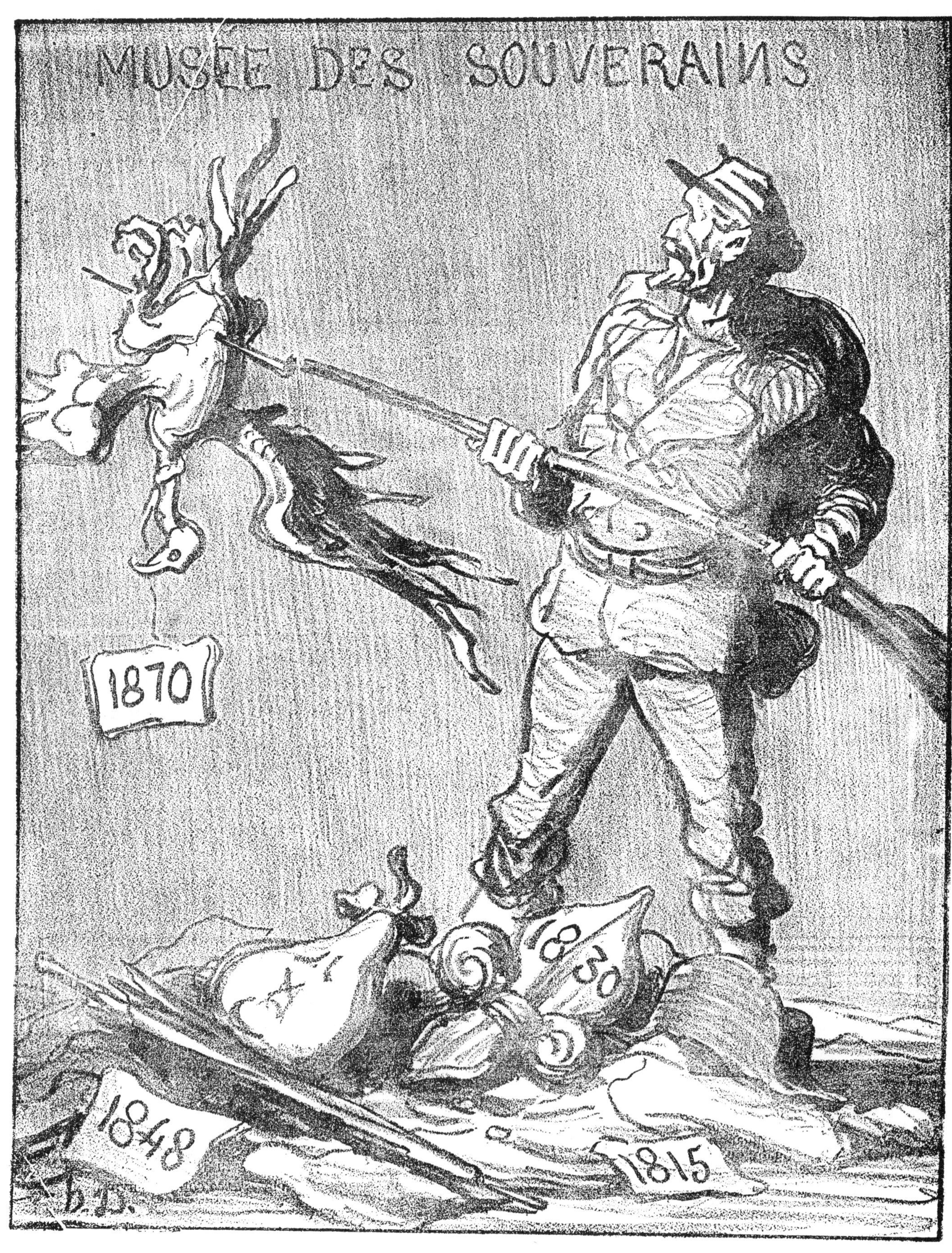

A qui le tour ?

116 Defeated in the Franco-Prussian War, the eagle of Napoleon III joins the relics of earlier nineteenth-century French regimes. [Oct. 31, 1870]

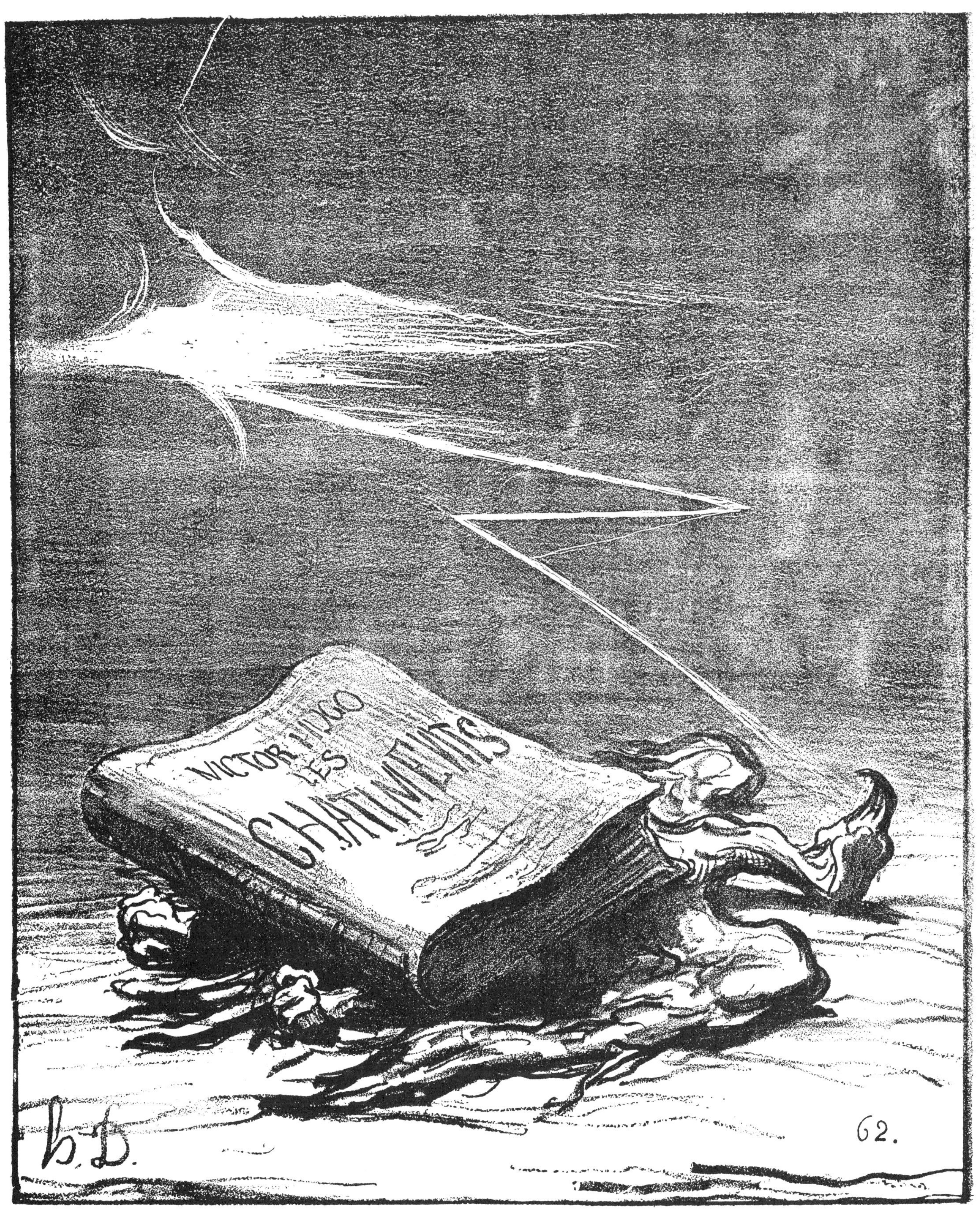

PAGE D'HISTOIRE.

117 Victor Hugo's poems of opposition finally overwhelm the Napoleonic eagle. [Nov. 16, 1870]

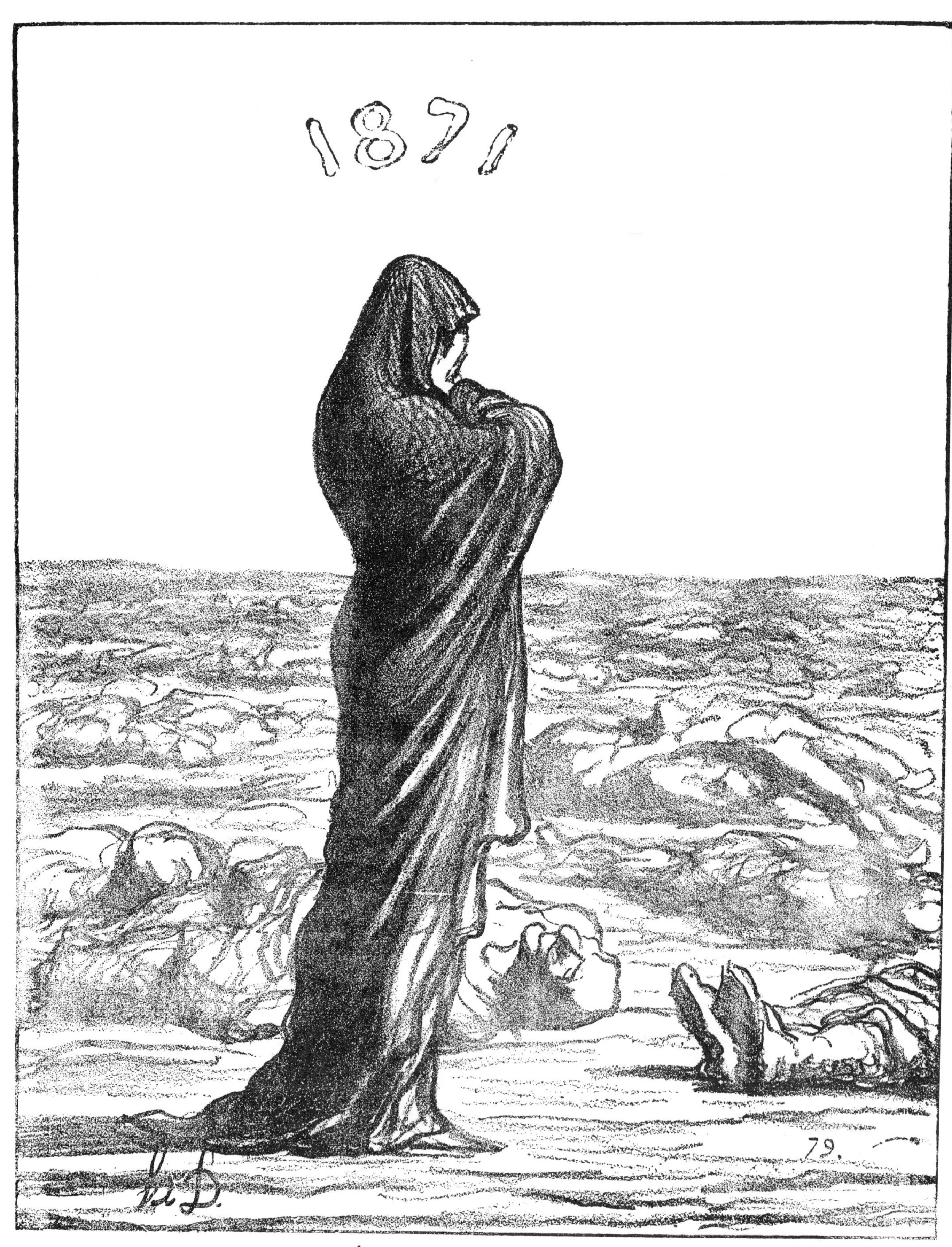

Épouvantée de l'héritage.

118 The year 1871 is appalled at the destruction wrought by 1870. [Jan. 11, 1871]

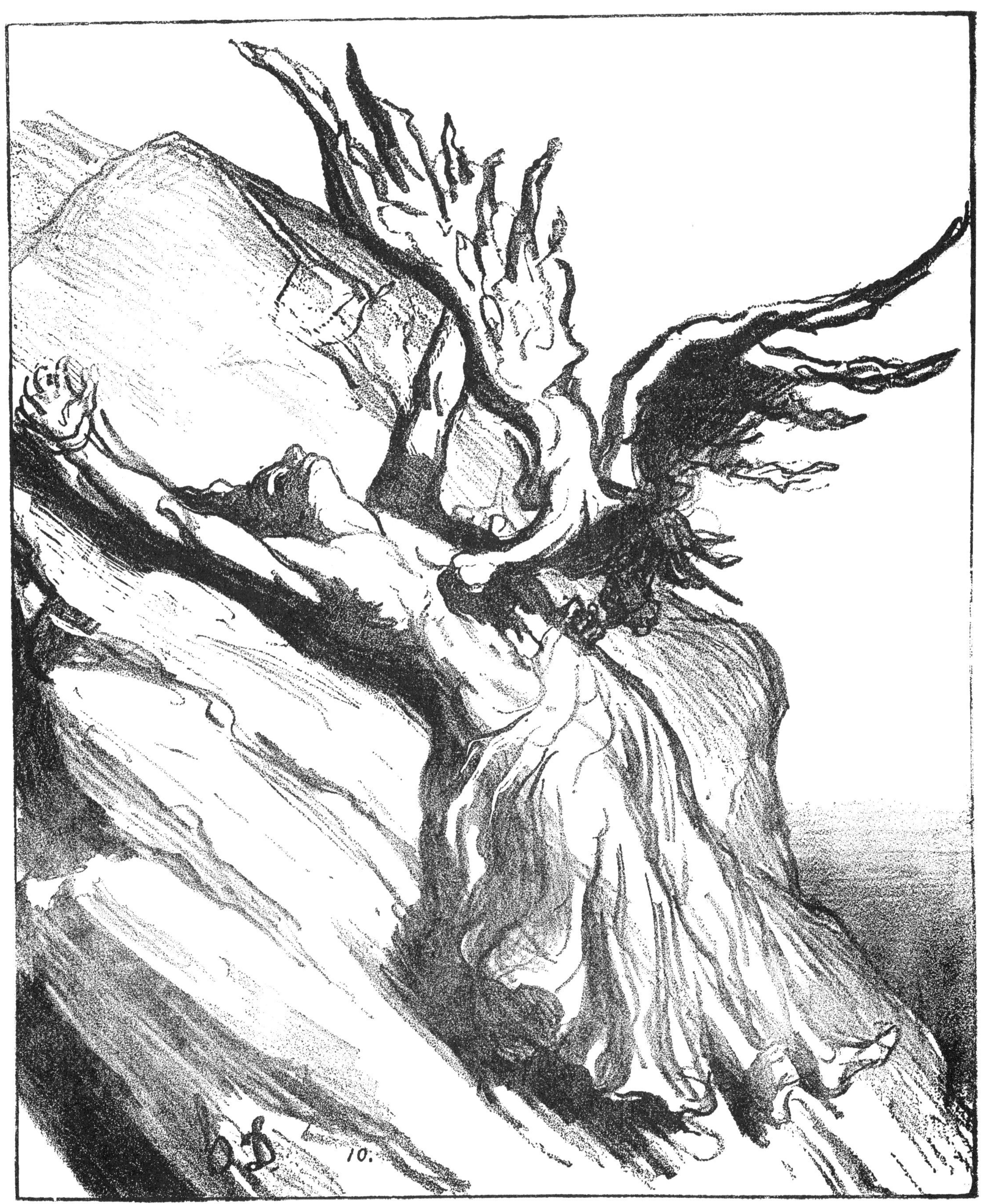

La France-Prométhée et l'aigle-vautour.

119 The vulture-like eagle of Napoleon III (or of Prussia) eats the liver of France, represented as Prometheus. [Feb. 13, 1871]

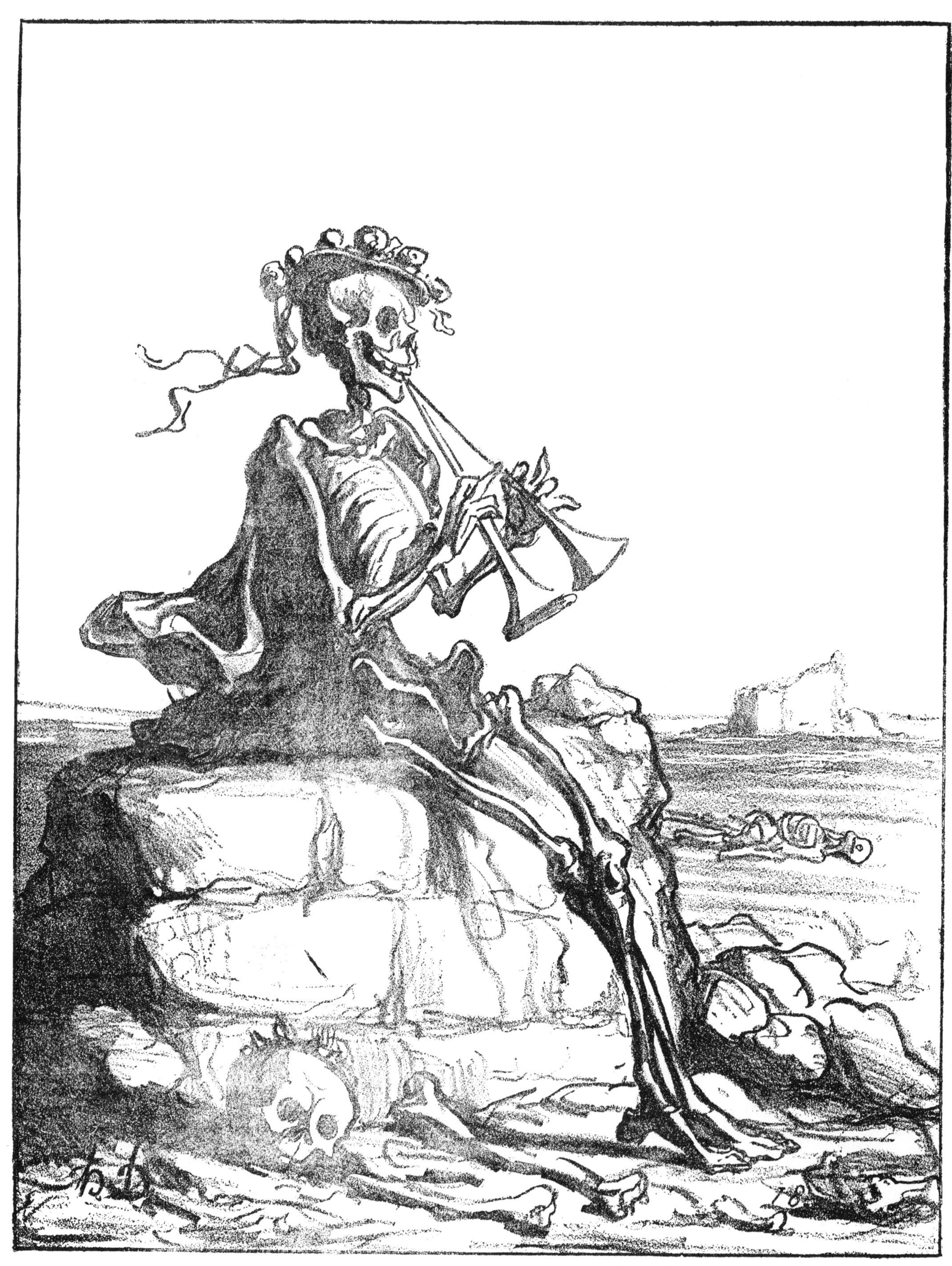

LA PAIX
Idylle.

120 The return of peace in 1871 will find France devastated. [Mar. 6, 1871]

NOTES ON THE PLATES

Each note begins with a short form of the French title, which is followed by a full English translation of the caption (in parentheses). The L.D. number that follows is the number assigned to the print in the standard catalogue of Daumier's lithographs, compiled by Loys Delteil (see Bibliography). Next, the particular state of the litho reproduced in this volume is indicated in the form "II/III" (second state of three). After this, wherever applicable, come the series number of the litho and the date and place of its original publication. All the prints shown are from the author's extensive collection and have been purchased since 1929 from the R. G. Michel Gallery in Paris.

1. Un héros de juillet, Mai 1831 (A hero of July; May 1831.) L.D. 23. II/III. Deposited* June 1, 1831.

This print was published and sold by Aubert at his print shop (Galerie Véro-Dodat) associated with the paper *La Caricature*, but did not appear in the paper. A crippled veteran of the July Revolution of 1830 stands in back view on a parapet of the Pont de la Concorde, where he is about to jump to his death. His greatcoat is covered with government pawnshop tickets, some of which are for his watch, his mattress and his clothes, while hung around his neck is a rope attached to a paving stone (always a principal element in a Parisian revolutionary barricade) on which one reads "Last resource." In the right background is the Palais de Bourbon, meeting hall of the Legislative Assembly. In this lithograph Daumier has thrown off earlier influences of other artists and has come into his own in both interpretation and technique.

2. Dup . . L.D. 45. Only state. *La Caricature*, Plate 171, from No. 85, June 14, 1832.

Philipon commissioned Daumier to do two series of portraits of the leading ministers and deputies of Louis-Philippe, one series of 18 standing portraits, the other of some 25 bust portraits. The bust of André Dupin is the second of five appearing in *La Caricature*. The contraction of his name in the caption could also signify "dupe," an appellation resulting from his unfortunate efforts to become one of the ministers. This old Voltairian, the whipping boy of the republican opposition press, was born in 1783 and died in 1865 after a long career as a lawyer and an astute and devious politician. He was implicated in the overthrow of Charles X, was president of the Chamber of Deputies for several years, and served again as a deputy in the Second Republic and the Second Empire. He had a vacillating tendency, as shown by the weathervane surmounting his lawyer-judge's hat in the mock escutcheon. The two scrolls, left and right, show his duplicity in pleading either for or against. The bag of money suggests bribes and his acquisitive desire for riches. The pair of shoes is an allusion to his peasant origins and to his renown as a tightwad who wore iron soles and heels on his boots that made a loud clatter when he attended court festivities. The press often referred to Dupin as "the savior of the country," since he was deeply involved in some of Louis-Philippe's nefarious schemes both before and after the latter's accession as "the Citizen King."

3. Mr. D'Argo . . L.D. 62. II/II. *La Caricature*, Plate 292, from No. 140, July 11, 1833.

The standing portrait of Count Antoine-Maurice-Apollinaire d'Argout was drawn by Daumier from the clay bust which he had made and which he used over and over to caricature this famous personage whom Nature had endowed with a phenomenal nose. D'Argout was known and satirized all over Europe for his giant proboscis, and the editors of both *La Caricature* and *Le Charivari* had great fun in making puns and writing long articles on the mishaps and predicaments of this poor minister, promoted but exploited by the Pear-Headed King. D'Argout (1782–1858) was a conniving politican, a financier, successively the Minister of Fine Arts, Commerce and Public Works, and later Governor of the Bank of France. Many references were made in the republican press to d'Argout's burning of the tricolor. and he was responsible for his special police bludgeoning citizens in 1833 in a street riot resulting from the government's persecution of the hawkers of newspapers on the streets.

4. La crise actuelle se complique! . . . (The present crisis is deepening! The horizon of subscriptions is being covered with fog! The political structure of *Le Constitutionnel* is cracking on all sides! . . . Long

*"Deposited" dates refer to the French *dépôt légal*, the system by which publishers register their works with a central government agency, in Daumier's time the Ministry of the Interior.

live the King, nevertheless.) L.D. 169. Only state? *Le Charivari*, Oct. 22, 1833.

This litho lampoons one of the favorite papers of the bourgeoisie, *Le Constitutionnel*, which expressed many of their feelings and sentiments. One of its editors, Charles Etienne (1777–1845), here personifies *Le Constitutionnel* as an old dotard sitting on a pile of oyster shells. This is a visual pun on the slang meaning of *huître* (oyster): dunce or blunderer. The spiderweb indicates the lack of activity in this newspaper office which, as the signs indicate, is for sale. One pen wiper is tied to the leg of the editor's table, and another is attached to the quill pen Etienne sleepily holds. Daumier used the cotton nightcap to emphasize the drowsiness. Note, too, in the vest pocket a snuffbox with the portrait of Louis-Philippe. The various portentous phrases in the caption indicate Philipon's hope for the collapse of an opposition newspaper. For more on Etienne, see No. 6.

5. LE PASSÉ. LE PRÉSENT. L'AVENIR (The Past. The Present. The Future.) L.D. 76. I/II. *La Caricature*, Plate 349, from No. 166, Jan. 9, 1834.

Philipon's earlier page of four sketches showing the transformation of the head of Louis-Philippe into a pear (*poire* = fool) provided Daumier and other artists with one of the most famous symbols in all caricature. It was to become the "monkey on the back" of the "King of the Barricades," as the opposition press often called Louis-Philippe. The pear began to appear on walls and sidewalks throughout France. Even a book was written by Peytel (see Bibliography), *Physiologie de la Poire*.

6. Melle ETIENNE-JOCONDE-CUNÉGONDE-BÉCASSINE DE CONSTITUTIONNEL . . . (Miss Etienne-Joconde-Cunégonde-Bécassine de Constitutionnel, indignant and choked with anger, in a flutter and antiquated at the performance of *Antony* in which that rascal Dumas has had the immorality to scoff at the noble family Bécassine de Constitutionnel.) L.D. 78. II/II. *La Caricature*, Plate 385, from No. 183, May 8, 1834.

This is one of the finest contributions in the realm of caricature, a caustic depiction of Etienne, editor of *Le Constitutionnel* (seen in No. 4), himself a playwright, a censor under Napoleon who converted himself into one of Louis-Philippe's "improstituted" deputies, as *La Tribune* labeled them. He was a famous man-about-town, a vain beau who had no preference between blondes, brunettes or redheads. Daumier shows him here as a loathsome old woman dressed in Rococo fashion, seated in a box at the performance of the play *Antony* by Alexandre Dumas the elder in 1831, later closed by the censor. Miss Etienne's puffy face is that of Etienne himself, as can be seen from Daumier's other portrait of him. Joconde and Cunégonde are old-fashioned names, while *bécassine*, literally "snipe," has the connotation of a naïve country girl.

7. VOYAGE À TRAVERS LES POPULATIONS EMPRESSÉES (A journey through the eager provinces.) L.D. 82. Only state. *La Caricature*, Plate 413, from No. 197, Aug. 14, 1834.

This is one of Daumier's most lashing attacks against "the common royalty" as it lampoons "Mr. Money Box" and his cheap visits to the provinces each autumn. On these trips a giant omnibus held all the royal family, while the King's speech writers went along in separate vehicles, as did the important flatterers of the court. Here Daumier portrays the tired "King of the People's Choice" slumped on the bony back of a jaded nag which looks quizzically at the prone corpse partly concealed behind the fence. From the standpoint of composition, the artist has carefully arranged the six bodies lying in the background and the flapping crows waiting to feed. As it became increasingly necessary to avoid fines, Daumier and other draftsmen of both *La Caricature* and *Le Charivari* began to indicate the person of the King by a three-quarters back view of his ponderous bulk.

8. RUE TRANSNONAIN, LE 15 AVRIL 1834 (On the Rue Transnonain, April 15, 1834.) L.D. 135. Only state? *L'Association mensuelle lithographique*, for the issue of July 1834, but delayed until Aug.–Sept.

Philipon began to publish the *Association*, with each monthly issue containing a large lithograph, in order to raise money for the ever mounting fines levied by the courts not only on his own paper but other republican journals as well. Philipon wrote of the bloody and senseless massacre of innocent residents of the tenement house No. 12 on the Rue Transnonain: "This lithograph is horrible to see, frightful as the ghastly event which it relates. Here lie an old man slaughtered, a woman murdered, the corpse of a man who, riddled with wounds, fell on the body of a poor child which lies under him, with its skull crushed. This indeed is not a caricature, it is not an exaggeration, it is a page of our modern history bespattered with blood, a page drawn with a powerful hand and dictated by noble anger. In creating this drawing, Daumier has raised himself to his full stature." The massacre, which occurred during the uprising of April 1834, was a reprisal by troops under the command of General Bugeaud and Minister of the Interior Thiers. The infantrymen, angered by shots from upper-story windows, stormed up the narrow stairways, smashed down doors, and killed or wounded some 14 old men, women and children. When this lithograph finally appeared in September 1834, the stone was immediately confiscated and most of the prints destroyed. Aubert's print shop briefly exhibited the lithograph, which angered all who saw it, and long lines of indignant citizens gathered day after day to view "Rue Transnonain." Daumier was acknowledged to be Philipon's greatest artist and Louis-Philippe's most dangerous critic. Daumier had drawn five of the lithos for the 24 issues of *L'Association* during its two-year existence, this one appearing in the final number. All critics and historians of Daumier are unanimous in praising it as one of the great masterpieces in the graphic field.

9. LA TENTATION [PARODIE D'UNE TOILE DE TENIERS] (The Temptation [a parody on a canvas by Teniers].)

L.D. 101. I/II. *La Caricature*, Plate 453, from No. 217, Jan. 1, 1835. Not signed.

This plate reveals the eclecticism of Philipon and his staff in taking many suggestions from old master paintings, in this case Teniers' *Temptation of Saint Anthony*. Louis-Philippe is shown as a hog in the garb of the Saint, with his hands piously clasped above an open volume of Machiavelli's *The Prince*. Clockwise, from the left, the ministers surrounding the King include Dupin giving advice, the grimacing Thiers holding up a building and old Marshal Soult with a scepter indicating the hope of the King's confederates for a more autocratic rule. To the right is Félix Barthe, the walleyed Minister of Justice, showering a sheaf of bills designated as Secret Funds, Endowments, Civil List (the King's yearly stipend for expenses) and Universal Suffrage (showing a total of two votes cast). In profile at the far right, the enormous nose of d'Argout projects over a padlocked money box (one of the typical insinuations by Daumier and Philipon of the King's being a miser; the parrot beak emerging from the lid of the box is another symbol of the monarch as a chattering parrot, used many times over in *La Caricature*). Appearing in the right foreground is Talleyrand, France's prize dissimulator, the breaker of oaths of allegiance to Church, Republic, Directory, Empire and Restoration, now offering the Saint a large crown. Note that all the bearers of gifts are represented as devils with horns.

10. Quand le Diable devint vieux, il se fit Ermite (When the Devil grew old he became a hermit.) L.D. 111. Only state. *La Caricature*, Plate 476, from No. 229, Mar. 26, 1835.

This excellent symbolic print is typical of the vicious caricatures and satires of nineteenth-century France. Louis-Philippe, as a monk, is solemnly telling his beads; his rosary is a string of coins, again an indication of his avarice. From the cord around his waist hangs a large medal, the Montyon Prize for virtue, while in front of him lies the Charter he had sworn to uphold, placed upside down to indicate he is neither reading nor following it. Kneeling at the right is Talleyrand, wearing a nun's coif and veil marked with a tricolor cockade while sprouting two devil's horns. His hands are clasped over his crutch, unmistakable attribute of this old diplomat, often called "the Limper." His white robe is tied at the waist by a rope to which is attached a string of medals indicating his services during the various regimes: the Bourbon crown of Louis XVI, the bishop's mitre showing his connection with the Church, the Napoleonic eagle of the Empire, the fleur-de-lys of the Restoration under Louis XVIII and Charles X, and finally the pear face of Louis-Philippe. The cat, symbol of nine lives, again emphasizes Talleyrand's numerous offices as it sits upon a protocol representing the many documents he issued. The altar is a fantastic summation of the Juste-Milieu (middle-way) regime of Louis-Philippe. On the padlocked money chest of the King stands a base of four pear heads supporting a column decorated with crossed swords. Above these, standing upon the hat of a police constable, is the figure of France-Liberty stretched on the cross, while over her head appears a large pear with figures 27, 28, 29, the dates of the "Three Glorious Days" of the Revolution of July 1830. Related to the title of this print are the sayings listed in the Larousse dictionary, "The Devil chants the High Mass," said of a hypocrite who assumes the mask of piety, or, again, "He is no more devout than the Devil is a saint," regarding a man who has not the least devotion. Daumier missed no chance to label as devils the King, who has claws for toenails, and Talleyrand, whose robe discloses a cloven hoof.

11. Principal acteur d'un Imbroglio-tragi-comique (Principal actor in a tragicomic imbroglio.) L.D. 235. II/II. *Le Charivari*, Mar. 29, 1835.

This superb satire, with its vitriolic attack full of a deep-seated spite, is one of Daumier's best, not only in the rich textures suggested but also in its superior interpretation of the duplicity of the King, ironically called "the most honest man of his realm." Note the adroit substitutions of autocracy, the hidden but ill-concealed monarchical desires, for the simple democratic virtues feigned by the hypocritical monarch. The King's cockaded high silk hat falls away and uncovers a crown. The paper wrapper around the scepter is not translatable in print. His bourgeois umbrella falls as his overcoat opens, revealing a royal costume. The smiling mask shows the angry face of the King underneath. His feet rest on a sheaf of papers, "Prerogatives of the Chambers," indicating the rights of the deputies usurped by the King.

12. Juges des accusés d'Avril (The judges of the April defendants.) L.D. 124. I/II. *La Caricature*, Plates 513–515, from No. 247, July 30, 1835.

During the "monster trial" following the uprising of April 1834, Daumier drew some of his finest portraits, depicting some 16 of the judges. At the left is the Marquis Charles-Louis-Huguet de Sémonville (1754–1839), a politician shown in his Peer's costume, with a Cross of the Legion of Honor on his breast. The seated figure is Count Pierre-Louis Roederer (1754–1835), a politician, economist and pamphleteer, also a Peer. The central figure shows the unmistakable features of Adolphe Thiers (1797–1877), statesman and historian, but the costume is that of Robert Macaire, the cunning rogue and swindler, leading character played by Frédérick Lemaître in the play *L'Auberge des Adrets*. Robert Macaire is the embodiment, the archetype, of the little rascal, cheat, charlatan, knave, confidence man. All of these appellations were likewise applied by the anti-government papers to the swaggering little dwarf Thiers, always audacious, blustering, boasting. Philipon and his staff, in depicting Thiers, added many uncomplimentary accusations such as juggler of the secret funds, shrewd manipulator of people and events, pupil of the wily Talleyrand. Soult called him *le foutriquet*, an epithet translatable as "the little whippersnapper," but with many less polite meanings. This print shows but one of the 111 representations of Thiers drawn by Daumier. (The humorous attribution on the print to "M.

Rosolin" refers to Prince Ferdinand, who occasionally drew pictures.) As Germaine Cherpin commented: "During the entire existence of *La Caricature*, from 1830 to 1835, Thiers appeared in all the political ensembles as one of the supernumeraries of this grotesque parade that was, in the eyes of Daumier, the government of Louis-Philippe." After the publication of this lithograph, the sections were cut apart and sold as individual prints at Aubert's.

13. LE PETIT CLERC, (DIT: SAUTE-RUISSEAU) . . . (The little law clerk, called the gutter-jumper. The little law clerk doesn't eat much, runs a great deal, strolls about more and returns as late as possible to the office, where he is the drudge. He is usually named Pitou, Godard or Galuchet.) L.D. 260. II/II. No. 1 of the series *Types français* (French Types), from *Le Charivari*, Sept. 23, 1835.

For this series of 31 plates, Daumier drew 11 and Traviès 20. Philipon envisioned these lithos, along with a series *Grotesques parisiens* by Grandville and the *Béotismes parisiens* (Parisian Stupidities) by Auguste Bourdet, as presenting a complete physical makeup of the nation, with the characteristics, appearances and costumes of the various classes of society. While some biographers have erroneously presumed this to be a drawing of Daumier when he was apprenticed to a bailiff, it shows no physical resemblance to his other portraits.

14. TU VAS PORTER CETTE NOTE AUX JOURNAUX . . . ("Take this note to the newspapers: 'A gentleman from the provinces, having accidentally swallowed a *blague* [means "pouch" and "hoax"], suddenly became bald and insolvent. The famous Dr. Robert Macaire concludes from this that if *blagues* ruin some people, then by the homeopathic system, they should enrich others. His medical treatment has been a complete success. Wig wearers take notice.' And since I am named in this article, by virtue of the law of September 9, 1835, I will demand that the following letter be printed: 'To the editor, Please state that the article in which you mentioned my name yesterday was not received from me. It is true that I am engaged in curing baldness (Rue Belle-Charge, No. 1), but I treat it in a manner different from the one you describe. Yours truly, Robert Macaire, Rue Belle-Charge, No. 1.' ") L.D. 421. III/III. No. 66 of the series *Caricaturana*, from *Le Charivari*, Nov. 5, 1837.

Here Robert Macaire, in one of his many guises as a charlatan, is shown as a quack handing a concocted letter to his stooge Bertrand to take to the editor of a paper. Philipon gave as his reason for publishing the Robert Macaire series: "Robert Macaire has disappeared from the stage. Since press censorship prevents us from stigmatizing the Robert Macaires of politics, we are obliged to turn instead to the Robert Macaires of the business world. We intend to publish a rogues' gallery of the many varieties of this species."

15. LE PUBLIC, MON CHER, LE PUBLIC EST STUPIDE . . . ("The public, my dear fellow, the public is stupid . . . we're bleeding it white, we're purging it to death, and it is not satisfied . . . it wants something new . . . well, damn it, let's give it something new! Let's turn into homeopaths . . . it likes hoaxes, so let's treat it according to like-cures-like. *Similia Similibus*." BERTRAND: "Amen!" [Macaire continues:] "Here's a prescription that sums up the whole system: 'Take a tiny grain of . . . of nothing at all . . . divide it into ten million molecules . . . throw one . . . just a single one, of these ten-millionth parts into the stream . . . stir, stir, grind it a lot . . . allow it to steep for a few hours . . . draw up a pailful of this salubrious mixture . . . filter it . . . cut it with 20 parts of ordinary water and wet the tongue with it every morning on an empty stomach. . . . ' And there you have it!" "Is that all?" "Yes . . . oh, damn! I was forgetting the main thing: 'Pay for this prescription!' ") L.D. 425. I/II. No. 70 of the series *Caricaturana*, from *Le Charivari*, Dec. 24, 1837.

16. POUR ALLER JUSQU'AU CŒUR QUE VOUS VOULEZ PERCER . . . ("To reach the heart that you want to pierce, this is the path your blows should follow.") L.D. 516. II/II. No. 48 of the series *Croquis d'expressions* (Sketches of Expressions), from *Le Charivari*, Mar. 28, 1839.

This was a series of 100 lithographs, of which Daumier drew 53. After the demise of *La Caricature* in 1835, Daumier devoted his lithos to the satire of manners, these Sketches of Expressions covering such topics as contrasting points of view, the daily misunderstandings between friends, married couples, family disputes, and legal and theatrical subjects. In many of his theater sketches, his inspiration came from the classic theater and from recalling plays read aloud by his father and those he attended on newspaper passes.

17. AYEZ PITIÉ DU PAUVRE PÉCHEUR! . . . (Have pity on the poor *pécheur* ["sinner," pun on *pêcheur*, "fisherman"]! The Seine Kingfisher. This type of kingfisher never gets any fish. Instead of flitting about pursuing his prey in a zigzag manner, the biped kingfisher remains motionless as a post in the water. The noises about him, the rain, the hail, the thunder, the lightning, the poor puns of the passersby, nothing excites him, nothing can make him turn aside from his line. Sometimes after a whole day of waiting he suddenly feels the tip of his rod bent by an unaccustomed weight; his eyes light up, his heart leaps with hope and happiness; carefully he pulls in the line and brings up . . . an old slipper or an old shoe. But, instead of fish, he is always sure of catching rheumatism or pneumonia. The kingfisher usually is located along the river banks in cold, wind and rain, plunged into the water up to his waist; thus he goes merrily down the river of life. And when death finally comes to seize him, he starts to doubt whether gudgeons really exist.) L.D. 524. II/II. No. 2 of the series *Cours d'histoire naturelle* (Course in Natural History), from *Le Charivari*, Mar. 15, 1838.

Although Daumier drew many series and individual prints devoted to hunting and fishing, there is no certainty whether he ever participated in these sports or was merely content to be an interested observer.

18. INTÉRIEUR D'UN OMNIBUS . . . (Interior of an omnibus; in between a drunk and a pork butcher.) L.D. 566. III/IV. Plate 8 of the series *Types parisiens*, from *Le Charivari*, Nov. 13, 1841.

This is one of a series of 50 popular genre subjects. The sign over the lady's head suggests that it was illegal to pick up intoxicated passengers. The idea of having public vehicles circulating throughout Paris following a set itinerary is credited to Blaise Pascal (1623–1662), and the first routes of these carriages or stagecoaches were established in 1672 for a brief period. Larousse states that it was only in 1828 that the idea was again taken up in Paris. A guide for foreign visitors in 1835 mentioned various lines, each company giving its omnibuses a different color and a different name. Among the early names were "Dames Blanches" and "Orléanaises," and later "Hirondelles," "Gazelles" and "Constantines." All the new vehicles had 15 places inside and additional seats on the open upper level, called the *impériale*. The first established fare was five sous; by the 1850s it was six sous inside and three sous on the *impériale*.

19. OH! . . . ABSOLUMENT COMME SI ON Y ÉTAIT . . . ("Oh! it's just like being right there; the big one is taking off her corset, and the little one is looking for a flea.") L.D. 583. IV/IV. No. 27 of the series *Types parisiens*, from *Le Charivari*, Dec. 1, 1841.

Daumier was apparently fascinated with Parisian types, odd individuals finding themselves in strange predicaments. Many of the lithos in this series were also printed in *La Caricature provisoire*, which ran from November 1838 to May 1840, and in the biweekly *Le Figaro*.

20. L'ODORAT (The sense of smell.) L.D. 594. IV/IV. No. 38 of *Types parisiens*, from *Le Charivari*, Jan. 18, 1843.

In its second state, this print had appeared as No. 1 of the series *Les cinq Sens* (The Five Senses) published in *La Caricature*, July 21, 1839. Prints of such general interest were often repeated in other papers, with slight variations in their titles.

21. LE MARI (LISANT): "NOUS ÉTIONS MOLLEMENT ÉTENDUS . . . (THE HUSBAND, READING: "We were lying softly on the sweet-smelling moss; the rays of the moon penetrated the boughs of the willow stirred by the evening breeze. Intoxicated with love, we hurled to heaven vows that sank back into our hearts." THE WIFE [*aside*]: "How can he read such things in a cotton nightcap and with a mug like his!") L.D. 634. II/II. No. 11 of the series *Mœurs conjugales* (Matrimonial Customs), from *Le Charivari*, Oct. 29, 1839.

Daumier drew 60 vignettes in this series, which appeared between May 1838 and October 1842. *Mœurs conjugales* marks the beginning of his richest and most prolific period. Some of the episodes in Balzac's *Human Comedy* of the same era are paralleled by the sorrows and laughter in Daumier's marriage comedy.

22. AH! TU TROUVES QUE TA FEMME NE TE SOIGNE PAS ASSEZ . . . ("Ah! so you think your wife does not take good enough care of you, you rascal, when you spend everything, you good-for-nothing! Well, I'm going to arrange my hair in lovelocks, you scoundrel! And I am going to buy bonnets, and I will give you corks to eat, you villain!" "My angel, I'm wrong, you are a good housewife . . . but you're breaking everything!") L.D. 661. III/III. No. 38 of *Mœurs conjugales*, from *Le Charivari*, June 6, 1841.

23. CE QUI PROUVE QUE QUAND ON FAIT LA PATROUILLE . . . (Which goes to show that when you patrol you should never pass your own house.) L.D. 692. II/IV. No. 9 of the series *Emotions parisiennes*, from *Le Charivari*, Oct. 24, 1839.

This series of 51 prints is, by common consent, one of Daumier's best groups of illustrations concerning the diverse feelings of typical Frenchmen.

24. COMMENT À CHAILLOT! . . . ("What do you mean, Chaillot? When you got on you said Bercy, you paid me and I thanked you." "Damnation! Come on, drive me back!" "Nothing doing, it's midnight, and there's no more service." "Damnation!") L.D. 701. II/II. No. 17 of *Emotions parisiennes*, from *Le Charivari*, Dec. 24, 1839.

Chaillot and Bercy are neighborhoods at opposite ends of Paris.

25. C'EST UNIQUE! J'AI PRIS QUATRE TAILLES . . . ("That's the limit! I've put my arms around four waists just like those in my life: Fifine, my first love; Cocotte, that tramp; big Mimi; and my wife up there in the corner.") L.D. 711. II/II. No. 27 of *Emotions parisiennes*, from *Le Charivari*, Feb. 7, 1840.

26. Mr TOUT AFFAIRES . . . (Mr. Business-Only, a lawyer without cases, pretending to be in a great hurry, knocks down a dozen urchins every day in the waiting room of the law court, tramples five or six mongrels, and hopes, by these gymnastic exercises, to make people believe he has a large clientele.) L.D. 758. IV/IV. No. 45 of *Emotions parisiennes*, from *Le Charivari*, June 30, 1840.

This print also appeared as No. 5 of the series *Les Parisiens*.

27. LA SALLE DES PAS PERDUS (The waiting hall.) L.D. 753. III/III. *Le Figaro*, Nov. 17, 1839, in II state. Embellished with an elaborate border of flowers, butterflies and birds, this III-state print appeared as one of 40 by various artists in an album titled *Paris au dix-neuvième siècle* (Nineteenth-Century Paris).

In the waiting room of the Palais de Justice a client is speaking to his lawyer, while the public scribe drowses behind his desk. (The French term for waiting room used here means literally "hall of wasted steps.")

28. LA SEINE EST UNE RIVIÈRE QUI PREND SA SOURCE . . . (The Seine is a river which has its source in the *département* of the Côte D'or and flows into the English Channel. It crosses Paris, and the inhabitants of this city, to avoid the heat of summer, seek the coolness and purity of its waters.) L.D. 762. II/II. No. 3 of the Series *Les Baigneurs* (The Bathers), from *Le Charivari*, June 26, 1839.

The Parisian public baths and washing places, the idea for which was borrowed from England, were intended to inculcate habits of cleanliness in the working classes by furnishing them at the lowest possible prices, sometimes even free, the facilities for taking baths and washing and drying their laundry. Both in England and in France, these facilities were run by private companies or by city managements, and in 1851, during the Second Republic, funds were voted for the expenses of these operations. Daumier drew 30 prints in this series, which was also published as an album, advertised in *Le Charivari* of August 2, 1843, as a bound volume at 16 francs.

29. EXCUSEZ; REGARD' DONC LA GROSSE FIFINE . . . ("Say, just look at fat Fifine! I would have sworn she was a Venus . . . What a disappointment she's turned out to be!") L.D. 771. III/III. No. 11 of *Les Baigneurs*, from *Le Charivari*, Oct. 4, 1839.

The two bathers furtively peer through cracks in the boards of the women's baths, one of the many bathing boats anchored along the quays of the Seine.

30. LE PÊCHEUR ACHARNÉ . . . (The inveterate fisherman, or, There's no accounting for tastes [pun on the homonymous *des goûts*, "for tastes," and *d'égout*, "of sewer"].) L.D. 817. II/II. No. 3 of the series of seven prints *La Pêche* (Fishing), from *La Caricature*, Aug. 16, 1840.

31. PIQUE-ASSIETTE . . . (The sponger, or dinner-hunter; "Well, well! A first-class wedding dinner at Véry's! The white gloves go on! I shall pay my respects to the bride as a friend of her husband . . . and to the husband as an acquaintance of the bride!") L.D. 830. III/III. No. 9 of the series *Bohémiens de Paris*, from *Le Charivari*, Dec. 25, 1841.

Daumier drew 28 plates in this series showing the Bohemian characters in the city.

32. LA GARDE-MALADE . . . (The sick-nurse; "It's a fact, there's no one like the fruiterers for getting you nice cases, an epileptic, a dropsical patient and a madwoman! . . . Now, if that grocer also gets me the consumptive he promised me, I would be doing very nicely!") L.D. 836. V/V. No. 15 of *Bohémiens de Paris*, from *Le Charivari*, May 22, 1842.

This print appeared under several titles, the old woman in the doorway at first representing a janitress, later a streetwalker (with the caption: "Psit!!!"). In the fourth and fifth states, she is a nurse. There exists also a painting of this subject which is attributed to Daumier.

33. L'ACTEUR DES FUNAMBULES . . . (The actor of the Funambules; "This sure is the kind of weather that makes you passionate! And in a few minutes I'll have to be blazing with Turkish love, and say: 'O Zulema, share my treasures and my throne . . . come, come and intoxicate yourself with pleasures and plenty!' And me with a penny's worth of French fries in my belly!") L.D. 841. IV/IV. No. 20 of *Bohémiens de Paris*, from *Le Charivari*, Feb. 19, 1842.

The Théâtre des Funambules was a small theater that owed its fame chiefly to the talent of its principal actor, the immortal clown Jean-Gaspard Debureau.

34. LE BAPTÊME D'ACHILLE . . . (The baptism of Achilles; As one tempers a weapon of war, Thetis, wishing to make a hero of her brat, dipped him in the Styx, as soon as he saw the light, which proves that a bath is good for all purposes.—*On the Influence of Baths*, poem by Mr. Vigier.) L.D. 946. III/III. No. 22 of the series *Histoire ancienne* (Ancient History), from *Le Charivari*, Aug. 28, 1842.

This series of 50 lithos on characters in ancient history and mythology appeared between 1841 and 1843. Daumier's irreverent satirizing of the sacred characters in Greek and Roman mythology contributed to the Romantic attack upon the Classical school in the continuing battle waged in the theater, literature and the arts. Philipon's contrived poems, as captions to this series, contain many veiled allusions to Louis-Philippe and individuals in his reign.

35. LA MÈRE DES GRACQUES . . . (The mother of the Gracchi; One day when a gay lady was shamelessly praising her jewels, which were worth a few cents, this Roman mother, showing her two sons, the hope of the country, said, "Behold my only jewels!"—Plutarch.) L.D. 970. IV/IV. No. 46 of *Histoire ancienne*, from *Le Charivari*, Dec. 23, 1842.

This well-known story provided Daumier the chance to portray two typical Frenchwomen with typical unruly children.

36. PYGMALION . . . (O triumph of the arts! What was your amazement, great sculptor, when you saw your marble come to life and, in a chaste and gentle manner, slowly bow down to ask you for a pinch of snuff.—Count Siméon.) L.D. 971. III/III. No. 47 of *Histoire ancienne*, from *Le Charivari*, Dec. 28, 1842.

37. UN HOMME À LA MER . . . (Man overboard; "Harpoon him more firmly . . . we can't get him otherwise! And you, hold his legs up in the air, that's the main thing! . . . There isn't anything that gives you a cold sooner than getting the soles of your feet wet!") L.D. 1036. IV/IV. No. 14 of the series *Les Canotiers parisiens* (Parisian Boaters), from *Le Charivari*, June 11, 1843.

In this series of 26 plates, the captions are by Louis Huart. Boating had become a very fashionable pastime in Paris around 1840, continuing so for several years.

38. VOUS CHERCHEZ VOTRE MALLE . . . ("You're looking for your trunk, sir, there it is! . . . and the lady's hatbox, too. . . . ") L.D. 1057. II/II. No. 15 of the series *Les Chemins de fer* (The Railroads), from *Le Charivari*, Dec. 19, 1843.

Although the railroads had been transporting people and material in France for some years, Daumier used the travel theme for this set of 16 lithos in the 1840s and would produce further series on the railroads during the 50s and 60s, with other occasional prints on the subject. Many of these were humorous depictions of the trials of the passengers, deluged by quick showers, getting cinders in their eyes, crowding into carriages, waiting at stations, riding on the car roofs or searching for their luggage.

39. LE CHASSEUR CHASSÉ (The hunter hunted.) L.D. 1075. II/III. No. 4 of the series of 12 prints *La Chasse* (Hunting), from *La Caricature*, Oct. 15, 1843.

Several prints in this series appeared in the revived *La Caricature*, the rest in *Le Charivari*. Here a country guard is irately chasing a frightened hunter who is trespassing. There are some nine other series on hunting and other occasional prints by Daumier on the subject.

40. LA NEIGE . . . (The snow; "Be quiet, Phoenix! How do you expect me to see anything coming? . . . Strange, and this is such a terrific spot!") L.D. 1079. III/III. No. 8 of *La Chasse*, from *Le Charivari*, Dec. 6, 1843.

41. UN SOIR DE FÊTE NATIONALE . . . (The evening of Bastille Day; "It never fails . . . you go out to see the fireworks, and all you get is waterworks!") L.D. 1107. II/II. No. 20 of the series *Les beaux Jours de la vie* (The Wonderful Days of Life, or, The Red-Letter Days), from *Le Charivari*, Aug. 21, 1844.

Like *Caricaturana*, this series also numbers 100 prints. It is one of Daumier's most consistently high accomplishments in wit, drawing and technique, not to mention his adroit representations and his extreme humanitarianism.

42. QUAND ON A SON PORTRAIT AU SALON . . . (When your portrait is hung at the Salon; "It's flattering, isn't it, Eudoxie, to be shown like this in public, and I don't regret the 200 francs it cost us . . . There's a man looking at us; he seems to think highly of us!" THE ART STUDENT: "How do they have the nerve to sit for their portraits when they have faces like that!") L.D. 1147. III/III. No. 59 of *Les beaux Jours de la vie*, from *Le Charivari*, Apr. 26, 1845.

43. UN PREMIER VOYAGE EN CHEMIN DE FER (Their first train ride.) L.D. 1178. II/II. No. 90 of *Les beaux Jours de la vie*, from *Le Charivari*, July 19, 1846.

This is obviously not the first train ride for the two men who are tranquilly dozing.

44. LA MÈRE EST DANS LE FEU DE LA COMPOSITION . . . (The mother is in the heat of composition, the child is in the bath water!) L.D. 1227. II/II. No. 7 of the series *Les Bas-bleus* (The Bluestockings), from *Le Charivari*, Feb. 26, 1844.

The term "bluestockings," applied mockingly to women who dabbled in literature, originated in England, where it first designated the members of an eighteenth-century literary circle. In Daumier's time in France the bluestockings were ridiculed for supposedly neglecting the care of their households while they occupied themselves with literature. This series of 40 lithographs on career women was to be followed by later series on *Les Femmes socialistes* (Socialist Women) and *Les Divorceuses* (Divorced Women).

45. MONSIEUR, PARDON SI JE VOUS GÊNE UN PEU . . . ("Pardon me, sir, if I disturb you a little . . . you see, I am writing a new novel, and I must look up a number of ancient authors." THE GENTLEMAN (*aside*): "Ancient authors! . . . humph! she should have looked them up when they were alive—she certainly must have been their contemporary!") L.D. 1233. III/III. No. 13 of *Les Bas-bleus*, from *Le Charivari*, Mar. 8, 1844.

One of the feminists' demands was for a reading room for women at the Bibliothèque Nationale.

46. FEMME DE LETTRE HUMANITAIRE SE LIVRANT . . . (Humanitarian woman of letters devoting herself to wonderfully philosophical reflections on man!) L.D. 1235. IV/IV. No. 15 of *Les Bas-bleus*, from *Le Charivari*, Mar. 10, 1844.

There is a pun on *crâne*, "skull," in the adverb *crânement* of the caption. Jacqueline Armingeat observes that "Daumier applied himself with vigour and evident satisfaction to producing the many drawings in this series which deal with the bluestocking's attitude towards her husband—scorn, indifference, rebellion."

47. [LA CAROTTE DE L'ÉLECTION (The Election Hoax).] MON CHER AMI, NE CROYEZ PAS . . . ("My dear friend, don't think that I come to ask you for your vote. I respect the indepedence of opinions too much for that. It is the Baroness who said to me, 'Go see that poor Galouzet, tell his little wife that she is neglecting me and that I am angry with her for it. Ask about their delightful children, and say that I absolutely must have them to dinner!' ") L.D. 1261. II/III. No. 1 of the series *Les Carottes* (The Hoaxes), from *Le Charivari*, Mar. 21, 1844.

This is a short series of only six drawings revealing the dissimulation, bamboozling and double-talk in everyday situations.

48. CE QU'ON APPELLE DÎNER AU RESTAURANT . . . (What is known as dining in a restaurant; "Waiter, I've been in your establishment an hour and a quarter without a chair . . . and so far you have only served toothpicks to my wife who is dying of hunger . . . you will make me lose my temper [pun with *assiette*, "plate"] and I'll wind up doing something violent [pun with *plat*, "dish"] . . . do you hear, waiter?" "Coming, sir . . . coming, coming, coming!!!") L.D. 1274. II/II. No. 3 of the series *Les Etrangers à Paris* (Foreigners in Paris), from *Le Charivari*, June 7, 1844.

This series of 20 lithos appeared through the summer of 1844, portraying the predicaments and inconveniences that confronted visitors to the capital: searching for sleeping quarters, buying new clothes, visiting the zoo, having their pockets picked, buying daguerreotype portraits of themselves to take home.

49. GRANDES EAUX À VERSAILLES [literally refers to a day on which all the fountains are turned on; here it refers ironically to the rainstorm]. L.D. 1285. II/II. No. 14 of *Les Etrangers à Paris*, from *Le Charivari*, July 28, 1844.

50. MON CHER MONSIEUR, IL M'EST ABSOLUMENT IMPOSSIBLE . . . ("My dear sir, it is absolutely impossible for me to take your case . . .you are lacking the most im-

portant documents [*pièces*] . . . (*aside*:) the coins [*pièces*] of 100 sous!") L.D. 1356. II/II. No. 20 of the series *Les Gens de justice* (The Men of Justice), from *Le Charivari*, Aug. 6, 1846.

Probably Daumier's most famous series, these 39 plates appeared from March 1845 to October 1848, all but one in *Le Charivari*. Several other lawyer subjects appeared only as proofs and a few in later series.

51. IL DÉFEND L'ORPHELIN ET LA VEUVE . . . (He defends the orphan and the widow—that is, unless he attacks the widow and the orphan.) L.D. 1358. II/II. No. 22 of *Les Gens de justice*, from *Le Charivari*, Sept. 1, 1846.

52. GRAND ESCALIER DU PALAIS DE JUSTICE. VUE DE FACES (Main staircase of the Palace of Justice. View of Faces [pun on *vue de face*, "head-on view"].) L.D. 1372. III/III. No. 36 of *Les Gens de justice*, from *Le Charivari*, Feb. 8, 1848.

Daumier used this theme again in a painting, *The Two Lawyers*, now in the art museum of Lyons.

53. LE DANGER DE VOULOIR VISITER UN SITE PAR TROP SAUVAGE (The danger of choosing to visit a place that is too unfrequented.) L.D. 1397. II/II. No. 10 of the series *Pastorales*, from *Le Charivari*, June 27, 1845.

In this long set of 50 delightful country scenes, Daumier again depicts everyday pleasures, joys, troubles and bad days, here transferring them to the country, with characters similar to those seen in Paris. Whereas this frightened visitor is robbed by two footpads in an out-of-the-way place, other scenes show cows and farmers accosting Parisians in their Sunday best, a couple stung by bees, an absentminded reader of an enormous newspaper walking into a swamp, the wind ruining a picnic, and country relations seeming less than pleased at the arrival of company!

54. ET DIRE QUE C'EST AUJOURD'HUI LA St MÉDARD! (And to think that today is Saint Médard's Day!) L.D. 1401. II/II. No. 14 of *Pastorales*, from *Le Charivari*, July 10, 1845.

Saint Médard, bishop of Noyon in the sixth century, is the patron saint of hay crops, and, according to peasant superstition, rain on the Saint's day predicts 40 days of continuous bad weather. Médard is also considered the patron of agriculture and horticulture, and is invoked in cases of toothache and migraine. His feast days, June 8, September 9 and October 1, are occasions for prayers for good weather.

55. UNE COURSE AU COUCOU (A trip in [or, A race for] the post-chaise.) L.D. 1430. II/II. No. 43 of *Pastorales*, not published in *Le Charivari*.

It is not known whether this print was barred by the censor or rejected by the editors of *Le Charivari*. Its date of deposit with the Ministry of the Interior was January 6, 1846.

56. UN JEUNE HOMME EN TRAIN D'ACQUÉRIR . . . (A young man in the process of acquiring what is usually called a pleasurable art.) L.D. 1466. II/II. No. 29 of the series *Professeurs et moutards* (Teachers and Pupils), from *Le Charivari*, June 4, 1846.

This is a series of 32 pieces, humorously depicting schoolboy antics, recalcitrant students rioting, throwing snowballs at teachers, mocking their instructors, and well deserving the special connotation of *moutards*—brats! Occasionally a print appears in which good students are given laurel wreaths as prizes for their studies.

57. C'EST DEMAIN LA FÊTE DE SA FEMME (Tomorrow is his wife's birthday.) L.D. 1480. II/II. No. 4 of the series *Les bons Bourgeois* (The Good Middle-Class Folk), from *Le Charivari*, June 18, 1846.

One of the best long series Daumier produced is this one, many items of which concern the same themes as in his earlier studies of Parisian life, but with new twists to the old scenes and episodes. Of the 82 prints in the series, 12 excellent ones were never printed in *Le Charivari*, for reasons known only to that paper's editors, since nothing in them would seem to offend the censors. In this series Daumier reveals his great understanding of the simple pleasures of the ordinary citizen, with many homely domestic scenes closely related to the series *Les Mœurs conjugales*.

58. DITES DONC, RAVIGNARD, SI NOS FEMMES NOUS VOYAIENT! . . . ("Say, Ravignard, if our wives could see us! . . . you must admit we're pretty wicked dogs!") L.D. 1493. II/II. No. 17 of *Les bons Bourgeois*, from *Le Charivari*, Sept. 28, 1846.

Daumier himself, with his artist friends, often visited the roadside inns beyond the gateways of Paris, or those cafés in the vicinity of his studio home on the Ile de Saint-Louis. In his biography of Daumier, Adhémar notes that Daumier, like most Frenchmen, was known to indulge in "bending the elbow," and that Cézanne once observed that Daumier drank too much.

59. VOTRE TABLEAU ME PLAIRAIT ASSEZ . . . ("I'd be quite satisfied with your picture . . . but there's no doubt about it, it's half a cane-length shorter than I need!") L.D. 1495. II/II. No. 19 of *Les bons Bourgeois*, from *Le Charivari*, Oct. 12, 1846.

While the "art patron" measures a painting to fit his wall, his small son behind him has scribbled a mustache on a portrait.

60. MAIS SI, MA FEMME . . . ("Oh, yes, dear, I assure you the gentlemen is drawing a landscape . . . aren't you drawing a landscape, sir?") L.D. 1499. II/II. No. 23 of *Les bons Bourgeois*, from *Le Charivari*, Nov. 13, 1846.

61. OH! LA . . . LA . . . LA . . . LA! . . . ("Ow . . . ow . . . ow . . . ouch!" "Good . . . good . . . that proves it's coming out!") L.D. 1521. II/II. No. 45 of *Les bons Bourgeois*, from *Le Charivari*, May 4, 1847.

62. UN JOUR DE CONGÉ (A day off.) L.D. 1571. III/III. No. 4 of the series *Les Papas*, from *Le Charivari*, Dec. 27, 1846.

Daumier's gentle irony becomes almost benevolent in this series of 23 plates. Three additional plates certainly intended for the series did not appear in *Le Charivari*.

63. UN PÈRE EST UN CHEVAL DONNÉ PAR LA NATURE! (A father is a horse provided by nature!) L.D. 1572. III/III. No. 5 of *Les Papas*, from *Le Charivari*, Jan. 4, 1847.

64. SEULE MANIÈRE DE FAIRE POSER UN ENFANT AVEC FRUIT (The only way to make a child pose with fruit.) L.D. 1582. II/II. No. 15 of *Les Papas*, from *Le Charivari*, Aug. 24, 1847.

65. DE CE CÔTÉ-LÀ, VOUS VOYEZ LA TOUR St JACQUES LA BOUCHERIE! ("In this direction you view the Tower of St. Jacques la Boucherie!") L.D. 1603. II/II. No. 10 of the series *Locataires et propriétaires* (Tenants and Landlords), from *Le Charivari*, Apr. 19, 1847.

This series includes 32 drawings, plus three more not published but doubtless intended for the series. Daumier does not neglect either side of the confrontation, showing the landlords' vexations with destructive tenants, nocturnal departures and late payments, as well as the tenants' dismay with crowded quarters, smoking fireplaces and leaking roofs. The tower mentioned here is a landmark remaining from a demolished church in the old butchers' quarter of Paris.

66. BRIGAND DE PROPRIÉTAIRE . . . ("This robber of a landlord . . . who only chooses to make repairs when the weather is fine!") L.D. 1605. II/II. No. 12 of *Locataires et propriétaires*, from *Le Charivari*, May 26, 1847.

Larousse quotes French writers as saying jocosely that the word *propriétaire* was at first synonymous with brigand or thief, and that it was invented as an ostentatious title since there was nothing lower to call a landlord!

67. JE NE LOUE PAS AUX GENS QUI ONT DES ENFANTS! ("I never rent to people who have children!") L.D. 1607. II/II. No. 14 of *Locataires et propriétaires*, from *Le Charivari*, June 24, 1847.

68. NAYADES DE LA SEINE (Naiads of the Seine.) L.D. 1629. II/II. No. 1 of the series *Les Baigneuses* (The Women Bathers), from *Le Charivari*, July 14, 1847.

As a counterpart to his series on male bathers, Daumier drew these 17 lithos, which give further evidence of his lack of interest in portraying attractive women. These visual jibes did nothing to endear Daumier to the bluestockings, who were the women's libbers of the time.

69. MA P'TITE ME DONNE BIEN DU MAL . . . ("My little one gives me plenty of trouble, Madame Radiguet . . . she doesn't take to swimming.") L.D. 1639. II/II. No. 11 of *Les Baigneuses*.

This plate was printed in August 1847, but did not appear in *Le Charivari*.

70. TIENS . . . VLA UN HOMME QUI S'EST DÉGUISÉ EN FEMME! ("Well! . . . there's a man disguised as a woman!") L.D. 1683. II/II. No. 37 of the series *Tout ce qu'on voudra* (Whatever You Wish), 1848.

This was a series of 70 charming and diverting lithos. Unfortunately, 14 of them, including this one, were not used by the editors of *Le Charivari* and are therefore extremely rare prints. Once more Daumier presents the old themes of bourgeois daily life, street scenes, picnics, doctors and patients, a lawyer or two, a magnificent theater scene, the omnibus, the park bench, the restaurant.

71. INCONVÉNIENT D'AVOIR UN PARENT QUI SE NOMME BABYLAS . . . (The disadvantage of having a relative named Babylas, so that one is obliged to bring him a bouquet on the 24th of January!) L.D. 1709. II/II. No. 64 of *Tout ce qu'on voudra*, from *Le Charivari*, Jan. 29, 1850.

Saint Babylas was patriarch of Antioch about 238 A.D. and was martyred about 251. His saint's day was January 24. According to French Catholic custom anyone named for a saint would receive flowers or small gifts on the saint's day, as well as on his own birthday.

72. DIRE QUE JE N'AI PAS PU TIRER . . . ("Just think, I haven't seen a thing to shoot at all day long!" "Oh, with me it's different . . . I've killed my dog!") L.D. 1729. II/II. No. 1 of the series *Quand on a du guignon* (When You're Unlucky), from *Le Charivari*, Feb. 18, 1848.

This series includes 11 vignettes showing unfortunate situations, with couples arguing, patrons in a restaurant, a luckless hunter with no powder, and a fisherman who has caught "not even a gudgeon."

73. MA FEMME RESTE BIEN LONG-TEMPS À CE BANQUET . . . ("My wife has really been a long time at that banquet . . . it's almost 48 hours since she left!") L.D. 1927. II/II. No. 10 of the series *Les Femmes socialistes* (Socialist Women), from *Le Charivari*, June 9, 1849.

With the collapse of Louis-Philippe's monarchy in the revolution of 1848, many radical groups began to form clubs, holding small conventions or political gatherings with dinner meetings, providing opportunities for the citizens to make many speeches. Daumier produced a series of 11 lithos on *Les Banqueteurs* (The Banqueters) and this series of ten on socialist women, who also had their banquets, forsaking their husbands and families, carrying on the feminist movement as had the literary bluestockings.

74. UN PARRICIDE (A parricide.) L.D. 2002. III/III. No. 106 of the series *Actualités* (Current Events), from *Le Charivari*, Apr. 16, 1850.

This drawing of Thiers and the press can be rated as one of the best that Daumier ever did. When the feisty little Frenchman Thiers from Marseilles came to Paris, he was first a lawyer, then a journalist on the liberal political paper *Le National*, and leader of the protests against censorship of the press in Charles X's Ordinances of 1830. Now in 1850, Daumier sees Thiers as about to murder his "parent" with his huge club labeled "Law on the Press." With Louis-Napoléon as President and Thiers a deputy, Daumier predicts the coming of more censorship of the press. Thiers is one of the politicians most often drawn by Daumier, appearing at least as often as Louis-Philippe, as he continually changes sides to support the party in power—

a fomenter of trouble, a dissimulator, a chameleon. (There were various series of *Actualités* in *Le Charivari*, and the numbering started afresh several times.)

75. EMPIRE, ORLÉANISME ET LÉGITIMITÉ . . . (Empire, Orleanism and Legitimacy race for the prize in a heated contest, forgetting the oft-quoted saying about "riding for a fall."—Quatrain found in the mailbox of the President's residence.) L.D. 2060. Only state. No. 11 of the series *Idylles parlementaires* (Parliamentary Idylls), from *Le Charivari*, Nov. 4, 1850.

This series of 16 lithos, plus 11 more not published in *Le Charivari*, were drawn with pseudo-Rococo frames enclosing the scenes and with a quatrain under each, presumably written by Philipon with tongue in cheek, pointedly explaining the circumstances. This idyll includes the characters General La Hitte, the orator-lawyer Berryer and little Thiers. La Hitte had fought in Spain (1811–1813) under Napoleon I; Berryer was a Legitimist supporting the claim to the throne of the Count de Chambord, grandson of Charles X; while Thiers was an Orleanist who continued to uphold the family of Louis-Philippe. All three men were in the Legislative Assembly in 1850, and were symbols in Daumier's mind of three factions, remnants of past regimes, now struggling in the race for power. As predicted in the quatrain, all three took an embarrassing and spectacular tumble when Louis-Napoléon assumed full power in December 1851.

76. BELLE DAME, VOULEZ-VOUS BIEN ACCEPTER MON BRAS? . . . ("Fair lady, will you accept my arm?" "Your passion is too sudden for me to believe in it!") L.D. 2153. II/II. No. 212 of *Actualités*, from *Le Charivari*, Sept. 25, 1851.

The character Ratapoil, unlike Robert Macaire, was invented by Daumier, who first created a statuette of him and then drew from it some 35 lithographs. Ratapoil (Hairy Rat), who personifies Napoleonic imperialism, acts as an agent hired by Louis-Napoléon to instigate trouble in order to place his master on the throne; he shows a strong resemblance to Louis-Napoléon with his sharp nose and pointed beard. Philippe Roberts-Jones calls the statuette one of the masterpieces of French sculpture in the nineteenth century. Jules Michelet, the illustrious historian and liberal professor at the Collège de France, while visiting Daumier's studio, saw the statuette and exclaimed, "Ah! you have completely hit the enemy! Here is the Bonapartist idea forever pilloried by you!" It is said that Daumier's wife, recalling the "prison vacation" her husband had been given for the litho "Gargantua," kept this statuette carefully hidden whenever she heard footsteps on the stairs to their top-floor lodging on the Ile de Saint-Louis.

77. UN MONSIEUR QUI S'ENFLAMME EN TOUTE SAISON (A gentleman who gets hot in any season.) L.D. 2219. II/II. No. 2 of the series *Les Parisiens en 1852* (The Parisians in 1852), from *Le Charivari*, Jan. 14, 1852.

With this series, Daumier revealed that he had lost none of his verve in character-rendering or imagination. Most of these 11 prints show two half-length figures in typical Parisian situations.

78. AUX CHAMPS-ELYSÉES . . . (On the Champs-Elysées. It has never been determined whether the music makes the beer go down or the beer helps to take in the music.) L.D. 2231. Only state? No. 3 of the series *Croquis musicaux* (Musical Sketches), from *Le Charivari*, Feb. 13, 1852.

This series of 17 pieces was printed in *Le Charivari* from February to May 1852. It contains interpretations of Parisian musical life, showing frustrations, elation, boredom with amateurs, singers straining to reach a high note, nose-blowing, throat-clearing, overpraising of talent, vexed musicians. Here the scene is a café-concert on the Champs-Elysées. This is one of Daumier's subjects and compositions that anticipate such later artists as Degas and Lautrec. Degas especially used similar divisions in his paintings and pastels of opera, ballet and café scenes, where the action on stage is seen over the shoulders and heads of musicians and spectators in the foreground, thus seemingly breaking the composition in half, though in reality the composition is united by adroit overlaps of music stands, fans and the like.

79. OUI, MADAME FRIBOCHON, IL Y A ÉVU ("Yes, Madame Fribochon, three weeks ago there was a very strong earthquake at Bordeaux, and not later than the day before yesterday, between midnight and three in the morning, I felt shocks in my bed that weren't natural . . . the herbalist, Mr. Potard, has explained this phenomenon to me . . . he claims it's because the government allows too much excavating of the earth in California and eventually we'll have a real disaster here in the Batignolles neighborhood!") L.D. 2263. II/II. No. 278 of *Actualités*, from *Le Charivari*, Mar. 17, 1852.

This print is one of Daumier's finest technical efforts in the 1850s; he masses his values with an extreme economy of means. It has a good dramatic presentation, with the strong value contrasts supplementing the drama.

80. UN JOUR OÙ L'ON NE PAYE PAS (Free-admission day. 25°C [77°F].) L.D. 2300. II/II. No. 10 of the series *Le Public du Salon* (The Salon Visitors), from *Le Charivari*, May 17, 1852.

Daumier drew 11 pieces in this series from April 24 through May 29, 1852, depicting groups of connoisseurs and crowds of curious and bewildered citizens. As early as 1834, Daumier had drawn for *Le Charivari* interpretations of two paintings appearing in the Salon of that year, and did several other Salon subjects in succeeding years. From time to time his friends had urged him to exhibit at the Salon, but it was not until 1851 that two of his paintings and a drawing were shown. The Salon, originating under the patronage of Louis XIV as the exhibition by the Royal Academy of Painting and Sculpture of the works of living artists, was first presented in April 1667, and was repeated annually or biennially, usually during Holy Week, celebrating the anniversary of the Academy's founding.

81. Qui diable se serait jamais douté qu'il neigerait encore à Paris! ("Who the devil would ever have suspected it would still be snowing in Paris!") L.D. 2362. III/III. No. 71 of *Actualités*, from *Le Charivari*, Feb. 21, 1853.

Daumier is one of the very few lithographers who really knew how to render snow—he neither overdid snowflakes nor scratched too few on the stone. He was always able to use his velvety blacks and ashen grays to good advantage in bringing out the softly falling flakes, as in this scene and in other earlier depictions of snow.

82. Bigre! . . . j'ai eu tort de me mettre toute l'Europe sur les bras! ("Confound it! I was wrong to take on all of Europe!") L.D. 2542. III/III. No. 146 of *Actualités*, from *Le Charivari*, Jan. 2–3, 1855.

Czar Nicholas I makes a desperate effort to hold the entire globe, which threatens to crush him, while in the background are faint silhouettes of French and English soldiers. During the Crimean War, Daumier contributed lithos to two long series of Current Events in *Le Charivari*, which also appeared in albums titled *Les Cosaques pour rire* (The Cossacks in Jest) and *Chargeons les Russes* (Let's Charge [also means "caricature"] the Russians). In some 86 lithographs Daumier proved that he had lost none of his skill at satire, as he depicted the stupidities of inadequate Russian generals, the ill-prepared soldiers, the frustrations of the angry Czar. At this time, the severe censorship of the Second Empire was relaxed, and caricaturists were free to interpret foreign politics.

83. Des dames d'un demi-monde . . . (Women of the half-world [demimonde], but not wearing half-skirts.) L.D. 2624. II/II. No. 190 of *Actualités*, from *Le Charivari*, May 11, 1855.

Daumier did very few drawings of fashion, never trying to emulate the magnificently sensitive and beautiful creations of Gavarni, but he did seize upon the ridiculous situations arising from the hoopskirt craze. At first the enormous crinolines were worn only by fashionable courtesans, as here, but they soon became the style. Daumier pictured women wearing them on crowded streets, on circular stairways, entering public conveyances and railroad cars, creating havoc in flower gardens, while the wire hoops provided convenient places to hang smuggled articles. An album entitled *Crinolomanie* contained 45 prints, a few by Daumier, others by Cham and various other artists contributing to *Le Charivari*.

84. Modes du printemps de 1855 . . . (Spring fashions, 1855—the latest rage.) L.D. 2625. II/II. No. 191 of *Actualités*, from *Le Charivari*, May 14, 1855.

Daumier draws the skirts larger and larger, until one print is titled, "These are not women, these are balloons!" In an article on crinolines, W. Born mentions that the great fashion designer Worth was blamed by some contemporary journals for the abnormal increase in the width of skirts during the 1850s, but that actually Worth and other dressmakers were following the prevailing trends of the times, creating a dress that was fantastic, impractical and highly extravagant, as befitted that age of conspicuous consumption among the newly rich of the Second Empire.

85. Comme quoi un jour d'entrée à quatre sous . . . (Showing how, on a day when the admission is four sous, you can't get away with paying less than 60 francs—for a new dress.) L.D. 2677. II/II. No. 14 of the series *L'Exposition universelle* (The World's Fair), from *Le Charivari*, June 12, 1855.

During the summer of 1855, Daumier produced a series of 41 lithos concerning the fair being held in Paris. These prints show gawking provincials and foreigners, annoyed and puzzled in endeavoring to find lodgings, tired, lost, staring pop-eyed at the wonders of progress. During Louis-Philippe's reign, three industrial exhibitions had been staged, showing new ideas and numerous inventions. After the Revolution of 1848, the government resolved to give more importance to the national fairs by also including exhibits on agriculture and the French colonies; this was done in 1849. In 1851, the Crystal Palace Exhibition—the first modern world's fair—took place in London, and in 1855 the French began the series of world's fairs which were to take place regularly thereafter in various countries.

86. Histoire de tuer le temps . . . (Just to kill time until the fair opens.) L.D. 2709. II/II. No. 192 of *Actualités*, from *Le Charivari*, May 15, 1855.

The crowd has climbed up to the gallery of the Vendôme Column, where they are admiring the panorama of Paris. Napoleon Bonaparte, not content with commencing the construction of the Arc de Triomphe on the Place de l'Etoile, ordered a monumental column in the Doric style, a conscious copy of Trajan's Column in Rome (113 A.D.), except that here the spiral reliefs were done in strips of bronze cast from the guns and cannon captured from the defeated Prussian and Austrian armies. Napoleon named it the Austerlitz Column, but it is commonly called by the name of the square, the Place Vendôme, where it was raised. At the time of the 1855 fair, the column was the tallest edifice in Paris, as the Eiffel Tower had not yet been constructed.

87. A la Bourse . . . (At the Stock Exchange. What is known as "the basket"—certainly not a flower basket.) L.D. 2805. II/III. No. 6 of *Croquis parisiens* (Parisian Sketches), from *Le Charivari*, July 25, 1856.

The *corbeille* is the central railed-off enclosure on the floor of the Parisian Stock Exchange within which the brokers transact their business. This group of 22 lithos is only one of the ten or more series Daumier drew under this same title, Parisian Sketches.

88. Quinze centimes un bain complet . . . (Fifteen centimes for a complete bath . . . that's a real bargain!) L.D. 2811. II/II. No. 12 of *Croquis parisiens*, from *Le Charivari*, Aug. 30, 1856.

This print is typical of the play on words often found in the caricatures: the *complet* on the omnibus indicates "filled" but also refers to the "full" bath in the drenching rain.

89. LE MAUVAIS CÔTÉ DES NOUVEAUX OMNIBUS (An unpleasant aspect of the new omnibuses.) L.D. 2812. Only state. No. 13 of *Croquis parisiens*, from *Le Charivari*, Sept. 4, 1856.

90. AYANT EU LA FÂCHEUSE IDÉE D'ALLER FAIRE LA SIESTE AU BORD DE L'EAU (The unfortunate idea of taking a siesta on the river bank.) L.D. 2850. II/II. No. 9 of the series *Croquis d'été* (Summer Sketches), from *Le Charivari*, Aug. 25 and Sept. 3, 1856.

This series includes 44 pieces, of which 35 were drawn by Daumier.

91. DIVERTISSEMENT AQUATIQUE RENOUVELÉ DES GRECS (Aquatic amusement borrowed from the Greeks.) L.D. 2860. II/II. No. 20 of *Croquis d'été*, from *Le Charivari*, Aug. 16–17, 1857.

This lightly sketched view of summer fun revives the pastimes of the satyrs and fauns of the classical world.

92. FAISANT SON APPRENTISSAGE AU TOURNIQUET DE LA BOURSE . . . (Serving his apprenticeship at the turnstile of the Stock Exchange, in order to become a road-mender for a Russian railroad.) L.D. 2915. II/II. No. 28 of *Croquis parisiens*, from *Le Charivari*, Feb. 6, 1857.

This witticism, aimed at the winter weather in France, again reveals Daumier's economy of means in depicting a snow scene.

93. DANGER DE PORTER DES JUPONS-BALLONS . . . (Danger of wearing balloon petticoats in the season of equinoctial squalls.) L.D. 2917. II/III. No. 383 of *Actualités*, from *Le Charivari*, Apr. 3, 1857.

This print also appeared as No. 26 in the above-mentioned album *La Crinolomanie*.

94. AH! . . . LES COMÈTES . . . ("Ah! . . . Comets! . . . they always predict some great calamities! . . . now I'm not surprised that poor Madame Galuchet died suddenly last night!") L.D. 2943. II/II. No. 573 of *Actualités*, from *Le Charivari*, Oct. 30, 1858.

Daumier drew a series of ten plates titled "The Comet of 1857," which appeared in *Le Charivari* throughout March of that year, when a comet trailed over Paris from March 4 to March 23. An earlier comet had appeared in February and a third, without a tail, appeared in April. Daumier's drawings portray the anxious citizens peering from windows, searching with their telescopes, staring into the skies, trembling, nervous, preparing for anticipated disasters. Since the subject was so popular with the frightened Parisians, Daumier drew ten more lithos relating to the comets with his characterizations of the worried observers. These later prints appeared within the series *Croquis parisiens* or, as in this case, *Actualités*, and the editors of *Le Charivari* continued using them through the following year, 1858.

95. UN ORCHESTRE DANS UNE MAISON TRÈS COMME IL FAUT . . . (An orchestra in a very distinguished home, where the whim of performing an operetta is being indulged.) L.D. 3038. III/III. No. 8 of the series *Les Comédiens de société* (Amateur Actors), from *Le Charivari*, Apr. 20, 1858.

In this series of 16 prints, Daumier humorously portrays amateur theatrical performances in homes. In one, a buxom housewife, practicing her role in an operetta, has no thought for her child who has overturned his high chair and crashed to the floor—a return to the *bas-bleus* theme.

96. RAPPELÉS AVEC ENTHOUSIASME! . . . (An enthusiastic curtain call! . . . and not a hired applauder in the house . . . that's a real success! . . . and people say dramatic art is dying . . . go on!) L.D. 3042. II/II. No. 12 of *Les Comédiens de société*, from *Le Charivari*, Apr. 30 and May 1, 1858.

97. LA CRINOLINE EN TEMPS DE NEIGE . . . (The crinoline in snowy weather. "My fine lady . . . must I give you a sweep with my broom?") L.D. 3089. II/II. No. 1 of the series *Croquis d'hiver* (Winter Sketches), from *Le Charivari*, Nov. 13, 1858.

As the hoopskirt craze continued, Daumier often enlivened the tedium of his days with a finely composed creation of such technical excellence as this study.

98. UN AMATEUR—MAIS QUEL EST DONC CE TABLEAU . . . (AN ART LOVER: "But what does this picture represent? It's nothing but blackness." THE AUCTIONEER: "It's the Emperor Soulouque, drawn from a daguerreotype!") L.D. 3129. II/II. No. 1 of the series *La Salle des ventes* (The Auction Room), from *Le Charivari*, Mar. 16, 1859.

Faustin Soulouque (1782–1867), who rose to general, president and then emperor of Haiti, was originally a slave and scarcely knew how to sign his name. He attempted to conquer the Dominican Republic, but this failed and caused his downfall in 1858. Because of the great interest in current events, the editors of *Le Charivari* had Daumier draw a group of nine lithos relating to the insane sadist emperor both in his native surroundings and on his visit to Paris.

99. MADELEINE-BASTILLE . . . (Omnibus on the Madeleine-Bastille line. A trifle, a mere nothing . . . and the omnibus is already filled!) L.D. 3243. I/II (before the addition of the title *Souvenirs d'artistes* [Artists' Recollections]). From *Le Boulevard*, Mar. 16, 1862.

The journal *Le Boulevard* was founded late in 1861 by Daumier's friend Etienne Carjat. The ten drawings Daumier contributed to it, from March 16 to September 21 of 1862, are thought by many to be among his masterpieces. The lithos in *Le Boulevard* were more carefully printed, on better newsprint, and in a little larger format than the prints in *Le Charivari* in the 1850s. *Souvenirs d'artistes* consisted of ten lithos; each of the five included here is in the rare first state. The drawing, value contrast, spacing and massing of the figures indicate just how much Daumier's style had grown. This is the first in the series.

100. LE NOUVEAU PARIS . . . (The new Paris. How fortunate it is for people in a hurry that the thoroughfares have been widened!!!) L.D. 3245. I/II (before

the addition of the title *Souvenirs d'artistes*). From *Le Boulevard*, Apr. 6, 1862 (third in series).

The city administrator Baron Georges-Eugène Haussmann (1809–1891) widened the boulevards and otherwise embellished Paris during the Second Empire.

101. A TRAVERS LES ATELIERS . . . (Through the studios. "The devil!" "Amazing!" "Damnation!" "Superb!" "The thing speaks!") L.D. 3246. I/II (before the addition of *Souvenirs d'artistes*). From *Le Boulevard*, Apr. 20, 1862 (fourth in series).

Some writers have suggested that the figure peering closely at the painting represents Daumier himself.

102. NADAR ÉLEVANT LA PHOTOGRAPHIE À LA HAUTEUR DE L'ART (Nadar raising photography to the level of art.) L.D. 3248. I/II (before the addition of *Souvenirs d'artistes*). From *Le Boulevard*, May 25, 1862 (sixth in series).

Félix Tournachon (1829–1910) took the pseudonym Nadar when he began at 22 to write for many Parisian journals. He studied painting and founded his own paper, *La Revue comique*, in 1849, while contributing both articles and caricatures to several other papers. In 1854 he opened a photography studio under the name of Panthéon-Nadar. His gallery of portraits of contemporary celebrities included the best-known photographs of Daumier. As photography became a great vogue, Nadar received large financial returns and medals of honor in various exhibitions. When he took up aerial navigation, he built an enormous balloon with a propeller, which he named "The Giant," and it is in this balloon that Daumier pictures him photographing all of Paris. During the Franco-Prussian War (1870) Nadar became head of the group of aeronauts observing the movements of the German armies from balloons above Paris.

103. PAYSAGISTES AU TRAVAIL (Landscapists at work.) L.D. 3251. I/II (before the addition of *Souvenirs d'artistes*). From *Le Boulevard*, Aug. 17, 1862 (seventh in series).

This is an amusing comment on the Impressionists' going out to paint the changing light and moods in nature. Despite Daumier's satire, Monet, Pissarro and others labored long hours on paintings which were too far advanced for the public to appreciate, much less understand. Many of Daumier's lithos of the 1850s and 1860s are forerunners of the Impressionist school and reveal that Daumier was not only one of the pioneers in the use of scintillating light that suffuses his pictures but was aware of the gradual changes becoming apparent in the art world.

104. UNE DISCUSSION LITTÉRAIRE À LA DEUXIÈME GALERIE (A literary discussion in the second balcony.) L.D. 3264. II/II. No. 4 of the series *Croquis pris au théâtre* (Sketches Made at the Theater), from *Le Charivari*, Feb. 27, 1864.

This piece from a series of eight is one of Daumier's best theater sketches, showing him as an undisputed master of gestures and facial expressions. The second gallery of a Parisian theater was often ironically referred to as "Paradise."

105. LE PUBLIC À L'EXPOSITION . . . (The public at the exhibition. "There's no denying it's me, those are certainly my fine contours; but I'll always be sorry that the artist stubbornly refused to put in my glasses and my detachable collar!") L.D. 3316. III/III. The second state was published in *Le Journal amusant*, June 18, 1864, at about the same time that this third state appeared in *Le petit Journal pour rire*, another of the small papers established by Philipon.

Joseph Prudhomme, the nineteenth-century French John Q. Public, was a theatrical character created by Henry Monnier (1805–1877) in his famous monologues. Monnier in his youth had been a clerk in the Ministry of Justice, and in government bureaus he observed many characteristics and mannerisms which he later incorporated into his skits, theatrical productions and drawings. He acted Prudhomme with pompous dignity and gullible stupidity, pronouncing commonplace phrases in stuffy language. Larousse called Prudhomme "a modern type of satisfied nullity and authoritative banality." Daumier satirized this amusing bourgeois character in some 40 different lithographs. Like Monnier, Daumier showed Prudhomme as fat, even portly, with his short figure tightly buttoned into a long coat, his enormous head emerging above a large, white collar, with a double chin, parrot-beak nose and round eyes behind round glasses. By gestures Daumier suggests the waddling gait of gouty feet, the assured manner of unbending dignity, the sonorous voice giving vent to grandiloquent remarks.

106. LES PAYSAGISTES . . . (The landscapists. The first one copies nature, the second copies the first.) L.D. 3439. II/II. No. 1 of the series *Les Artistes*, from *Le Charivari*, May 12, 1865.

The editors of *Le Charivari*, after the absence of Daumier's drawings for more than two years, belatedly realized how much these lithographs were missed by the subscribers. Daumier, as can be seen in this print, was well aware that copyists endeavored to duplicate his works in order to benefit financially from his great popularity. K. E. Maison, in a 1958 article on Daumier's watercolors, says that numerous drawings purported to be studies for watercolors are obvious copies *after* the lithographs, lightly washed with color. Maison continues, "More than one French bourgeois must have amused himself in his leisure hours, between 1840 and 1870, by drawing à la Daumier!"

107. CETTE ANNÉE ENCORE DES VÉNUS . . . ("This Year Venuses again . . . always Venuses! . . . As if there really were women built like that!") L.D. 3440. II/II. No. 2 of the series *Croquis pris au Salon* (Sketches Made at the Salon), from *Le Charivari*, May 10, 1864.

In this series of nine scenes at the Salon, Daumier shows some artists congratulating each other on new works, others sneering at the ignorance displayed by the public, citizens complaining of the new landscapes in the Impressionist manner, and a curious family open-mouthed before a painting by Manet.

108. RENOUVELÉ DES PETITES DANAÏDES (The Danaïdes up to date.) L.D. 3509. IV/IV. The third state ap-

peared in *Le Charivari*, June 26, 1866, with the title, "Traités de 1815, faux équilibre" (Treaties of 1815, an improper balance). This fourth state was reprinted as No. 107 of *Actualités* in *L'Album de la guerre* (The War Album).

The Danaïdes were the 50 young daughters of Danaus, King of Argos, who were sentenced to Tartarus (the underworld) for the murder of their husbands, their eternal punishment being to carry water in a sieve and continue to pour it into a broken vase or cask. Here the powers of Europe vainly fill with gold the bottomless cask labeled "Treaties of 1815." With the gradual relaxation of censorship during the Second Empire—a period of much graft and corruption and a laissez-faire attitude, the French believing that they were invincible—Daumier was again able to enter the political field in caricature. Between 1866 and his retirement in 1872, Daumier drew some 417 lithos relating to internal happenings and the politics of foreign powers, with many warnings of the rise of the Prussian war machine.

109. L'Equilibre Européen (The European balance of power.) L.D. 3540. III/III. No. 231 of *Actualités*, from *Le Charivari*, Dec. 1, 1866.

This travesty of the unstable situation in Europe is only one of many ironically using the notion of equilibrium. A number of these subjects derive from the popular circus and variety acts of the day: a madly spinning top balanced on a saber blade; Europe, personified as a woman in a flowing gown, performing a balancing act on a ball which is, in fact, a smoking bomb; the enormously fat character Budget walking a tightrope.

110. Les cadeaux de Noël de 1868 (The gifts for Christmas 1868.) L.D. 3683. II/II. No. 280 of *Actualités*, from *Le Charivari*, Dec. 25, 1868.

At the fireplace where Europe has placed her slippers to await the Christmas gifts, she finds only cannon, guns, bayonets and bullets. In the pathetic figure of Europe, Daumier expresses his deep concern and bitterness over the events he foresees, just as a year earlier, he showed Europe dispensing her New Year's gifts of bayonets to the various nations. Again in 1870 he was to portray the little girl "New Year 1870" about to receive from the woman "1869" four marionettes on strings with the faces of the leading politicians.

111. Pauvre vieux! (Poor old fellow!) L.D. 3691. III/III. No. 6 of *Actualités*, from *Le Charivari*, Jan. 26, 1869.

The old man in eighteenth-century costume, broken with age and injuries, succinctly symbolizes the shaky European balance of power. He is attended by the equally aged and battered old woman Conference, the courtesan, the coquette of a departed century, a toothless old hag with powdered hair and Rococo costume. The same old woman is seen in another cartoon as Diplomacy, aghast at the little child Mars rising in his cradle with sword in hand; elsewhere she performs a balancing act walking on a ladder among eggs labeled variously "German Question," "Roman Question," "Oriental Question"; again, she attempts to leap across a chasm between the cliffs of Italian Issue and Oriental Issue; or she is ready with scissors in hand to cut up and rearrange once more the cloth map of Europe, before the group of astonished European states. Occasionally this same old crone symbolizes Austria and the waning Hapsburg power, which had been a stabilizing influence from the time of Napoleon's defeat at Waterloo in 1815. In her last appearance as Conference, Daumier portrayed the old woman in a painter's swing desperately trying to give a new appearance to the Temple of Peace with a coat of whitewash.

112. Comme Sisyphe (Like Sisyphus.) L.D. 3694. II/II. No. 27 of *Actualités*, from *Le Charivari*, Feb. 25, 1869.

Sisyphus, a king of Corinth, angered the gods and was sentenced to the eternal punishment of rolling a huge stone uphill to a height from which it immediately rolled down again.

113. Je voulais la lui jeter . . . ("I wanted to fling it at him, and I'm the one who got soiled.") L.D. 3737. III/III. No. 210 of *Acualités*, from *Le Charivari*, Sept. 22, 1869.

A Jesuit who wanted to spatter the statue of Voltaire with ink has broken the bottle and spattered only himself. The Jesuits had been driven out of France in 1762 but officially returned in 1865. Daumier's personification of the Jesuits was Basile, who first appeared in a lithograph of 1867 and is to be seen in some 19 satires in Daumier's later work. Roberts-Jones describes the character as tall and angular under his priest's robes, his face strongly marked like that of Bertrand, the accomplice of Robert Macaire. "Bertrand is the individual with no scruples, cunning, mercenary, and it should not be surprising that the Jesuits, in the eyes of Daumier, may have had the same characteristics. Daumier, a militant Republican, was, for that reason, anticlerical." In an earlier litho, Daumier had drawn Basile attempting to stop a sculptor from carving a statue of Voltaire, saying, "I don't want him to have his statue when I don't have mine!" Voltaire, with his anti-Church doctrines, was the natural target for many Jesuit attacks. On the day following the end of the Franco-Prussian War, March 14, 1871, *Le Charivari* published Daumier's drawing of an army of Jesuits marching into France, while the Prussians disappear into the background, with the caption, "One invasion replaces the other."

114. A l'instar de Pantin (Just like Pantin.) L.D. 3740. II/II. No. 225 of *Actualités*, from *Le Charivari*, Oct. 12, 1869.

The village of Pantin, France was the scene in 1869 of a tragic incident that received international attention: an itinerant laborer named Troppmann massacred and mutilated the entire Kink family, burying their corpses in a shallow common grave. Here the helmeted Prussian Bismarck is crushing the Duchy of Baden, while his other victims, Saxony, Hanover and Hesse, are already piled on the ground. Count Otto von Bismarck (1815–1898), who entered Prussian diplomacy in 1851, became Minister of State, Minister of Foreign Affairs and President of the Council, all in 1863. He was not long in putting into operation his plan to enlarge Prussia by any and all means. From 1866, with the formation of the German Confederation, this became a clear threat to France, and Daumier drew some 55 lithos caustically depicting the rise of the German Empire. Repeatedly Daumier offered his warnings against this menace, showing the Year 1867 placing a crown over the spiked helmet of an enormous woman, Prussia, with the caption, "First Prize for Growth!" Another time he turned to the fables of La Fontaine, showing a wolf in shepherd's garb and Prussian helmet about to devour the flock of small German states.

115. UN CAUCHEMAR DE M. DE BISMARK (Bismarck's nightmare. "Thanks!") L.D. 3802. II/II. No. 183 of *Actualités*, from *Le Charivari*, Aug. 22, 1870.

The German Chancellor, asleep in his chair under his tent, sees Death grasping his arm to show him the ghastly results of his campaigns, a plain strewn with corpses. This striking composition is one of Daumier's most dramatic, with the outstretched arm and the blade of the scythe leading the viewer's eye toward the battlefield. It was Daumier's warning of the tremendous loss of life France was to suffer. This print appeared only one month after the French declaration of war on July 19, and already the Germans, in their advance toward Paris, had overrun the French forces in a dozen encounters.

116. A QUI LE TOUR? (Whose turn now?) L.D. 3816. II/II. No. 240 of *Actualités*, from *Le Charivari*, Oct. 31, 1870.

A militiaman, before a wall marked "Museum of the Rulers," runs his bayonet through a plucked eagle, signifying the utter destruction of the imperial regime of Louis-Napoléon, who had joined the troops in July but surrendered to German forces September 2, following the Battle of Sedan. The Eagle of 1870 is soon to fall onto the pile of rubbish indicating a century of deposed sovereigns: the tricorne of Napoleon, 1815; the fleur-de-lis of the Bourbon Restoration, 1830; the pear and the umbrella of Louis-Philippe, 1848.

117. PAGE D'HISTOIRE (A page of history.) L.D. 3820. III/III. No. 234 of *Actualités*, from *Le Charivari*, Nov. 16, 1870.

A bolt of lightning rending the clouds strikes the plucked eagle, already buried under the weight of Victor Hugo's book of poems *The Castigations*. Hugo (1820–1885), the most famous poet of France in the nineteenth century, was at first a royalist, celebrating Napoleon's victories in "Ode to a Column" (the Vendôme) and welcoming the return of the Bourbons, but became a liberal under Louis-Philippe, who had created him a Peer in 1845. He became the chief orator of the democratic and socialist left, opposing the reelection of Louis-Napoléon and never fearing to ridicule him. When the coup d'état was announced making Louis-Napoléon Emperor on December 2, 1852, Victor Hugo's name was at the head of the proscription lists. He fled to Belgium and then to the island of Jersey, continuing his protests in two great, majestic works, *Napoléon le Petit* (Napoleon the Little; Brussels, 1852) and *Les Châtiments* (The Castigations; Brussels, 1853). The very rare second state of this print carried signatures of both Victor Hugo and Daumier.

118. EPOUVANTÉE DE L'HÉRITAGE (Appalled at the heritage.) L.D. 3838. II/III. No. 280 of *Actualités*, from *Le Charivari*, Jan. 11, 1871.

The female figure, representing France as well as the New Year, stands weeping, aghast at the sacrifices—not only the loss of life but also the devastation of property and the destruction of morale—that are the disastrous legacy from the Second Empire, and at the enormous reparations to be exacted by Prussia from the young Third Republic. All France, as well as Louis-Napoléon, was to suffer the punishments.

119. LA FRANCE-PROMÉTHÉE ET L'AIGLE-VAUTOUR (France as Prometheus and the eagle as vulture.) L.D. 3847. II/II. No. 309 of *Actualités*, from *Le Charivari*, Feb. 13, 1871.

Prometheus, in Greek mythology, angered the gods by carrying celestial fire to the mortals on earth. He was punished by being bound to a rock in the Caucasus mountains, where a vulture daily consumed his liver, which renewed itself every night. With a sick heart, Daumier saw France as Prometheus, being torn to pieces by the Imperial Eagle of Napoleon III, always depicted by Daumier as a vulture. With the capitulation of Paris on January 28, 1871, this vulture also might well be a portent of the coming reparations to be demanded by the new German Empire under the Prussian eagle.

120. LA PAIX; IDYLLE (Peace; an idyll.) L.D. 3854. II/II. No. 324 of *Actualités*, from *Le Charivari*, Mar. 6, 1871.

This is one of Daumier's most ironic lithographs, with the skeleton Peace oblivious of the surrounding devastation and gaily playing on the pipes. For New Year's Day, 1872, the last year of his long career, Daumier again showed a skeleton driving a hearse as it carried off the Accursed Year 1871. In one of his final works, no doubt intended for the series of Current Events but not published, perhaps because it was thought too horrible to use, a group of skeletons—a woman, a child and three men (one headless)—rush toward a door of the Council of War. The only known proof of this print, titled "Les Témoins" (The Witnesses), is owned by the Metropolitan Museum of Art.

SELECTED BIBLIOGRAPHY

BOOKS

Adhémar, Jean, *h. Daumier*, Editions Pierre Tisné, Paris, 1954.

——, *Daumier: Les Gens de médecine*, Editions Vilo, André Sauret, Paris, 1966.

——, *Daumier: Financial and Businessmen*, Editions André Sauret, Léon Amiel, Paris & New York, 1974.

Alexandre, Arsène, *Honoré Daumier: l'homme et l'œuvre*, H. Laurens, Paris, 1888.

Banville, Théodore de, *Mes Souvenirs*, D. Charpentier, Paris, 1882.

Baudelaire, Charles, *The Mirror of Art: Critical Studies*, Doubleday, Anchor Books, Garden City, N.Y., 1956. Translated and edited by Jonathan Mayne from two collections of Baudelaire's art criticism: *Curiosités esthétiques* (1868) and *L'Art romantique* (1869).

Bechtel, Edwin De T., *Freedom of the Press and L'Association Mensuelle: Philipon versus Louis-Philippe*, The Grolier Club, New York, 1952.

Beik, Paul H., *Louis-Philippe and the July Monarchy*, Van Nostrand, Anvil Original, New York, 1965.

Beraldi, Henri, *Les Graveurs du XIXe siècle*, 12 vols., L. Conquet, Paris, 1885–1892.

Blanc, Louis, *The History of Ten Years, 1830–1840*, 2 vols., Lea and Blanchard, Philadelphia, 1848.

Bouvy, Eugène, *Daumier: l'œuvre gravé du maître*, 2 vols., Maurice Le Garrec, Paris, 1933.

Cain, Julien, *Les Gens de justice*, Editions du Livre, André Sauret, Monte Carlo, 1971.

Canaday, John, *Mainstreams of Modern Art*, Holt, Rinehart & Winston, New York, 1962.

Champfleury (Jules Husson), *Histoire de la caricature moderne*, E. Dentu, Paris, n.d. (1870s).

Cheney, Sheldon, *The Theater: Three Thousand Years of Drama, Acting and Stagecraft*, Tudor Publishing Co., New York, 1936.

Cherpin, Jean, *Daumier et le théâtre*, L'Arche, Paris, 1958.

——, *L'Homme Daumier: un visage qui sort de l'ombre*, Arts et Livres de Provence, Marseilles, 1973.

Cobban, Alfred, *A History of Modern France*, Vol. 2, *1799–1871*, Penguin Books, Ltd., Harmondsworth, Middlesex, England, 1970.

Cormenin, Timon, *Livre des orateurs*, Vols. 2 & 3, Libraire Pagnerre, Paris, 1869.

Delteil, Loys, *Le Peintre-graveur illustré*, XX–XXIX bis (10 volumes and index), Loys Delteil, Paris, 1925–1930.

Dreyfus, René G., *Lithographies originales par Daumier*, Auction Catalogue, Hôtel Drouot, Paris, December 7 & 8, 1966.

Escholier, Raymond, *Daumier: la vie et l'art romantiques*, H. Floury, Paris, 1923.

——, *Daumier et son monde*, Editions Berger-Levrault, Nancy, 1965.

Foyer, Jean le, *Daumier au Palais de Justice*, La Colombe, Paris, 1958.

Fuchs, Eduard, *Der Maler Daumier*, Albert Langen, Munich, 1930.

——, *Daumier: Holzschnitte, 1833–1872*, Albert Langen, Munich, 1920.

Gobin, Maurice, *Daumier sculpteur*, Pierre Cailler, Geneva, 1952.

Hazard, N.-A., & L. Delteil, *Catalogue raisonné: l'œuvre lithographié de Honoré Daumier*, Orrouy, Oise, 1904.

James, Henry, *Daumier Caricaturist*, Miniature Books, Rodale Press, Emmaus, Pennsylvania, 1937.

Larousse, *Grand Dictionnaire universel du XIXe siècle*, 17 vols., Librairie Larousse, Paris, 1867 and following.

——, *Grand Larousse encyclopédique*, 10 vols., Librairie Larousse, Paris, 1963 and following.

Lejeune, Robert, *Honoré Daumier*, Clairefontaine, Lausanne, 1953.

Lemann, Bernard, *Honoré Daumier*, Reynal & Hitchcock, New York, 1941.

Maison, K. E., *Honoré Daumier: Catalogue Raisonné of the Paintings, Watercolours and Drawings*, 2 vols., New York Graphic Society Ltd., New York, 1968.

Melcher, Edith, *The Life and Times of Henry Monnier (1799–1877)*, Harvard University Press, Cambridge, 1950.

Murray, Alexander S., *Manual of Mythology*, Tudor Publishing Co., New York, 1935.

Parturier, Françoise, and Jacqueline Armingeat, *Lib Women: Blue Stockings and Socialist Women*, Léon Amiel, Paris & New York, 1974.

Peytel, Sébastien Benoît (pseudonym Louis Benoît),

Physiologie de la Poire, Librairies de la Place de la Bourse et du Palais-Royal, Paris, 1832.

Roberts-Jones, Philippe, *Humors of Married Life*, Boston Book & Art Publishers, André Sauret, Paris, 1960.

Thackeray, William M., *The Paris Sketch-Book of Mr. W. A. Titmarsh*, John B. Alden, New York, 1883.

University of Southern California, *Honoré Daumier: Histoire Ancienne*, Exhibition Catalogue, J. Paul Getty Museum, Malibu, California, May 1 to June 15, 1975.

Vincent, Howard P., *Daumier and His World*, Northwestern University Press, Evanston, Illinois, 1968.

Wasserman, Jeanne L., *Daumier Sculpture: A Critical and Comparative Study*, Exhibition Catalogue, Fogg Art Museum, Harvard University, Cambridge, May 1 to June 23, 1969.

PERIODICALS

Adhémar, Jean, "Daumier et la médecine," *Aesculape* (Société Internationale d'Histoire et de la Médecine), Vol. 41, Dec. 1958, pp. 2–4; Vol. 42, Jan. 1959, pp. 1–4.

Bechtel, Edwin De T., "Les Lithographies de jeunesse," *Arts et livres de Provence*, Marseilles, Daumier issue, 1948, pp. 40–56.

Born, W., "The Crinoline and the Bustle," *Ciba Review*, Basle, Vol. 46, May 1943, pp. 1658–1689.

Cherpin, Germaine, "Les cent onze Figurations de Monsieur Thiers," *Arts et livres de Provence*, Marseilles, Daumier issue, 1948, pp. 35–41.

Cherpin, Jean, "Le quatrième Carnet de comptes de Daumier," *Gazette des Beaux Arts*, Paris, Vol. 56, July–Dec. 1960, pp. 353–362.

Duranty, Louis Edmond, "Daumier," *Gazette des Beaux Arts*, Paris, Vol. 17, Jan.–June 1878, pp. 428–443 & 528–544.

Geoffrey, Gustave, "Daumier sculpteur," *L'Art et les artistes*, Paris, Apr.–Sept. 1905, pp. 101–108.

Ivins, William M., "Daumier: The Man of His Time," *The Arts Magazine*, New York, Feb. 1923, pp. 89–102.

Jones, Philippe [Roberts-], "Daumier et l'impressionnisme," *Gazette des Beaux Arts*, Paris, Vol. 55, Jan.–June 1960, pp. 241–250.

——, "Les Femmes dans l'œuvre lithographique de Daumier," *Médecine de France*, Paris, Vol. 23, 1951, pp. 29–32.

——, "Quelques personnages symboliques chez Daumier," *Aesculape*, Paris, Vol. 41, Dec. 1958, pp. 34–50.

Larkin, Oliver, "Daumier and Ratapoil," *Science and Society, Marxian Quarterly*, John Jay College of C.U.N.Y., New York, Vol. IV, No. 1, Winter 1940, pp. 373–387.

JOURNALS

Microfilm copies, *La Caricature*, all issues from Nov. 1830 to Sept. 1835, Bibliothèque Nationale, Paris.

Microfilm copies, *Le Charivari*, all issues from Dec. 1832 to Dec. 1836, Bibliothèque Nationale, Paris.

Xerox copies, *L'Association mensuelle lithographique*, all issues from Aug. 1832 to Aug.–Sept. 1834, Metropolitan Museum of Art, New York.

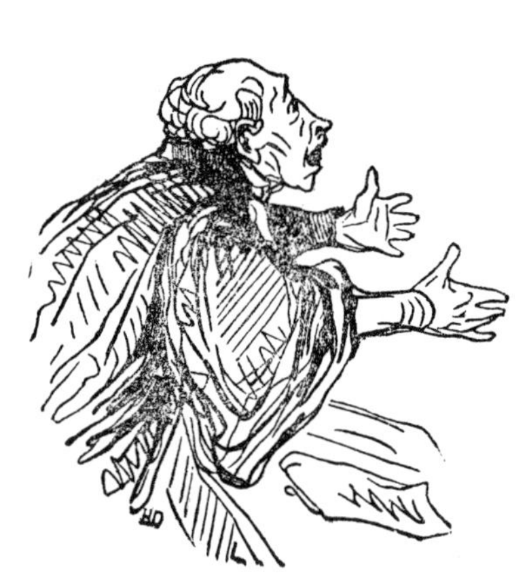

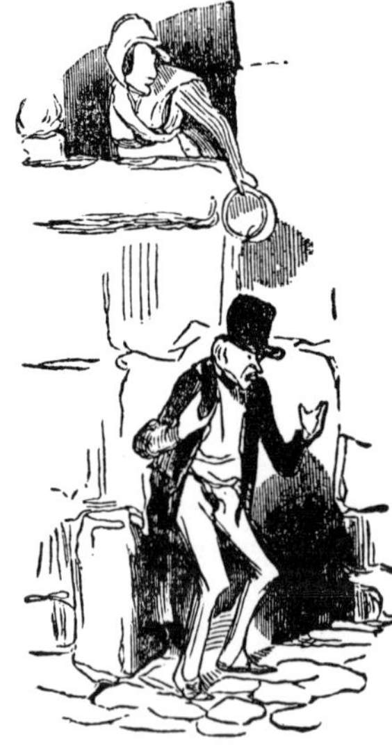

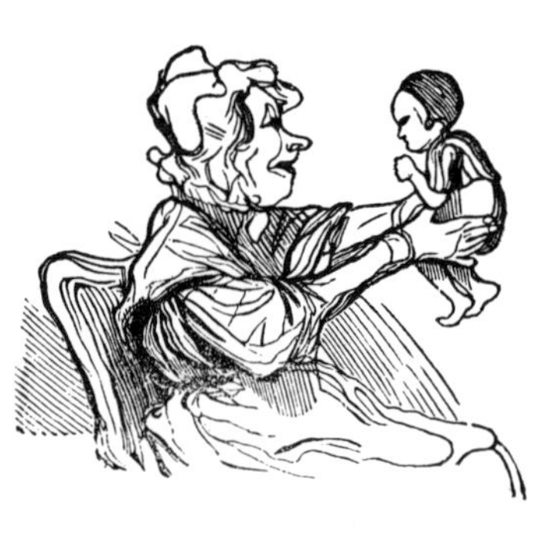

Illustrations from *Le Charivari*. LEFT: "Lawyer Pleading His Case." B.113. Nov. 6, 1839. CENTER: "Free Sprinkling." B.190. Mar. 25, 1839. RIGHT: "Old Woman and Tiny Tot." B.262. Aug. 8, 1839.